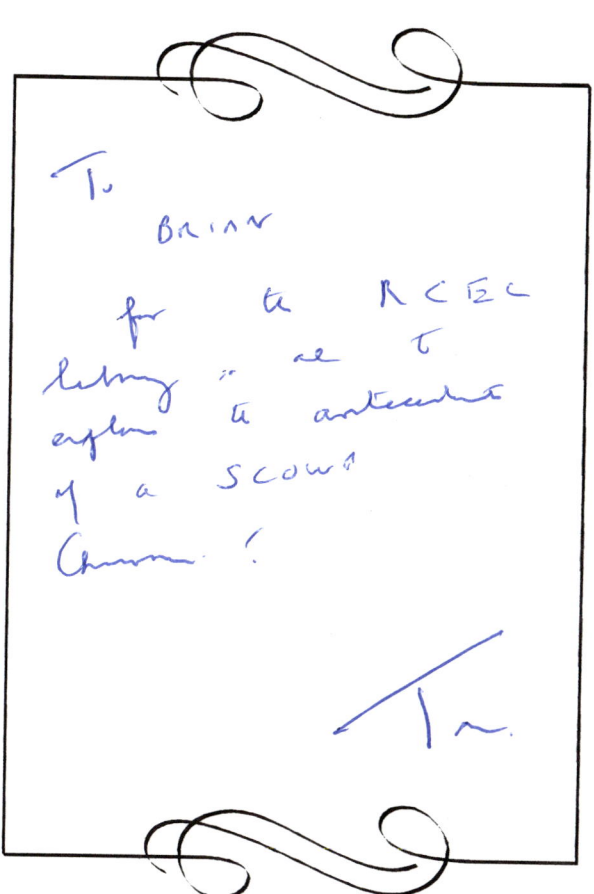

I Have The Honour To Be

I Have The Honour To Be

by

TOM RUSSELL CMG CBE

A memoir of a career covering fifty-two years
of service for British Overseas Territories.

I have the honour to be,
Sir,
Your most obedient servant

*(Concluding salutation of a
dispatch to the Secretary of State,
The War Office, 1943.)*

I have the honour to be,
Sir,
Your most obedient, humble servant

*(Concluding salutation of a
dispatch to the Colonial Secretary,
The Colonial Office, 1953.)*

The Memoir Club

© Tom Russell 2003

First published in 2003 by
The Memoir Club
Whitworth Hall
Spennymoor
County Durham

British Library Cataloguing in
Publication Data.
A catalogue record for this book
is available from the
British Library.

ISBN: 1 84104 047 9

Typeset by George Wishart & Associates, Whitley Bay.
Printed by Bookcraft (Bath) Ltd.

*Dedicated to my former colleagues
in the Western Pacific, the
Cayman Islands and London.*

Contents

Illustrations

Acknowledgements

I AM GRATEFUL for the assistance of Mike and June Hamilton, Jenny Manderson and Mary Chandler-Allen for auditing my memories of events in the Solomon Islands, the Cayman Islands and London, for making helpful suggestions and for providing valuable factual information. I much appreciate the provision of the foreword by Anthony Kirk-Greene, one of the leading historians of H.M. Colonial and Overseas Civil Services.

Finally I record my thanks to the Memoir Club, and particularly to my editor, David Bourke, for their helpful advice and encouragement.

Foreword

by Anthony Kirk-Greene, CMG, MBE
Emeritus Fellow, St Antony's College, Oxford

THE PUBLICATION of memoirs written by former members of the British Colonial Service, reconstituted in 1954 as Her Majesty's Overseas Civil Service (the Service itself came to a close in 1997, the year in which Britain's remaining colony, Hong Kong, was handed back to China), has created a certain niche for itself in the autobiographical literature of the past two decades. Partly this is because by the 1980s an interest in Britain's imperial era, particularly in who those expatriate civil servants were, what they did and how they managed to do it, was beginning to replace the fashion of a post-empire blackout on Britain's colonial past as something best forgotten, or at least not talked about. Partly too the renaissance is due to the realization by members of HMOCS that they are indeed the final generation, the last men and women of a civil service that could trace its origins back to the 1830s. Today the history of Britain is still searching for its proper role in school and college curricula, but at least an interest in our national past has been rekindled. Memoirs and museums play a significant part in this revival.

Tom Russell's memoir is an important contribution to the study of the Crown's overseas civil servants as well as to the story of the new nations where they once worked. It is also a memoir which extends beyond the standard setting of so many such contributions. Rather than the backdrop being Africa, which accounted for some three-quarters of Britain's colonial administrators, Russell's dual scenario is the lower profile but equally problematic Western Pacific, and later the long-standing Caribbean. His credentials are indeed impressive. Instead of a normal length Colonial Service career, Russell served overseas governments for a probably record-breaking fifty-two years, twice the length of the average career, in defiance of all kinds of retirement age regulations. Instead of retiring at the end of his already renewed appointment in the prestigious post of a colonial governorship, he went on to serve the government of that same territory, the Cayman Islands, in the new post of its official representative in London...for a further eighteen years! At that time there were only three other Representative Officers of Britain's Overseas Territories, as they came to be known after the closure of the Colonial Office in 1966: Hong Kong, Gibraltar and the Falkland Islands. The Cayman Islands thus made history in its innovation.

Tom Russell's memoir opens with a charming and compelling picture of pre-war family life in the Scottish Borders, where his mother (who was to live till she was just a few months short of her hundredth birthday) never for a moment doubted that for a good housewife to offer a 'bought' cake for afternoon tea was socially shameful. Unlike many family-centred introductions to a memoir, this is one not to be skipped. After war service in the Parachute Regiment, Russell joined the Colonial Service in 1948 and was appointed to the islands of the Western Pacific High Commission. His first posting was to the British Solomon Islands Protectorate, an archipelago of islands stretching for a hundred miles whose inhabitants spoke just about the same number of languages. Before 1939 the Solomon Islands had been something of a colonial backyard, but the battle of Guadalcanal brought them onto the world stage in 1943 and into the American folk-memory for ever. By 1978 the Solomon Islands were independent.

The bulk of Russell's memoir rewardingly narrates his years as a District Commissioner in Malaita, including his encounter with the famous Marching Rule uprising. This section of the book concludes with his promotion to the Secretariat in Honiara, first as Financial Secretary, then as Chief Secretary (later redesignated Deputy Governor). His service included appointments as Acting High Commissioner for the Western Pacific as well as a posting to Fiji and secondment to the Colonial Office in London. These Solomons chapters offer a rich insight into the work of a colonial administrator in the Western Pacific, light miles removed from, yet immediately familiar to, the District Commissioner and his life in the better-known context of East or West Africa. As such, Russell's contribution assumes an added value in filling out our understanding of the bewildering, almost unbelievable, range of work, responsibility, location and conditions in which the colonial administrator had to operate, wherever he was posted round the globe.

In a further extension of the up-and-coming colonial administrator's career, Russell found himself, at the age of 54, selected for transfer across the Pacific to the Caribbean, to head the government of the Cayman Islands. Here was a colony already far more politically advanced than the Solomon Islands, though the keen-eyed reader may detect an echo of

pre-war Pacific 'underdevelopment' in the 1970s' administration of the
Cayman Islands, where, Russell assures us (p. 174), before a Gazette Law
had been enacted, laws were published by pinning a copy of the laws
with a drawing-pin to a notice board outside post offices. The Cayman
years occupy less space than the rest of the memoir, yet still with the
same detail of activities and the same dedication to – a bonus for any
historian – naming names of colleagues and other acquaintances. By
Russell's setting of his time in Government House against his District
Commissioner years in the Solomon Islands, the reader is enabled to put
both periods together and construct the enormous variety of work and
interest offered by a career in the post-war Colonial Administrative
Service.

The memoir closes with a meticulous account of Russell's unique
pinnacle to his career, namely his remarkably prolonged term as the
Cayman Islands' trusted and respected Representative in London. The
final chapter sets forth a number of miscellaneous reflections, among
them an insider and important consideration of the future of Britain's
remaining handful of Overseas Territories, all but one of them islands,
spread across four of the world's oceans. Russell takes his story right up
to the publication of the proposed partnership arrangements in the
Foreign and Commonwealth Office's White Paper of 1999 and the
current constitutional proposals for the Cayman Islands.

Tom Russell's enjoyable memoir will be of interest to a whole range
of readers. Historians of the Solomon Islands and of the Cayman Islands
will find a narrative of extensive and informative detail. Those whose
careers overlapped with Russell's in either the Pacific or the Caribbean
can, as the lengthy index of personal names indicates, anticipate an
investigative field-day. To those whose central interest lies in the history
of the Colonial Service, the memoir offers an excellent account of what
the life of a District Commissioner was all about, a narrative all the more
valuable in the literature because it is located in the rarer and non-
African – markedly quite different, despite the curious prevalence of the
post-prandial ritual of 'looking at Africa', described at p. 77 – context of
colonial administration in the post-war Pacific. Colonial Service readers,
too, will appreciate the validity of Russell's verdict that 'only families
who have led the nomadic life which we led in the Overseas Service can
appreciate fully the deprivation felt by wives and mothers constantly on
the move' (p. 200). To the constitutional enthusiast, Russell's personal
experience of the sometimes fraught relationship between the British
government and the Cayman Islands, derived from his twenty-five years

first as Governor and then as London Representative, allows an insight into the problems of the post-colonial territories as well as the new proposed solutions.

Finally, there is the general reader, who can be confident that here are the reminiscences of and reflections on a career and lifestyle which, sought-after and fulfilling in its day, will not be seen again. *I Have The Honour To Be* is at once a memoir of and a memorial to a life which is no more.

St Antony's College   May 2003
Oxford

CHAPTER ONE

The Formative Years

I WAS BORN in the parish of Melrose, in the Scottish Borders, on the 27th May 1920. The date is important only as serving as the datum line for an archaeological dig through eighty-three years of existence. Twin brothers, John and Jim, were born in 1923.

Hassendean, the house where I was born, was built in 1760 in the village of Gattonside, sited on the other side of the River Tweed from Melrose. Gattonside was said to have provided the orchards and the gardens for the monks of Melrose Abbey in former times. An old suspension bridge over the Tweed links the two communities.

My parents married in 1919 after my father returned from service in World War I. He was educated at George Watsons College in Edinburgh and initially employed in the Royal Bank of Scotland. His father died, however, in 1912 and he then took over the family draper's business in Melrose. Enlisting in 1915, he was commissioned into the Motor Machine Gun Regiment. In trench warfare this was used to secure breaches in the line. Vickers machine guns were mounted on the side-car of a motor cycle. Ideally the guns were dismounted, but in case of need could be fired from the side-car as the unit swept into action. He was awarded the Military Cross, being severely wounded by shelling in the last weeks of the War. He enlisted again in World War II in 1940, joining the 13th Battalion of the Cameronians (Scottish Rifles) as a Lieutenant, reaching the rank of Lieutenant-Colonel in 1943 and Colonel in 1945. He was transferred to the R.A.F. Regiment in 1942 and took part in the Normandy landings. He was twice Mentioned in Dispatches. He took the German surrender at Lubeck Airfield and on the island of Sylt.

After the War, having sold his business, he was appointed by the Foreign Office as a British Resident in Germany, serving in Rhine-Westphalia until ratification. He was then appointed by the Army to the Joint Services Liaison Organisation, serving in Germany for a total of fourteen years until 1961. Earning commendations from both German and British sources, he was awarded the OBE. On returning to Gattonside, he was immediately elected a County Councillor for

Roxburghshire and served in this capacity for a further fourteen years. He retired, aged eighty-two, when Regional Local Government was introduced. He had served as Convener (Chairman) of the Education Committee and of the General Purpose Committee. He had been a member of several national bodies, such as the Scottish Teachers Salaries Committee and the Executive Council for the Scottish Commonwealth Institute. He was an elder of the Church of Scotland for 63 years and held many senior positions such as Moderator's Elder on the Moderator's annual visits to London. One of his Church memories was assisting Tubby Clayton to construct the original Toc H church in Flanders in the first World War. The 'stained glass' windows were made of coloured cardboard soaked in margarine.

My father was a tall man, six feet three inches in stature. He had the long nose and sympathetic eyes typical of many Border faces. Soft-spoken, he could talk with authority when required. He was undemon-strative and I can never recall being embraced by him, as I was by my French father-in-law. Perhaps this was the only subtle lesson in sex education I received at home or in school. Tactile contacts between men, or the shedding of tears, were to be avoided. Today's shenanigans on the football field after a goal has been scored would have drawn his dis-approval. We had great love and respect for each other.

My mother was the younger daughter of John Wilkie, a baker in Galashiels, who was prosperous enough to indulge his love of horses by running a small farm for them at Pilmuir, near St Abbs Head in Berwickshire. He also rented Hassendean as a holiday home. My uncle continued to farm Pilmuir between the two wars.

My mother's life was devoted to being a good wife, a good mother, a good Christian and a good Scot. She had inherited her father's skill as a baker. She considered it a social gaffe to serve a 'bought' cake for afternoon tea. She read widely and completed crossword puzzles until she died. She had a sweet singing voice and played the piano by ear. I came to know her best in her old age – she lived to the age of ninety-nine years and nine months – after both my father and my wife died. Although working in London, I kept in touch with her by telephone on a daily basis. I also took her a motoring holiday in Scotland each year, her preferred choice. After thirty-four years abroad, I explored my own country. She would say, wryly, that Robert Louis Stevenson had stolen my opportunity to write *Travels with a Donkey*. Until she was in her nineties, she was well known in Melrose, cycling across for her shopping. This involved wheeling the bicycle across the suspension bridge, which was closed in a high wind. On one occasion, having crossed the bridge to go to Melrose, she found it closed on her return. 'I was not going to cycle to the Toll Bridge' (The road bridge a mile upstream), she said, 'so I made sure no-one was looking. I put my bicycle on the other side of the gate. I then hoisted my skirts up and climbed over.' Freedom of movement, after all, is one of our fundamental rights.

At the age of four I went to the village school in Gattonside. The teacher was Jean Thomson, who taught all classes to the age of eight. She was an austere spinster who lived to the age of one hundred. Affectionately known as Auntie Jean by most of the villagers she had taught, she became very deaf in her old age. I was expected to call on her whenever I returned to the village. An aged relative was her companion. I was never sure who was looking after whom.

After this introduction to the educational system, pupils were sent to the Melrose High School, which taught pupils up to the school-leaving age. Gattonside School was lit by kerosene lamps and there was a healthy smell of kerosene from a large drum standing in the entry hall. Teaching was mainly of the three 'R's. The mathematical tables were drummed into us. We had counting frames for arithmetic. Nearly all pupils received a prize of some sort at the end of the year.

Play was important at that age and we battled each other with chestnuts in the autumn and marbles (boules) in the summer. The boy whose turn it was to flick the marble would cry, 'Pers and onnies' – Pairs and choice of any target. The opposing player would cry, 'Nae ups nae clears' to prevent the player raising his marble off the ground or moving it to one side to avoid another 'boule' which was in the way. Cowboys and Indians was somehow converted into Scots and English and there were few volunteers to be on the English side. The winters were harder then. We sledged on the brae behind the school. We also skated, with insecure skates screwed on to existing boots with a spanner.

The school doubled as the village library and during school hours the books were locked in handsome cupboards with copper-wire latticed doors. These somehow conveyed the impression that books were valuable and created a desire to have access to them.

When I left the school, Miss Thomson presented me with a magnifying glass and a copy of *The Heroes* by Charles Kingsley. Coincidentally, I later went on to take both Science and Classics.

We Scots tend to boast of a good Scots Education. I certainly received that at Melrose High School. In English classes we were steeped in Sir Walter Scott and Burns. In School Assembly we sang the Psalms and

Paraphrases and in singing lessons, Scottish Ballads and the songs of Burns. In the History class Bannockburn and Flodden took precedence over Agincourt and the Somme. One was made conscious of the contribution to civilisation of Scots missionaries, explorers, administrators, engineers, doctors and Scottish Regiments. The Greenyards, home of the Melrose Rugby Cub, which gave birth to Seven-a-side Rugby, was adjacent. As pupils we did not need much convincing that we had the ball at our feet. Discipline was strict. Few of us escaped the tawse, a leather strap administered on the hand. According to legend, a small piece cut off the end would act as a talisman and prevent chastisement. It did not provide me with much benefit.

Most of the masters had nicknames. The science teacher was called 'Spinle', the music mistress 'Mary O.T.' and the headmaster 'Hairy Macgreegor'.

> Hairy Macgreegor's a very guid man
> He gans tae the kirk on the Sundays
> And prays tae the Lord tae gie him the strength
> Tae wallop us bairns on the Mondays

'Hairy' earned respect because he gave the tawse properly. He stood at right angles to the offender and administered the 'strap' across the hand. 'Spinle' did not play according to the rules. He faced the pupil, and the 'strap' fell not only on the hand, but up the wrist and the lower arm. But discipline meant discipline in the classroom. Teachers were relaxed about students' factions in the playground. There would be a buzz of excitement because there was going to be a fight at the back gates after school on a particular night. Most of the age group concerned awaited it eagerly. The teachers leaving school would pass through this assembled gathering on the way home with a look of: 'We know what you are up to'. We were careful not to start proceedings until they had left. I had challenged Tommy Richardson to a fight because he had bullied my young brother. This was bare knuckle stuff. By luck rather than by science, I caught him an early blow on the nose. Blood gushed forth. Blood had been spilt and the fight was over. I put an arm round his shoulders and asked if he was all right. We went home. I waited in trepidation the next day, wondering if an irate mother was going to attack me for ruining his shirt.

We spoke two languages, English in the classroom and at home, and the Roxburghshire dialect, closely related to the language of Burns, in the playground. The latter stays in the memory throughout life. The

Scotsman speaking English in Scotland will unconsciously interject traces of dialect into everyday speech, such as 'Aye' for 'Yes', I'll 'no' for I'll 'not', 'bairn' for 'child' or 'Its gey cold today' for 'Its fairly cold today'. For the returning resident a knowledge of the dialect is a precious commodity for reabsorbtion into the community.

Most of the pupils at Melrose High School left after three years' secondary education, while a few passed on to the main High School in the county, Hawick High School. I had an excellent preparation for this at Melrose in Science, Mathematics English Literature, History, Geography and Latin.

In the best Scottish tradition, education in the home was taking place at the same time. My father being an elder of the Kirk, the three Russell boys, clad in kilts, went regularly to church twice on Sundays. The Christian ethic was gently inculcated both in the home and at church. Truth, neighbourliness, duty were virtues to strive for. Hell-fire, however, never seemed to be a rational long-range punishment. Besides the teaching of right and wrong, with the implication that God sees all, there was a faint flavour of 'What would the neighbours say?' All in good Scottish tradition according to the precepts of a line in the Auld 100th Metrical Psalm:

> For it is seemly so to do.

We were a close family and social contacts were mainly with relatives, particularly the Mitchell family in Dingleton, the Hossacks in Galashiels, and families from the congregation of St Aidan's church to which we belonged.

As boys, we had duties in the house which we were expected to perform without reward, although we had modest pocket-money each week. From the age of five I walked every night, sometimes in blizzard conditions and without street lighting, to collect the milk from the old toll-house on the far side of the suspension bridge. We also had to clean the lamp chimneys and keep the lamps filled with kerosene. Bedrooms and bathrooms were unheated. We were not expected to complain about the frosted designs on the windows, nor about clothing lightly starched with frost in the early morning. We were also expected to help in the garden and with shopping.

We looked forward each year to summer, and sometimes Easter, holidays on my uncle's farm at Pilmuir in Berwickshire. At the age of ten, accompanied by brothers aged seven and a half, I cycled the 36 miles to Coldingham. Again the work ethic. 'You can have a good holiday but you must work for it.' According to season we singled turnips and brought in potatoes. In those days we forked sheaves of corn into stooks, turned the hay and forked it into ricks. In the cold nights of the lambing season we stuffed our pockets with hot potatoes filched from the cauldron boiling potatoes and bran for the pigs. We accompanied my uncle round the fields, assisting with lambing if necessary. In the summer evenings we walked across neighbouring farms to Coldingham Sands to swim.

The two farm labourers, Jimmy Logie and William Elliot (Wull), taught us their trade. Wull's proud boast was that he had paid personally for his wife's funeral. 'It took fifteen poun' tae bury auld Nell, an' I nivver had a penny aff the pairish.' He also derided another farm worker for being 'near' or ungenerous: 'He's that mean, gin 'e 'ad a box o' bogles he wadna gie y' a gliff.' (He is so mean that if he had a box of ghosts he wouldn't give you a fright).

The year 1930 saw the three boys standing in a field on the farm. A cow had died. Beside the body was the grave being dug by Wull and Jimmy. The hole was about as deep as Jimmy's height. Wull rested on his spade, pulled out his time-piece from his waistcoat pocket, looked at the time, and carried on digging. A little later he did the same, stopped digging, removed his cap and stood at attention. His weatherbeaten red-brown face was in stark contrast to the white pate normally covered by his cap. 'Whit wey (Why) ye no diggin?' said Jimmy. Said Wull: 'It's the Keeng. Deid. Bein' buried the day'. Jimmy spat. He was thinking. He then said what a countryman would have said on learning of the death of a stranger. 'Was 'e ever married?' His simplicity was almost touching.

Not far from the farm was St Abbs Head. The coast is subject from time to time to dense fog. As well as a lighthouse, there is a fog horn. This had sounded irregularly throughout the whole of Jimmy's life. One day a look of comprehension flooded across his face. 'D'ye ken, Wull, it's a funny thing, Whenever that horn's blawin' its aye foggy.'

As boys we regarded them with something like reverence.

Rugby was our main sport and we played this with teams of indeterminate number in the field in front of the house, with the goals and try lines marked by jackets. Each year the local villages competed at the Greenyards in a seven-a-side competition called the Crighton Cup. Gattonside was badly beaten one year thanks to a youngster called Charlie Drummond. He was later to be capped for Scotland.

But to return to formal education. I had to travel to Hawick each day by train. There was a walk of a mile at each end. At my first day of school we were asked to list the subjects which we wished to take. Perhaps mindful of Charles Kingsley's *Heroes*, I wrote down 'Greek'. Later, when I was in the English class, the door burst open and the Classics master burst in. Where is this boy who wants to learn Greek?' I was his only Greek pupil. He succeeded in coaching me to Higher standard in three years. I had excellent tuition. In English I was introduced to Shakespeare, Lamb and Goldsmith as well as the longer poems, Beowulf, Matthew Arnold's Sohrab and Rustum and the Prelude. In my sixth year the Roxburghshire Education Committee decreed with foresight that both male and female students should undergo one term of domestic science. They foresaw that men in future would have to perform a greater share of domestic duties. Hence we were taught how to sew on buttons, iron and cook. With University entrance in my sights, I studied hard and eventually gained entrance to St Andrews University with Higher Physics, Chemistry, Mathematics, History, English Literature, Latin and Greek. On appearing before the Interview Board for the Bursary Competition, I was surprised to find all members of the Board laughing as I entered the room. 'Tell me, Mr Russell,' said the Chairman, 'Why have you presented yourself in such a bizarre choice of subjects, English Literature, Chemistry and Greek?' I looked at him in astonishment and said, 'They are my best subjects, Sir!'

I enrolled at St Andrews in autumn 1938. War was looming and I enlisted in the Officers Training Corps, to which I gave priority over sport, although I played Rugby, Tennis and Squash. I had enrolled for a Master of Arts degree with the indefinite aim of joining the Colonial Administrative Service. The three subjects in my first year were Greek, Latin and English Literature.

I elected to stay in rooms – a bunk, as it was called – rather than one of the University Halls. This was in 42 South Street, which is now a listed building near the Byre Theatre. From memory, the rooms cost 17/6d per week with 2/6d for Sunday lunch and 2/6d for laundry. Wearing of Scarlet Gowns was compulsory. A vivid memory is the Sunday procession after Chapel when students, lecturers and professors walked along the cliff-top, along the lower level of the pier at St Andrews harbour and back along the higher level.

The summer vacation, spent at home, was overshadowed by the threat of war. On the 3rd September, a Sunday, we heard Chamberlain's speech to the nation saying that we were at war. We set out for the church and at the church door my mother broke down. The reason was abundantly clear a year later when her husband and myself were both in the Army, one twin in the Merchant Navy and the other in the Royal Air Force. During the service the air raid siren wailed. The Minister suspended the service. It was, however, a false alarm.

I returned to University and enlisted, receiving the King's shilling. To my chagrin I was told that I would not be called up for service until my twentieth birthday towards the end of term. University Rules were altered because of the War. I was allowed to take the two Special subjects, in my case Greek and English Literature, normally taken in the third year, together with Philosophy as a General subject. All my spare time went into the Officer's Training Corps, in which I gained Certificate B, qualifying for commissioning after call up. As Corporal T. Russell, I was awarded the Brockie Prize for the best cadet of the year.

Although it was the time of Dunkirk, the War Office wisely decreed that although Certificate B holders would be sent to an Officer Cadet Training Unit (OCTU) for Commissioning, they would serve a period in the ranks first. Hence sixty St Andrews students were told to report to the Queen's Barracks in Perth for enlistment as private soldiers. Ninety regular reservists were called up at the same time for re-training and to teach us soldiering.

My education was about to begin.

CHAPTER TWO

Wartime Service up to Captivity

I REPORTED TO THE Queen's barracks in Perth as a private in the Black Watch in July 1940, about six weeks after Dunkirk. The remainder of a battalion of the regiment which had been evacuated had been posted back to Perth. Accommodation was scarce. Recruits were housed in the dyeworks, emptied of machinery, unheated, stark. We had frequent parades but there were not enough rifles for each man.

My reservist buddy, Tommy Davidson, was from the Gorbals of Glasgow. He greeted me by saying: 'The polis pulled me in for the Clydebank murder but they couldnae pin anythin' on me.' If I had been looking for a minder, I could not have chosen better. Few of his civilian friends could have possessed his intense hatred of the establishment. But a fierce loyalty had developed among them. He brought this to the barrackroom. If a stranger entered without knocking, an army boot flew at his head. Reputedly he distilled Brasso when no other form of alcohol was available. He was a marksman. Noticeably, he was treated with respect by the platoon sergeant. He could outlast any of us on the wallbars in the gym. He could hang with his legs at right angles to his body for long periods. From years of toil, his abdominal muscles rippled under the skin. He took my drill and arms drill in hand by coaching me behind the dyeworks. He polished my boots and bayonet scabbard to mirrored perfection. My guard eventually won the monthly competition for the best guard. I was singled out to be stick orderly (the privilege of standing outside the Commanding Officer's door for a day), as the best recruit on parade. Then Davidson showed the platoon how to celebrate.

We had a magnificent figure of a man as Regimental Sergeant-major. He would strut over the parade ground and, poking me in the stomach with his pace-stick, demand: 'What are the three S's that make a unit?' On receiving no reply he would shout scornfully, 'Sentries, Salutin' and Esprit de corps'. He liked to create the impression that the smallest departure from military perfection would not escape him. One frosty morning, before I had undergone Davidson's instructions in drill, there were almost a score of platoons on the drill square. They were under the individual command of their platoon sergeants. My platoon was marking

Lt Thomas Russell Junior after joining 10th Cameronians.

time. A bellow rang out in the crisp morning air: 'Sergeant Curry. Halt that squad!' We halted on command. The Sergeant Major strode over, and with military correctness, said, 'May I take over, Sergeant?' 'Mark time,' he commanded. 'Rear rank, Halt!' 'Centre rank, Halt!' 'Number one to number five in the front rank, Halt!' Five of us were left wearily pumping our legs up and down. He then pointed at me with his pacestick and said. 'That's 'im, Sergeant Curry. Puttin' 'is feet down wrong.' This had encouraged Davidson to give me special tuition.

We had many exercises by day and by night, route marches and hardening training, range and grenade-throwing practice, gas and bayonet drills and inspections. Then off to Officer Cadet Training Unit (OCTU) at Pwllheli, North Wales.

By this time my father was a Major in the Cameronians (Scottish

Rifles). I was commissioned into the same regiment, and, in spite of the War, had to have references to join. I must have possessed bovine qualities as one letter said that I came from good Border stock. I was posted to the 10th battalion of the Cameronians, then in 15th (Scottish) Division. After serving in the area of Newcastle and Durham, my battalion was allotted a stretch of coast near Walberswick in Suffolk to guard against German landings. It was a dreary part of my service. I was sent on a course for 3-inch mortars. For someone who had studied at University, mastering a thirty-page manual took about forty-eight hours. I gained a 'Distinction' on the course. As this was regarded as creditable for the battalion, I was sent on course after course without having the time to pass on the new skills I had learnt. In rapid succession I took courses in Infantry Rangefinders, Infantry Battlecourse, Two-pounder and Six-pounder Anti-Tank Gunnery, and other specialist subjects.

By early 1943, the 15th (Scottish) Division was reorganised. My battalion was to become a draft-finding unit training up soldiers to replace casualties in fighting formations. I was told that, with my specialist training, I was well cast for this role. At the age of 22, however, this had little appeal. At the time recruits for the Parachute Regiment were being sought. My Company Commander, John Frost, later to achieve fame at Bruneval, Sicily and Arnhem, had already volunteered and I followed his example. I was interviewed by Brigadier Down of the Second Parachute Brigade, who made it clear that joining was a privilege and that recruited officers were on trial.

Although the 10th Cameronians had a static role, our training had been arduous to the extent that I was not unduly challenged by the hardening training course at Hardwick Hall in Derbyshire. This took place prior to undertaking the requisite seven parachute jumps from Ringway, now Manchester Airport, into Tatton Park. Training for the jumps themselves was a tougher prospect.

We were first taught how to fall by emulating our instructors in the gym. Then we jumped from the backs of moving trucks. There was an ingenious merry-go-round where we hung, suspended in parachute harness, rotating individually as the contraption gained speed. The instructor had a release mechanism for each trainee. He chose to release us when he adjudged we were likely to hit the ground most awkwardly. But the 'Fan' was the device which would weed out the faint-hearted. First, the trainee had to scale a vertical fifty-foot ladder and climb on to a wooden platform in the rafters of an aircraft hanger. Many of the planks had been removed, so that there was a good view of the cement floor far

Colonel Thomas Russell Senior OBE, MC.

below. A foam-rubber landing-mat looked the size of a postage stamp. At the edge of the platform, a U-shaped aperture had been cut with vertical metal poles on each side of the jaws of the U. These were about three feet high and connected by a stout metal rod. There was an elongated roller round the rod, similar to a cotton reel with a pencil through the central tube. Wire cable, wound around the roller, was attached to a harness dangling in space at the jaws of the U. The trainee sat down in the aperture, leant forward to grasp the harness, and put it on. At the end of the roller was a small propeller – the fan. As the trainee jumped on the word 'Go', his increasing velocity spun the roller round faster and faster. The propeller bit into the air and acted as a brake. Ingenious engineering of propellers allowed the hapless trainee to descend at different speeds.

The legend was that the first time this device was tried, a pile of foam-rubber landing mats was heaped below the aperture and a member of the Army Physical Training Corps made the first jump. The propeller, however, had been fixed the wrong way around. Thus there was no braking action whatsoever. To the horror of the onlookers he bounced several times on the landing-mats before picking himself up. Reputedly he said, 'I think that it still needs some adjustment.'

There were as many refusals to submit to this experience as to make the first parachute jump. We were told that vertigo is only experienced when there is a vertical connection between the individual and the ground. Be that as it may, the barrage balloon with basket beneath, from which we were to make our first two jumps, took a long time in gaining six-hundred feet. The basket has a circular hole in the bottom and four parachutists sit around the hole, legs along the side.

A nonchalant instructor straddles the hole as the balloon ascends. He fastens the static lines to a metal bar over the hole. The other end of the static line is fixed to the bag containing the parachute worn on the jumper's back. On jumping, he falls first to the end of the static line where the bag is fastened to the apex of the folded parachute. The falling parachutist pulls out the liftwebs of the parachute attached at the shoulders to his parachute harness. The fall continues. The parachute cords, fastened at one end to the perimeter of the parachute and at the other to the lift webs, snake out from loops in the bag holding them loosely in position. When the parachute cords are at full length, the folded parachute canopy then snakes out until the tie connecting the apex to the bag snaps. The parachutist floats free. The bag connected to the static line remains behind. On an aircraft jump, it is whipped up underneath the plane by the slipstream, to be hauled in later, before the aircraft lands.

I was so relieved that the canopy had opened on my first jump that I started singing on the way down, to be sternly rebuked by the instructor. 'Keep your feet and knees together, Number one!' Immediately on hitting the ground, one collected another parachute. After a mug of tea came the second jump, said to create more apprehension than the first. But there was a psychological element in training in that we were trained in 'sticks', which were competitive. No individual wanted to let down his team-mates.

As we were to discover later, the balloon jumps were less agreeable than jumping from an aircraft. From a balloon, one initially dropped like a stone. From an aircraft the jumper seemed to slide down a chute in the slipstream. The canopy appeared to develop quicker. Initially we jumped from Whitleys, which, like the balloon basket, had a hole in the floor. This had a claustrophobic feeling which made me keen to get out! The fuselage was very constricted, with a smell of 'dope' from the interior walls. We sat in one row on the floor, seven each side of the hole. Our bottoms were on the floor: helmets touched the ceiling: feet touching one wall and backs against the other. There were no windows. It was dark so that we could see the warning red and green-for-'Go' lights. There was an unmilitary shuffling motion sideways along the floor until it was the turn to jump. We had to grasp two handles, swing feet-first into the hole, about three feet deep, and jump, all in one clean motion. At the bottom of the hole, nearest the nose, was a curved shield protruding below the bottom of the aircraft. This was designed to protect the jumper from the slipstream. If, however, he did not exit properly, he was likely to hit the side of the hole with his head. He would be thrown back violently in the opposite direction hitting either head or neck on the edge of the shield. Sometimes blood was drawn. This was known as 'Ringing the bell'. The change when we parachuted in North Africa from Dakota aircraft, and exited through a door in the side, was very popular. It was natural to walk through a door even at 1300 feet. For most of us exhilaration replaced the apprehension of sitting in the basket of a balloon.

On qualification as a Parachute Regimental Officer, I joined the 5th (Scottish) Parachute Battalion in the 2nd Parachute Brigade in the 1st Airborne Division.

In April 1943 we embarked for North Africa, landing at Oran, Algeria We were briefed before landing by an ex-warrant officer in the Regular

Army, who had been commissioned and promoted to captain after the outbreak of war. He had served in foreign parts before and spoke with experience. As the French fleet had been attacked by the British Fleet at Mers El Kebir at Oran, and the fortifications ashore had been shelled, we could not expect to be popular with the French population. In addition foreigners were not to be trusted. We could expect to be dealing with an untrustworthy lot who would 'even steal the sugar out of your tea'. We got ashore in early evening and embussed on large American lorries driven in the main by jovial Afro-American drivers. They drove inland like demons. I was in the cab with the driver, who took the corners at speed and said with white teeth flashing, 'My mammy done say I die in a motor accident'. Dawn broke. We were travelling through a land bathed in sunshine, with rows and rows of vines traversing the red soil. Gleaming white farm buildings and small muslim temples – Marabus, I think they were called – dotted the landscape. Sometimes we passed through densely-populated villages. Houses were small and in poor repair. Arabs, clad in long bournous and seated on donkeys or camels, paid little attention to traffic. Eventually we arrived at Tisi, on a dry barren plain, where a tented camp had been prepared for us. 'The middle of nowhere', it could have been called. But between it and Mascara, the nearest town, was a traditional oasis. With plenty of water, date palms and greenery, it presented a stark contrast to the surrounding terra-cotta landscape. Sidi Bel Abbes, the headquarters of the French Foreign Legion, was not far distant.

Although we were on standby for the endgame of the North African campaign, we were not, in the end, required. Before crossing into Tunisia, near Sousse, I met my wife-to-be, the daughter of a fourth-generation French settler. She later claimed to be my only piece of loot from the War. Her father had an open invitation for Scottish officers to visit his house and I used to walk about ten kilometres to Mascara to take up the invitation. The house, gleaming white in the sunlight, had walls about four feet thick, and in the afternoons the shutters were drawn to keep out the sunlight. This was before the days of air-conditioning. The house was not only cool, but had an air of tranquillity and distance from war. When the move to Tunisia was planned, contacts with the local population were discouraged. I had to invent the recovery of a watch put in for repair at Mascara to say an unspoken goodbye. I had to feign lack of knowledge when my father-in-law-to-be, who had organised the rail transport for the Brigade's heavy baggage, said: 'I know that you are leaving for Tunisia and have come to say goodbye'.

In Tunisia we carried out both day and night parachute drops, one at brigade strength, at that time a novelty.

> Parachute jumps by the pale white moonlight
> Standing like a god on the edge of space:
> Leaping like Mercury from Mount Olympus
> With night air cool on a pulsing face.

We were on the American supply line and were dropped from American Dakota or DC3 aircraft. We soon learnt that we were training for the invasion of Sicily. To our chagrin, after we had been briefed to drop near the port of Augusta for operation 'Glutton' and had waited at the airport for orders to emplane, the operation was postponed for twenty-four hours. It was then cancelled. We recommenced training with Italy as the next objective. I was in charge of the Mortar Platoon in Headquarters Company. We carried out live firing with ample supplies of ammunition to sharpen our performance. By indenting for spare parts over a period, we had assembled two extra mortars and were able to bring six instead of four into action if need arose.

On the ninth of September 1943, the battalion embarked on the cruiser H.M.S. *Dido* for Italy. The Welsh Battalion of the Parachute Regiment was on H.M.S. *Abdiel*. The 4th Battalion was on H.M.S. *Ajax*. The flotilla was accompanied by the battleships H.M.S. *Howe* and *King George V*. At sea we were told that we would disembark at Taranto. Later news was that the Italians had declared an Armistice, which would complicate our landing. As we neared Taranto, the Italian Grand Fleet put to sea. 'Battle stations' was ordered and battle ensigns hoisted. It is not often that 'pongos', as soldiers were called by the Navy, were going to have the opportunity to witness a naval battle. Gun turrets were rotated to face the direction of the enemy. Damage parties rushed towards their stations and we to the rails, to have a grandstand view of the battle. We were immediately escorted below, as we should have been blown off the decks if any of the heavy calibre guns had fired a salvo.

Fortunately for us, but to our disappointment, the Italian Fleet surrendered. It was escorted into Malta by the two battleships.

We scrambled down nets into small craft in Taranto Harbour and went ashore. As we landed, there was a massive explosion. The Germans, before leaving after the Armistice, had left acoustic mines in Taranto harbour. H.M.S. *Abdiel* was severely damaged, with many deaths and casualties in the Welsh Battalion. Our landing, however, was unopposed. We marched inland, eerily passing roadblocks manned by fully armed

Italians, whom we simply bypassed. The larger Italian towns were carrying on as best they could, but some, like Foggia, which we reached later, showed evidence of substantial bombing damage. Many villages were relatively unscathed, the town halls still bearing bronze Fascist emblems. At any formal function to welcome us, or to celebrate our entry into the town, half a dozen Italian Admirals in full uniform tended to appear, even in mountain country. Our intelligence section had the bright idea of telephoning various towns and asking if there were any Germans there. We were able to make rapid progress north to San Georgio and Palagano on foot and to Aquaviva by train. By the end of September we had advanced to Barletta and had a brief stay in Foggia before reaching Manfredonia. By this time the rest of the 1st Airborne Division had been returned to England to train for D-Day. We had become the Second Independent Parachute Brigade under Brigadier Down. While in Manfredonia, we carried out an elaborate feint by faking a landing north of the German lines at Termoli, embarking on landing craft and heading north into the Adriatic. The Germans were also using telephone lines and other forms of intelligence. They were expected to move troops to combat the landing. On coming opposite Termoli, we returned to port.

By December we were north of the River Sangro and in position south of Perano. This was a tough period for the battalion, with patrols probing German positions on the next ridge. There was gradual forward movement, with heavy shelling on both sides. Our battalion, with a complement of less than six hundred men, was about one hundred and fifty below strength. This compared with nearly a thousand in a regular infantry battalion. Reduced numbers increased the frequency of patrol work. Patrolling at night and endeavouring to sleep in extreme winter conditions inevitably created fatigue. This would have affected the morale of a less dedicated unit. But soldiers were on edge. Two patrols were fired upon by our own sentries as they returned to our lines.

During shelling of a village street, I sprinted into a house and threw myself down on the floor of the second storey. As I lay there, a frightened dog dashed up the stairs and stretched itself out beside me. When the shelling stopped, it resumed its walk through the village. Shelling was worse than aerial bombardment. Returning up the line after hospitalisation in Bari for infective hepatitis, which was common at the time, I was unable to reach the forward units before dark. I spent the night with B-echelon, the heavy trucks which bring forward ammunition and food. But the Germans had their position marked and we came under very heavy and accurate shelling during the night. I was scared and that worried me. It occurred to me that I had then only myself to think about. Responsibility for others shielded one to some extent from personal concerns. A few nights later we brought down mortar fire by arrangement, when a patrol got into difficulty. It successfully extricated itself as a result.

On the 4th February 1944, an artillery officer, myself and my platoon sergeant, Sergeant Grant, went forward with a night patrol to a ridge in front of our positions, ready to start ranging at dawn. There were seventeen in the party. We occupied a house which was being used by the Germans as an observation post by day. It was a dark night. The patrol commander placed two men with a Bren gun to guard the path leading to the house. Shortly afterwards two men approached who looked in the dark like parachutists but who gave a password in German. The Bren opened fire, dropping one of them. The other escaped, and shortly afterwards most of a German company attacked the house. They opened heavy fire with tripod-mounted machine guns. Despite return fire, some of them got close enough to fire rifle-grenades through the windows. Sergeant Grant and I climbed a ladder to the loft, but the only aperture was the one used by the Germans as an observation post facing our lines. As the firefight was intensifying and grenades were exploding beneath us, we decided to join the members of the patrol below on the first storey. As we approached the trapdoor, someone shouted: 'The bastards are in the roof'. We looked down into the muzzle flashes of a sten gun before a string of profanities left no doubt as to our identity.

At the moment we moved from the bottom of the ladder, a grenade exploded which struck me lightly on the buttock and, as I learnt afterwards, severely wounded Sergeant Grant in the throat. Only seconds later a machine gun bullet struck me at the top of the left thigh, breaking the femur and bringing me down among the debris on the floor. The muscle went into spasm and I passed out from pain and loss of blood. Fortunately the bullet missed the femoral artery. I came to in silence, followed by a peculiar wailing sound as someone came up the stairs. It was a German soldier with a hand-operated dynamo torch. He shouted. Two parachutists appeared to help me down the stairs, with my broken leg bouncing down the steps. They told me that the house had been overrun as ammunition, including grenades, diminished and that the occupants were prisoners. Of seventeen in the patrol, three, including Sergeant Grant, were killed and seven wounded, including two of the three officers. The Germans did not waste time in returning to their lines, avoiding roads and paths and going across country. I was carried on a makeshift stretcher, a blanket tied between two poles, and was dropped several times as it was dark and muddy. Eventually we arrived at the German battalion headquarters, where the Commanding Officer said in English that we had put up a good fight but that someone had to win. He looked down at me and said: 'You are in a bad way and are going straight to hospital. I have excused you interrogation.' I was operated on by a German surgeon in a field hospital where five other operations were in progress in the same theatre. Obviously we were not doing too badly. When I recovered, a few German soldiers recuperating from wounds offered me cigarettes and schnapps. Potter, the Artillery Officer, was also in the hospital. We were taken north to a *krankensammelstelle*, a collecting place for casualties. There we joined an ambulance train which took us through Parma, the Brenner Pass and Munich to a prisoner-of-war hospital at Königswartha, near Dresden.

CHAPTER THREE

Prisoner of War Experiences and Demobilisation

THE HOSPITAL AT Königswartha was run by an Edinburgh doctor with an interest in surgery. He too was a prisoner. He was assisted by a French anaesthetist and a Middle-Eastern radiographer. Many casualties from the Anzio beachhead owe their lives to his skill. While there, I was given a postcard to be sent to my next of kin. It had several printed pieces of information, such as being a prisoner of war, being severely/lightly wounded, being well cared for. One could delete what was inappropriate, but was only allowed to sign and address the card. I wanted to say that I had been shot in the leg. I addressed my mother as 'Mrs L' Russell and signed it 'E.G.' Russell. On receiving this, my mother telephoned her brother to say that I was alive – I had been reported missing until then – a prisoner of war, and had been wounded. She went on to say 'But the poor boy must have been shot in the head. He doesn't even know his own name!' Fortunately the mystery was explained.

A fellow patient at Königswartha was Vic Moore, a Canadian, who had about three inches of shinbone shattered by a mortar bomb. We were both placed in a narrow room with beds back to back. Hence we could not see each other when we conversed. He was a linguist and set himself the task of teaching me French and German. He was later to be repatriated because of his wounds, joined the Canadian Foreign Service, and was to attain the rank of High Commissioner. When we said goodbye in Germany, neither of us expected to see the other again. But we were to meet in Cambridge after the War, and in Germany when he was posted to Bonn. I had married and, together with my wife, we made a joint visit to Berlin. Some years later, when he too had married, my wife and I stayed with him and his wife in Karachi on our way home to England on leave.

Vic published poetry in Canada and persuaded me that this might be good therapy in prisoner-of-war conditions. After the War, in 1947, we both submitted poems for the Poetry Society's Greenwood Competition and I was gratified to be awarded second prize for a poem entitled 'The Well', which I reproduce below:

The Well
by
Thomas Russell

It is quiet down here.
With solitary baleful eye
I peer
Into my slimy telescope
Up to the distant disc of sky.
Long, long it is since spinning rope
And bucket clashed from wall to wall
Reverberating hollowly.
I brood on quietness and death
Where silence, like a muted breath,
Freezes the starlings' colloquy,
The plaintive curlew's lonely call.

A child came here to play.
I saw him looking down at me
Today.
He spoke his name. With bell-like tone
I sang it back. Till suddenly
He laughed, and dropped a small round stone
Which sifted to my rocky floor.
Kaleidoscopically bright
The plate of sky-space spun around
In ecstasies of light and sound,
In phantasies of sound and light,
Until the ripples rolled no more,

And when my eye was clear
I stared at him, as if to say,
Come here,
Where it is secret, dark and cold.
For every pleasure man must pay,
The debt is new, the stipend old.
Nor did I call to him in vain.
With limbs close-pinioned down he fell
Precipitous as stooping hawk,
As straight as withe or lily stalk –
Within the fastness of the well
It is quiet down here again.

The following was the critique by William Kean Seymour:

My choice for Second Place is *The Well*, an irregular rhymed poem of thirty-six lines by Thomas Russell, which has for me – and I think it will have for our readers – the appeal of something magical and inexplicably haunting. In its economy of words, in its evocation of cool shadowed beauty encompassing chill horror, its pictorial precision and reticent statement of swift tragedy, it appears to me to be a perfect short poem and one which will find its way into the anthologies.

But to return to the narrative. After about two months, when I had my plaster cast removed, I had about three centimetres shortening of the left leg. I was escorted across Germany to Stalag IV A at Lamsdorf in the vicinity of Breslau. It was a huge camp with nearly all nationalities hostile to Germany in separate compounds. We received Red Cross parcels once a week. The camp boasted a number of orchestras of different sizes, including a pipe band. The musical instruments were supplied by the Red Cross.

I had been there for about three months when the Germans realised that four of us were officers. We should not have been sent there. There followed a fascinating journey across wartime Germany by train to Oflag VA in Weinsberg near Heilbron am Neckar. We were escorted by a Feldwebel, (a Warrant Officer) and two privates. We had to change trains late at night at Stuttgart, which was still smoking from an allied air raid. On leaving the train, we were disconcerted to see two platoons of SS marching along the platform. They sensed our unease and grinned as they passed us. The Feldwebel took us into a Red Cross canteen full of German soldiers. He arranged for us to stay the night and took us to a table for the meal that was on offer. He was confronted by a German of his own rank who shouted that this canteen was for German soldiers. Our Feldwebel calmly retorted that the Red Cross was international and that he was responsible for us. We eventually reached Oflag VA.

The following is an extract from the diary I kept at the time:

28 July 1944 Arrived Weinsberg
Life at Weinsberg first few weeks
    School. Church. Bank. Library. Carpenter's shop.
    Mess. Barber's. Cobbler. Tailor. Gym. Bar.
    Committees covering every subject under the sun.
    Jockey Club and their 'horses'. Gambling. Bets 1000 marks.
    £66 in an afternoon.
Meals
    (Red Cross) Parcel issue every Tuesday

1/5 of a German loaf per day.
Brew up at 0800 and 1100
Communal meal at 1230 (Two sittings)
Brew up at 1430
Communal meal at 1730 (later discontinued)
Brew at night
Big meal on Sundays

Entertainments

School sessions
Theatre: practically continuous shows
Games. Softball the main game. Games run on club system
Very keen. Very systematic. Batting, pitching and fielding averages available
for reference
Exhibition of Arts and Crafts
Sketch clubs
Parole walks

News

1. German newspapers. Censored if necessary.
2. Newsletter service collated from letters from home
3. New arrivals
4. Translated German communiques and broadcasts in English at 1430
5. Usual sources (Explanatory note: only one clandestine radio was used at any time to listen to BBC. One person per bungalow rendezvoused at a different bungalow each night and the news was read out in the shower room with all taps and showers turned on. This was repeated in each bungalow with one person per room attending.)

Restrictions

1. Shooting-towers, Double barbed wire fences with approach wires. Double gates.
2. Two roll-calls – was three. About 0800 and at dusk
3. Locked in bungalow after evening roll-call. Patrols with dogs through the night. Bars on windows. Searchlights at night.
4. Anti-tunnelling (sand-filled) ditch round perimeter.
5. Exterior patrols
6. Searches for illicit articles
7. Stools and methods of finding out what we are doing.

Until the opening of the Second Front, we enjoyed one food parcel per week. These grew infrequent, however, and finally ceased. We ate in messes of two in rooms holding about twelve prisoners sleeping on two-tier bunks. My mess-mate was Bill Cormack, of the Argylls, with whom I had swum at Coldingham Sands pre-war. The communal meal each day was eaten in a large refectory. This might consist of two or three small potatoes, boiled dried cabbage and meat twice a week. This was tolerable while we had Red Cross parcels. When we brewed up tea, we preferred Red Cross supplies, even if used several times. The German variety was herbal. Following the opening of the second front and the massacre of Stalag Luft 3 prisoners, the word went round that escapees would only embarrass advancing forces. They had to be fed, interrogated and repatriated. They would arrive in England too late to be recycled and retrained for further active duty. We refused to believe this but the rumour may have been authentic.

With time on my hands, and books available through the Camp library and the Red Cross, I continued my studies in English Literature. My diary records about fifty titles of the English and American classics. Some colleagues passed accounting and law examinations invigilated in the camp.

My mother was helping to pack Red Cross parcels in one of the depots which were to be found throughout the United Kingdom. The Scottish Borders depot was at Hawick. Sometimes we received a parcel with the Hawick stamp. Unpacking his parcel, a POW found a wedding ring in the shavings separating the tins, noted the packing depot, and handed the ring to the next Red Cross visiting team. A grateful acknowledgement of its safe return was eventually received.

We were allowed to go for exercise on parole walks outside the wire accompanied by two German guards. The parole was only valid for the time of the walk. We could do nothing, however, which might assist a future escape. We were on the edge of legality, purloining apples from orchards and potatoes and root crops from farms through which we passed. This was often with the connivance of German farmers. One day there was a camp notice suspending parole walks for a fortnight. 'A hundred kilos of mixed fruit and vegetables' had been confiscated when we returned to camp.

We were within the area in which flares were dropped for a massive night air raid on Heilbron on the 4th December 1944, but few bombs dropped near us. The guards, many of them in their seventies, had to stay at post while their families were obviously in mortal danger.

The pace of advance by Allied troops after D-Day was disappointingly slow for us, but by April 1945 it was clear that the end was coming. We were aware that a train was being assembled near the camp. My diary records:

> 31/3/45 Train arrived in station. Seems certain that we move tonight. Sky
> still pretty overcast but looks like clearing. Praying for aircraft. Our forces

very near and coming down the Neckar valley. Heidelberg fallen. Planes started coming over in the afternoon apparently taking no notice. But at four o'clock, accompanied by the cheers of 1000 hysterical officers, train was divebombed by five Mohawks. Unfortunately it is still serviceable. Germans in complete state of flap. Officers drunk and all the guards want to be captured. Both Germans and British doing everything to delay the move. (One ploy was to insist that all the stage props for the drama clubs were taken with us.) Promised no move tonight.

But at eight o'clock it is fixed and we march in truckloads to the station. Very efficiently guarded to station by Volksturm and Wehrmacht. Dogs as well. Accommodation 30 officers and 8 guards to a cattle truck. Three benches. Rations for journey one loaf and 1/3 Limburger cheese (Factory in the area and no transport to take it away.) Mess rations one half parcel and half tin bully beef. Escaping. An official ban until we detrain at Einstatt in case Germans lock the doors. Bill Cormack and I register in case ban is lifted before Einsatt. Train moves by about midnight.

On the 5th April We duly arrived at Moosburg, where we had to have showers before being allowed into filthy quarters. It was a very large camp which had not been designed for the numbers being crammed into it. My diary continues:

5/4/45 Conditions 260 to a bungalow of which there were four with two large rooms holding 130 each. In the middle is a washroom with one tap for 130, off at certain times each day. Four lights in each half. Nearest to me is 24 feet away: a 40 watt bulb. Sleep in blocks of twelve bunks: three tiers up next to Bill Cormack. Much too dark to read by day or night. Latrines are of the squatter variety, emptied by a 'honey-wagon' daily if we are lucky. No clean straw for palliasses, which are flea- and in some cases louse-ridden. In very high spirits on arrival, although some are very depressed and some very angry like Padre Jamieson.

By 11th April rumours were spreading that officer prisoners were to be moved further south to Bertesgaden and packed into the courtyards to prevent Allied bombing. Bill Cormack and I decided to make a 'hide' under the floor and spray the camouflaged lid with pepper to keep dogs from getting too curious. My diary records:

11/4/45 Sawed a trapdoor under my bunk, and together with Bill Cormack started a slit-trench 4ft x 1½ ft x 4ft to be roofed and camouflaged. Took four afternoons. Carrying away and camouflaging spoil was difficult as distance between ground and floor was only a foot maximum. Began saving food to accumulate about three weeks rations. Bought hammer and saw from American GI for eight cigarettes.

The camouflage was a tray of earth of the same colour as the ground with ventilation provided by a pipe protruding through the lid into a rusty can lying on the surface.

Fortunately this was not required. Fighting was reported at Augsburg, 24 miles distant. The Germans knew it was a matter of time. We negotiated with the guards to obtain our individual prisoner-of-war documents. An American relief column reached us at the end of April. We swarmed outside, looted the German ration stores and waited for the American supplies to come in. And waited. In number we represented the equivalent of about ten divisions on their supply line. On day three of our relief we had a spoof demonstration with prisoners marching about with placards: 'Bring back the Germans'. Meanwhile the American Engineers were lengthening a fighter airstrip nearby. When the evacuation began, the Dakota aircraft were arriving like a flock of starlings. After waiting at the airfield to emplane, we realised that we should not get away until the following day. We were given the choice of returning to camp or sleeping rough at the airfield. We elected to stay and Bill Cormack and I rigged a bivouac under a scarlet Hudson Bay blanket left to me by Vic Moore. As 'werewolves', teenagers recruited by the Germans at the end of the War, were taking pot shots at the airfield during the night, we wished that our camouflage had been more discreet. We took off for Brussels in the morning. On arrival we had our clothes confiscated while we went into showers smelling strongly of carbolic. We then entered a clothing store where we were issued with complete new uniforms. Lastly a small squad seized us and thrust tubes up our sleeves and trouser legs before releasing a cloud of DDT powder under pressure. The following day we flew back to England in Lancasters to the south of the country and I heard Churchill's speech announcing the end of the War in Europe over the intercom.

And what happened when we reached England? Our new clothes were removed and we went through exactly the same routine as in Brussels. When we emerged like bakers after the DDT treatment, there was a smiling WVS lady standing with a mug of tea saying, 'Welcome home'. The reception arrangements were extremely efficient, however. We were on our way home with railway warrants in our hands within twenty-four hours.

I reported back to Hardwick Hall, where I commanded Parachute Training Company, although I was personally unfit for parachuting, with a short leg. I had the rank of Captain. I briefly took over the job of adjutant of No 1 Parachute Regiment ITC until September 1946. I revisited St Andrews, having decided to apply for the Colonial Administrative Service.

In the belief that a second degree would enhance my chances of acceptance, I made tentative approaches to return. I also took and passed the written examination for the Home Civil Service. However an active campaign for the different branches of the Colonial Service was taking place and I was accepted for the Administrative Service. My first appointment was to the Western Pacific High Commission, which then comprised the British Solomon Islands Protectorate, Gilbert and Ellice Islands Colony, the New Hebrides Condominium, Tonga and Pitcairn. My first posting was to be to the Solomon Islands but several of us were nominated to be the guinea-pigs for the first Devonshire Course for Colonial Administrators. Half of us were to go to Cambridge and half to Oxford for an academic year. This was to be followed by a term at London University to study regional anthropology and the language of our individual territories.

I went to Cambridge and matriculated at Peterhouse. Post-war Cambridge was surprising both for the students and the authorities. There were undergraduates, who had been too young for war service, and had won the few places then available for normal entry, These were rubbing shoulders with demobilised ex-service students who were older. They had not much time for undergraduate frivolities. The authorities were surprised by the dedication and the determination of most ex-service students to put time at University to best scholastic advantage. Yet there was little effort to adapt University rules to cater for a predominantly different student component. Students had to be back in college by a certain time each night, for example. Graduates of other universities were still undergraduates as far as Cambridge was concerned. The colleges continued to be subject to wartime rationing. Peterhouse, which had access to farms and supplies of game, was reputed to have one of the best cuisines in Cambridge. It still enjoys this reputation.

The Colonial course was specially designed. As most of us would be magistrates, Law was the main subject. We also had History of the Colonies, Colonial Geography, Tropical Medicine and Diseases, Accounting, Surveying, Anthropology. After my first week, I felt that there was nothing, except Law, into which I could get my teeth. I discovered that although a Diploma in Anthropology was normally a two-year course, the examination could be taken in one year. I enrolled, and had a hard year of study, which I enjoyed. I was awarded the Diploma as well as passing the Administrative Service requirements.

We had a term at the School of Oriental and African studies in London, although no-one then knew any of the Solomon Island languages to teach us. But if we were going to the Pacific, it might be useful to know something about boats. I was thus sent for a course in diesel engines in Manchester. All I remember was that it spanned Gilbert and Sullivan week. I eventually received, after tuition and examination, a Certificate of Competence in Coastal Navigation. I had never been to sea. I did, however, use the time to study the anthropology of the Solomons under Professor Firth. This was of great subsequent benefit.

In the Christmas period of 1947 I paid a visit to Gelsenkirchen in the Ruhr to say goodbye to my parents, who were resident there. There were to be many more such visits to Germany in subsequent leaves, as they did not leave until 1961

On return from Germany I packed up for my new career.

CHAPTER FOUR

Colonial Service
The Western Solomons

AIR TRAVEL WAS in its infancy in 1948. My journey to the Solomons was by boat: by small cargo-ship with twelve passengers via Curaçao, Jamaica and the Panama Canal to Auckland, New Zealand; by M.V. *Matua*, a small passenger-ship, from Auckland to Suva in Fiji and finally by very small cargo vessel, the M.V. *Tamatea* to Honiara, the capital of the British Solomon Islands Protectorate. I left England on the 24th January, 1948 and arrived on the 24th May. I spent a fortnight on a farm in Rotorua in New Zealand, waiting for the next ship to Suva. I assumed duty for six weeks at the Headquarters of the Western Pacific High Commission in Fiji until the M.V. *Tamatea* was due to sail. Peter Cameron, another administrator, was a fellow passenger.

Peter had also served in the Parachute Regiment during the war. He had a shock of black hair to hide the scar of a wound in the head. We shared a cabin with most of the floor-space filled by boxes of whisky consigned to Honiara. On one of these, next to his bunk, was an enamelled basin in case he was seasick. On another was a glass of water with a neat row of four pills. When I asked what these were, he said: 'This one stops me from getting scurvy. This one stops me from getting seasick. This one stops me from getting malaria. And this one stops me from going mad'.

There was little doubt that the captain's wife, in her late sixties, was the navigator. She had the aid of a New Hebridean at the masthead when she thought that we were nearing land. He had the features of one of the stone heads from Easter Island, silhouetted against the sky. The Captain however, on whom we stood guard over the cases of whisky, occasionally emerged from his cabin. Impressively, he purported to take a sight with a battered sextant, looked at his chronometer, an ancient alarm clock, and retired again to bed. On sighting land the lookout shouted dramatically and pointed in its direction. We had arrived. There was a small crowd waiting on the old American forces' jetty at Kukum. We thought at first that it had assembled to welcome us. It was to make sure, however, that basic commodities like sugar, rice, tinned food – and whisky – were aboard.

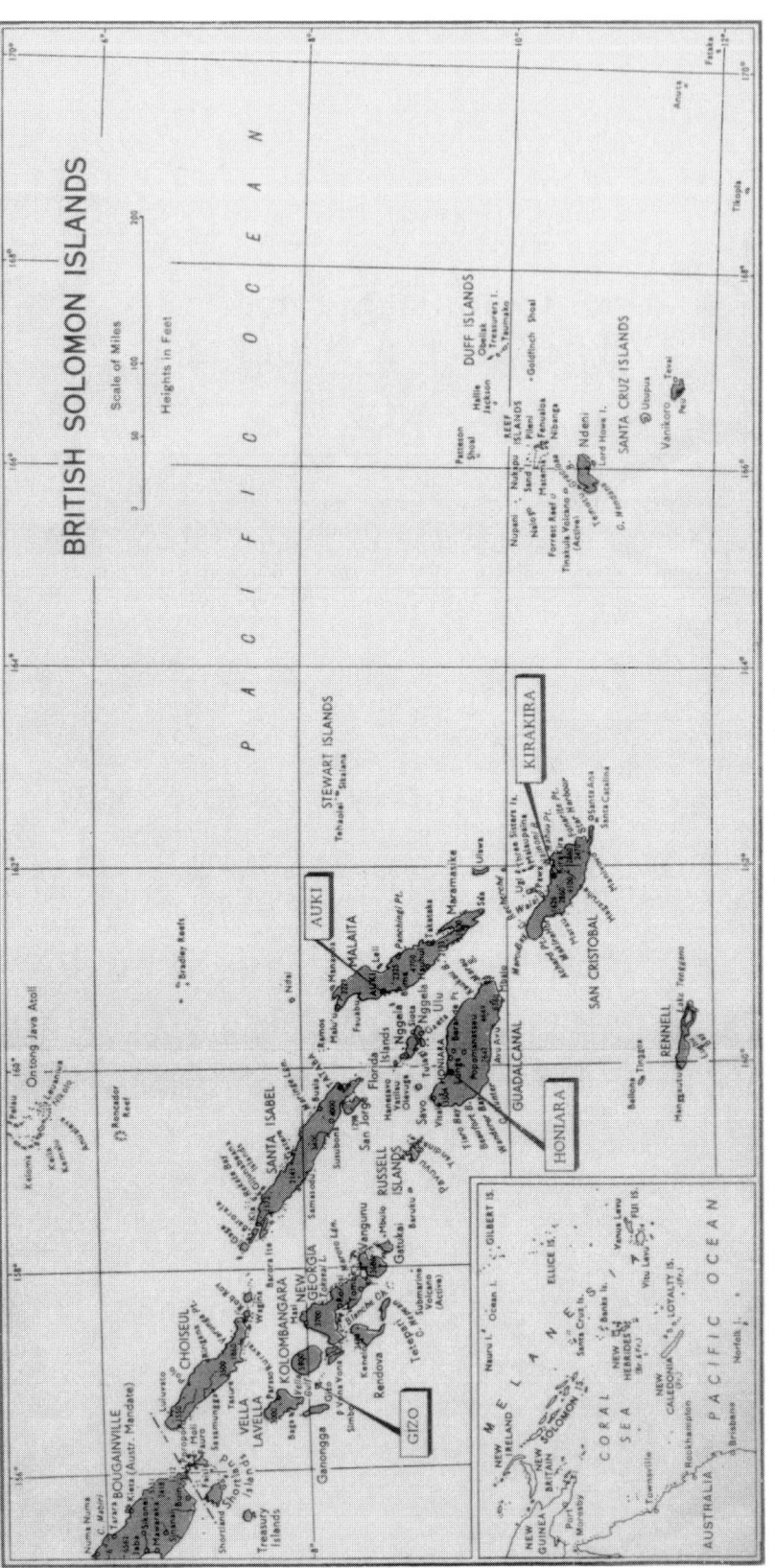

Map of the Solomon Islands.

The Solomon Islands, colloquially called 'the Solomons', are a large archipelago of islands lying between Papua New Guinea and the New Hebrides (now renamed Vanuatu.). They cover an area similar to that occupied by the West Indies from the southern end of Trinidad to the southern end of Jamaica. They stretch in a south-easterly direction for more than a thousand miles. Large islands or groups of islands are each surrounded by about four hundred miles of coastline. The largest is Guadalcanal. In 1948 the most populous, with a population of about 60,000, was Malaita. Administratively, the Solomons were divided into four Districts, each under a District Commissioner responsible to a Resident Commissioner in Honiara. A Secretariat served the Resident Commissioner and the usual Departments such as Health, Education, Police, Public Works, and Forestry. The Resident Commissioner had then an Advisory Council of members nominated from the public service, the missions and the business community.

Geographically the islands form a double chain south-east of the Shortlands and Choiseul. Vella Lavella, the New Georgia group, the Russell Islands and Guadalcanal lie to the west; Santa Ysabel and Malaita to the east. At the other end is the island of San Cristoval. The sound dividing the western and eastern islands is known as the Slot. This was the scene of several naval battles in World War II. Several hundred miles out from the main chain are a number of outliers: Lord Howe or Ontong Java, Sikaiana or Stewart Island, Tikopia, Anuda, Rennell and Bellona. The residents there are Solomon islanders of Polynesian ancestry. They are believed to have been descended from the crews of canoes forming part of the Maori immigration to New Zealand. Raymond Firth, my Professor of Anthropology in London, had made a study of Tikopia and was able to make himself understood in Maori when he first arrived. Far out towards the New Hebrides lies the Santa Cruz group, due east of San Cristoval. The islands of Rennell and Bellona are about a hundred miles south of Guadalcanal.

Before the war the Solomons had been a colonial backwater. Along with other Pacific islands, they had been brought under British administration in 1893 for their protection. They had suffered from illicit recruitment to work on the sugar plantations in Queensland and from distribution of arms and liquor to further the labour trade. Inter-island fighting and headhunting were still rife.

With thousands of miles of coastline, and with a large proportion of the population living in mountainous, heavily wooded, terrain, pacification of the islands was difficult. In 1927 the District Commissioner of

Malaita, whose name was Bell, and his District Officer were murdered while collecting a small headtax which had been imposed. This followed a period in which Bell, travelling in a rowing boat, had endeavoured to collect rifles and shotguns which were compromising public order. The island of Choiseul was not fully brought under administration until 1937. On some islands the missions preceded government officials. Remaining there for extended periods, they became proficient in local languages, while officials seldom remained long in one place. Consequently missionaries often had more influence than district administration staff. Tax collection, law enforcement, collection of weapons were seen in negative terms. The head of the Methodist Mission in Western District was an austere man of strong character called Goldie. The inhabitants of the District were said to place Goldie, God and Government in descending order of importance. There were very limited financial resources before the War to improve what infrastructure existed. Money from the United Kingdom was limited to supporting a very basic administration. It was only after the War that Development Funds were recognised as essential.

War in the Pacific had a profound effect on the Protectorate. The Administration was evacuated in advance of the Japanese arrival. A number of administrators were recruited as coastwatchers under Australian command. Later in the conflict a few served in the Solomon Islands Defence Force or Labour Corps. But administration ceased. Where the islanders had seen Europeans in tens and hundreds, suddenly there were thousands of Japanese and Americans. Great naval and air battles were taking place in their homeland. Masses of material, bulldozers, and trucks opened their eyes to what was available in the outside world. One of the District Headquarters, Gizo, in the Western Solomons, had been destroyed by the Japanese. Laulasi, an offshore island in Malaita, had been bombed in error by the Americans. Tulagi, the previous capital on the island of Ngela, had been destroyed. The American base on Guadalcanal, Honiara, was well equipped with roads, an airfield, a port, a hospital and a plethora of adaptable buildings. This was taken over by the returning British administration as the new capital. The port was later replaced and the airfield brought up to civilian aeronautical standards.

Fortunately the War had instilled a new realisation in Britain as to what was needed in its dependencies, whether for reconstruction or development. The Colonial Development and Welfare Act after the War released funds hitherto unavailable. Even by 1948, ships had been purchased in greater numbers to augment the small pre-war fleet. Ships were essential to allow government officers to get about. As some of the larger pre-war enterprises were reluctant to return to the Protectorate, the Government had set up a Trade Scheme to sell retail goods. It also provided wholesale services for smaller stores established on the different islands.

This was the situation when I arrived. Shortly afterwards I met Roy Davies, the District Commissioner of Western District, who was going on long leave, and had an hour's chat with him. After receiving some handing-over notes, I left for the island of Hombu Hombu near the former American base at Munda, on the island of New Georgia. I was to act as District Commissioner and Magistrate for the Western Solomons. I was the only non-Solomon Islander in government service in the District. I would be three hundred miles from headquarters and communication was by wireless, when it worked.

Hombu Hombu was indescribably beautiful, lying off the main island of New Georgia. It lay outside the reef which fringed the Roviana Lagoon and looked over to the island of Rendova. In the other direction the lagoon was dotted with small islands. My thatched house was at one end of the island, segregated from the parade ground and offices, store buildings, the hospital and police barracks. All buildings were constructed of local or salvaged materials.

The people of the Western Solomons are generally short of stature and mostly jet black in colour. Usually the features are fine, with few negroid characteristics apart from crinkly hair. Young women are strikingly beautiful but age quickly. Lifespan is shorter than that of Caucasians. Because of the higher level of education, at that time provided by the Methodist Mission, Westerners were recruited for the Civil Service in greater numbers than young Solomon Islanders from elsewhere. They were generally efficient and hard-working. Malaita, by comparison, supplied labourers for the coconut plantations. Stevedores and general workers employed in the capital were mainly Malaitan.

My territorial jurisdiction extended to the most northerly islands in the district, the Shortland Islands, which were adjacent to Bougainville in Papua New Guinea. The islands of Vella Lavella, Ganongga and Simbo were grouped as a sub-district. Choiseul lay to the northeast of Vella Lavella. Further to the southeast lay Gizo, Kolombangara, New Georgia and Rendova. The languages of the Shortlands and Choiseul were distinct. While Marovo was part of New Georgia, to which Roviana belonged, the two languages, although having similarities, were different.

On Vella Lavella a proto-Melanesian language was spoken, an anomaly which was shared by Savo, near Honiara.

Only three or four generations before, headhunting had been rife. Choiseul sent raiding canoes to New Georgia and Kolombangara. Santa Ysabel and Roviana also sent out reciprocal war parties. Accordingly, although the District was an administrative unit, there were traditional enmities not far below the surface. These extended to relations between other islands in the Solomons such as Malaita, Guadalcanal and San Cristoval.

After I had taken stock, and heard some court cases which had awaited my arrival, I planned a rotation of tours to different parts of the District. The first was to Marovo Lagoon. The island of New Georgia boasts three lagoons, Wana Wana, Roviana, and Marovo. These are fringed by a reef which in places may be a mile offshore, with blue-green water not more that three fathoms deep, studded with coral on the sandy bottom. Hundreds of small islands rise from the floor of the lagoon. Some of these are inhabited. Others are planted with coconut palms. A few have thousands of white orchids growing on the rocks. As the population had moved their village sites during the War for a variety of reasons, there was no map of villages to be visited. Sasabule, the captain of the M.V. *Mary*, my flagship, ascertained locations from villagers as we went round. I acted as cartographer in retrospect.

Sasabule was a taciturn islander from Simbo. As a youth he had worn a nose-stud, the hole being visible at the end of his nose. He had also worn two bone cylinders as ornaments, about a quarter of an inch in diameter, through holes punched in his earlobes. These had stretched with the weight. Without the ornaments, the earlobes hung down the side of his face He was round-faced and bald, his teeth discoloured from chewing betel. He had a peculiar dignity. He was respected throughout the Marine Service as a superb navigator. On one occasion, on a pitch-black night, we were sailing down a stretch of the Choiseul coast which is fringed by a reef. He gave the order to turn hard to port. Only the black mass of the island was visible against the night sky. I said, 'Do you see the breakers at the entrance?' He said 'No'. He then tapped his cheek and said 'But you can feel the wind coming down the Vurulata river valley.' In a few minutes the breakers on each side of the passage showed up white in the gloom. He had probably heard them before they came into view.

There was a post-War lethargy about keeping villages clean. Cleanliness was important. Mosquitoes bred in tins or half-coconuts.

Mosquitoes bring malaria. I laid down dates by which I expected defects to be rectified and said that I would be coming round again in a few months. All government clinics and schools were visited, with courtesy calls on any mission stations or plantations. I was fascinated by the various artefacts and fishing and building methods which I saw. I subsequently wrote an article, 'The Culture of Marovo', which was published in the *Journal of the Polynesian Society*. The following is a description of a kitchen in the area:

> The kitchen (Marovo *Vanua reco*: Roviana *Vetu oputu*, literally 'house-oven'), where most of the social life of the household takes place is always apart from the house, built of leaf, with an earthen floor. The floors are swept clean, with two or three circles of stones (M, *reco* R, *oputu*) about two feet in diameter where most of the cooking takes place. A stout batten of wood often keeps the stones in position. Outside there are sometimes stone-lined pits and large square platforms of stones forming a bed some nine inches deep where pigs can be cooked whole. In villages where the Seventh Day Adventist faith holds sway, the pig is considered unclean and these have disappeared. The interior of an old kitchen is black with smoke, and a miscellaneous collection of artefacts is tucked away in the staging above the fire where the *gnali* nuts (Canarium spec.) are smoked in their season. This staging is called *Calea* in Marovo and *Hapehape* in Roviana, and forms a small loft slightly above head level, where fishing spears, rods, baskets and odd belongings are stored. A few innovations are made of wire netting. A low staging similar to that in the sleeping rooms and known by the same name (M, *Pade* R, *Hatara*) stretches along one or both walls: a few mats are scattered on them where the family sit and talk while the meal is being prepared. Personal property is stacked indiscriminately on these platforms, resting against the wall: cooking pots, pudding-mortars and nut-pounders lie anywhere which is easy to hand. Occasionally a smoke-grimed row of pig's jaws or bonito fish heads is tucked along one of the roof-poles.[1]

Towards the end of the tour I came across a small hamlet where all the inhabitants were suffering from yaws, with pustular eruptions on mouth, nose, eyes and face. Today this is quickly cured by penicillin injections, which were not then available. I transported all the villagers to the Hombu Hombu hospital. I repatriated them three weeks later, after treatment, virtually unblemished.

On return, I planned to move the District Station from Hombu Hombu back to Gizo. This had been approved, but no money had been

---

1. See T. Russell 'The Culture of Marovo', *Journal of the Polynesian Society*, Vol. 57, no.6, 1948.

set aside for a move that year. I reckoned that by using prison labour to demolish buildings on Hombu Hombu, I could re-erect them on Gizo. With thatch cut from the island of Simbo, I could make a start. The priority at the Gizo end was to erect prison accommodation, a dormitory, a bond shed, a police barracks and an office building. I obtained modest funds from a vote for reconstruction and put this in hand.

My next tour was planned to Vella Lavella, Ganongga and Simbo Islands. I notified the headmen of the islands of the dates when I should visit. I had decided to reconstitute the Native Councils in each sub-district as these each had forty or fifty members. This was too numerous for decision making. The District Council of Vella Lavella was at Doveli in the north of the island and the various councillors had to make their way there by foot or by canoe. Three days before I was due to set off, I was told that my ship, the M.V. *Mary*, which had been sent to Tulagi for servicing, would not be ready. I had no means of getting a message to Doveli in time to keep the Councillors from coming in. Being a greenhorn, I decided that if I could not go by ship, I could use local transport, a canoe. I ordered the biggest ocean-going canoe in the Wana Wana lagoon, with paddlers. We set off on a journey of about a hundred miles, most of it by open sea. The monotony and fatigue of paddling was eased by having a variety of paddle strokes, tapping the thwart between strokes, alternating long strokes with short ones, and having a sprint stroke, sending up a stream of spray, when entering port.

We slept the night on the sand on an island near Gizo and crossed a very treacherous strait between Gizo and the southern tip of Vella. After spending a second night ashore, we finally arrived at Doveli, with much blowing of a conch shell, in time for the meeting. We left to come down the other side of the island and had almost circumnavigated it when we sighted the M.V. *Mary* coming to meet us. We hoisted the canoe and paddlers on board and returned to base,

On my first tour of Choiseul, the first undertaken there post-war, the villages were filthy. I used powers in the Public Health Law to set fire to a derelict house which had been abandoned. It had mosquito larvae in pools of water in the accumulated rubbish. News of this preceded me and I could trace my route down the coast by smoke rising from the bonfires of rubbish in the villages to be visited. Walking across the island, I visited the last pagan village to convert to Christianity. An old man had taken to the bush for fear that he might be poisoned by strangers. He alone had resolved to remain a pagan. The village had apparently held a meeting and decided that they should adopt Christianity. The main question was from which denomination they would derive the most benefit. The Seventh Day Adventists won. They had built a small school on an eminence above the village. It looked like an army pillbox threatening the past. At the end of the tour I was warmly welcomed by the missionary at Sasamunga, who approved of my cleaning-up efforts. He endeavoured to inveigle me into the pulpit to preach a sermon on the theme of cleanliness coming close to godliness.

On the island of Simbo there was a small extinct volcano and in pre-Christian days the souls of the dead in the Western Solomons were believed to congregate there. There were two villages on Simbo and, having disembarked at the first village, I had ordered the ship to go around the island to await us at the second. It was growing dark when we set off on foot. I realised, as we were passing the dark shape of the volcano, that the pace of the party was quickening. Melanesians do not like the dark, when spirits are believed to be at large. By the time we entered the second village, we were at a slow canter and I was moving as quickly as the rest of the party.

The building programme at Gizo was taking shape. I obtained the plans of a house from the Public Works Department for the District Commissioner's house. I sited this on a high spur overlooking the entry to the harbour through an opening in the reef. It had a view of 360 degrees with islands in all directions. One of them, Kolombangara, another extinct volcano, towered to about 2000 feet. A long chain of islands ran from it towards Gizo harbour. This included Plum Pudding, renamed Kennedy, Island where the former President of the United States was rescued during World War II. The colours on the reef, bright iridescent blues and greens, changed throughout the day. These, together with the soothing sound of the sea breaking on the reef, created one of the best house sites in the Solomons. I was to leave the District before the house was finished.

In March, 1949 I had to visit Headquarters to take examinations in Law and Pidgin English This was the lingua franca of the Solomons, in which there were about eighty different languages. I passed and later was to have the grandiloquent title of Chairman of the Pidgin English Examination Board.

The building programme was going well. I discussed with a Solomon Islander mechanic whether we could dam a spring at the foot of a cliff to get sufficient head of water to supply water to the flat area of the station. We sailed to the island of Ballalia in the Shortlands and loaded supplies of piping, valves and taps, abandoned by the Japanese before they left the

Solomons. On a visit to Gizo in the 1990's I was gratified to find that the system was still working. I had also to renovate the beacons which guided ships into the harbour in time for a visit by a British frigate.

Eventually the time was ripe to move stations. A Japanese tug was renovated and a Chinese storekeeper pressed into service as tug-operator. Stores were loaded on an ex-American flat-top barge and tons of building materials, government supplies and files were ferried to Gizo. We finally moved and government services ceased at Hombu Hombu on one day and opened at Gizo the next. I was then acting District Commissioner, Magistrate, Harbourmaster, in charge of Police, Customs, Immigration and Public Works, Queen's Proctor in a divorce case, and coordinator of educational and medical policies in the district. I was being quietly tutored in these duties by my Solomon Island chief clerk, Willie Paia. On arrival, I hung some blankets across one end of the bond shed to demarcate my quarters. At least I had running water.

My respect for Willie Paia was justified by his future career. He was one of the first Solomon Islanders to be appointed a member of the Advisory Council. He was subsequently elected a member of the Legislative Council. He went to the United Kingdom for training in administration and to a conference in Edinburgh. My parents had agreed to meet him there. My father remarked that he thought it appropriate to find him under a potted palm in the North British hotel. I met him at Munda on a return visit to the Solomons. He had retired from public life and remained the unassuming gentle character I had known. I had arranged to climb to the top of Nusa Roviana Island to revisit the dog-god which used to give warning of approaching headhunters. This was a piece of coral in the shape of a dog's head, said to turn to face the danger and alert the warriors to the direction from which the attack was coming. Willie asked to come with me as he had never seen it. He must have known that his days were numbered as, in the canoe coming back from the island, he gave me a copy of his curriculum vitae. His daughter Kuria was married to Tony Hughes, an administrative officer. He later became the Governor of the Solomon Island Central Bank and an expert on the post-Independence economy of the Solomons.

On the 23rd June Roy Davies returned from leave and I was posted as District Officer, Malu'u. This was a station which had been opened on North Malaita specifically to deal with the Marching Rule movement. The ensuing chapter will say something about this so that my next assignment is more easily understood.

CHAPTER FIVE

The Marching Rule Movement

T HERE ARE THREE RACES in the Pacific: Melanesian, Polynesian and Micronesian. The former Western Pacific High Commission included the Gilbert and Ellice Islands. The Gilbert Islands were Micronesian while the Ellice Islands were Polynesian. This was recognised at the time of Independence, when the Gilbert Islands became Kiribati and the Ellice Islands the separate country of Tuvalu. The New Hebrides, called Vanuatu after Independence, was Melanesian, as were the Solomon Islands, apart from the Polynesian outliers already mentioned.

Melanesian culture is very old, carbon dating taking the Solomon Islands back at least six thousand years. In pagan days – and in the 1950's not all Solomon Islanders had converted to Christianity – the people practised ancestor worship. This is a very logical religion. Simply explained, 'My wordly goods are inherited from my father, and his from his father'. A recitation of the genealogy of the 'line' will follow. Eventually one reaches the supernatural progenitor, who was not a man but a 'devil'. This is the Pidgin English for spirit or 'akalo' in North Malaita languages. He was reputed to have come in a canoe with a pig, dog, coconut, and edible tubers, taro, and yams. From the ancestors all good things in life are descended. The skulls of the dead were consequently revered. In Roviana and Vella Lavella they were placed in a coffin-shaped repository standing on four legs, each skull decorated with a network of shell discs. On Malaita the skull was placed in a basket of bamboo strips tied at each end to secure the skull inside.

Approached from the sea, Malaita, even on a sunny day, has a sinister look. Mountainous and densely wooded down to the edge of the sea, with mists usually obscuring the mountain tops, it has an air of mystery. To the Malaitan of previous generations, it was full of spirits. These had to be propitiated for agriculture, fishing, fecundity in marriage, before a war party left, or to cure illness and wounds. Superimposed on this background of religion and superstition was a highly pragmatic way of life. At home the two principal means of livelihood were subsistence agriculture and fishing. Yet a steady flow of young men left the island to work and to earn money. They left behind a strong Malaitan culture. This was expressed in dances, in distinctive artefacts such as body ornaments, decorated food-bowls, fishing floats, clubs and finely crafted weapons. There was a rich body of folklore and song. Malaitans had evolved systems of justice in which every crime was an offence against an individual. This could be extinguished by payment of native money, which was hand-made on the island. Native money could also be used as currency for purchases and for payment to the father of a prospective bride.

This pattern of existence was known in Pidgin English as 'Custom', the code of the indigenous way of life.

Melanesia was generally male-orientated. In pagan villages there was a man's house where the men slept. Sexual relations took place in the gardens or the family house where the wife and children slept. There were male secret societies throughout Melanesia, particularly in Papua New Guinea, the Solomons and the New Hebrides. There was a history of male cults throughout the Pacific as a whole. One existing in Fiji before the First World War was named The Water-Babies. In Western Samoa during World War I the German Battleship *Emden* was hunted down and sunk. When the excitement died down, the effect was to create a movement called the Mau Movement. This became so disorderly that troops had to be called in from New Zealand, the Colonial power responsible, to restore public order.

I have previously referred to the profound effect which the Second World War had on the population of the Solomon Islands. In the face of the Japanese threat, most of the administration and many missionaries, planters and businesses were evacuated from the Solomons. Although a skeleton administration remained, it operated in hiding in the bush. Consequently the islanders felt abandoned and defenceless. It was the Americans who came to the rescue after the Japanese landings on Tulagi, the capital, and Guadalcanal. It was true that some members of the British administration had returned as Coastwatchers and to establish the Solomon Island Defence Force and the Solomon Islands Labour Corps. But the sheer numbers and scale of the American war effort were beyond both knowledge and imagination. Nearly three thousand Solomon Islanders were employed in the Labour Corps, being paid the basic wage of the time of £2 per month plus accommodation and rations. But the GIs were generous with army supplies. They would trade a case of meat, worth several months' pay, for a good piece of carving. Nor were the GIs economists. Solomon Islanders often had to unload heavy cargoes, frequently under Japanese bombardment. Yet, to Americans, they received small recompense. 'Why don't you go on strike?' one would say. The ill-informed Solomon Islander would reply: 'What's that?' Colonialism being anathema to the average American, the odd GI may also have voiced the thought that such meagre reward was due to Colonial oppression. But it was the sight of thousands of Europeans, hundreds of aircraft, ships, trucks, and bull-dozers, field hospitals, cargo sheds and hutted camps which made the most impression. If, in several months, port facilities, airfields and roads could be constructed, why had so little been done by the British authorities before the War? The Americans were sinking Japanese battleships and supply vessels and shooting down Japanese Zeros while the British had walked away. The grand strategy agreed between Churchill and Roosevelt, that America should concentrate its war effort in the Pacific while Britain prepared for war in Europe, did not percolate down to this level.

Then silence. The War in the Solomons was over. The British administration came back and took over the American bases at Munda in the Western Solomons and Honiara on Guadalcanal. It was time for the Labour Corps to go home and they had to be repatriated in the few ships which the British administration had available. The Malaita labourers had assembled large quantities of possessions legitimately acquired from American dumps of abandoned material. They were told to leave these behind as there was no space on the ships. This caused deep rancour and compensation was being sought twenty-five years later.

Before the War there had been a cult movement on Ngela and Santa Ysabel named the Fallowes Movement, after an Anglican priest who had urged the formation of local Councils and Courts and greater infrastructure development by the Government. It did result in a greater emphasis on local government but was overtaken by the outbreak of war. In the district of Kwara'ae in central Malaita, two more primitive cults have been recorded[2]. In the first a woman, Ko'ogiri, urged people to build a special house for her, construct roads leading to it, and provide her with food for the dead. If they did, their deceased fathers and mothers would return to earth. Following an epidemic, the people became disillusioned and the cult died. In the second cult, a man called Niusuri cajoled the people to cook food and place it on the roadside. If they did so, a 'devil', Bulu, would send them lots of money, rifles and cartridges. Their dead fathers and mothers would come to take the food.

---

2. See Colin H. Allan, 'Some Marching Rule Stories', *Journal of Pacific History*. Vol.9, 1974. Also based on my own personal knowledge.

They would bring these gifts in return. When this did not happen, Nusuri said that if he were given a girl to marry, all would be well. Nothing happened. The people were then told to go to the coast and build canoes and a wharf. They should prepare heaps of firewood to cook the porpoises they were to catch. After three days of fishing, no porpoises were caught. The people were disillusioned and the cult died.

These two different stories exhibit that in a customary setting people can be induced to believe that something impossible is going to happen. When the prophecy fails, they can then be further persuaded. This was to happen in Marching Rule.

By 1946, after the War, a system of Native Councils and Native Courts had been reintroduced in Malaita. In each subdistrict there was also a Headman, a man of traditional influence in the area, who reported directly to the Administration. Public order was maintained by the Armed Constabulary. As there were no armed forces in the territory before the War, the Police Force had been armed with Lee-Enfield rifles. This policy continued after the War, a few sub-machine guns being added to the armoury from wartime surplus equipment.

In 1943 members of the Solomon Islands Labour Corps collected money to pay to the Americans to persuade them to take over the administration. The Americans properly reported this to the British Administration and the compromise was that the money was credited to the American Red Cross.

By the end of 1944 the political cauldron on Malaita was beginning to simmer. The Americans had virtually left. There was strong resentment at the paucity of development which had been achieved on the island before the outbreak of hostilities. The Native Courts and Councils were not considered effective. The system of appointed headmen was resented. In Are Are, a sub-district in the south of the island, paganism and 'Custom' were strong. There was a traditional chiefly system. Thus it seemed logical to appoint one of their own leaders to be a chief who would speak for the people. As money conveys power, they started to collect money which would make their movement and their chief 'high'.

The two protagonists of the movement were Nonohimae, a traditional chief, and Nori, neither of whom were fluent in English. Nori, however, was a good Pidgin speaker. The movement came to be known as 'Marching Rule'. Michael Foster, however, District Commissioner at the time, and steeped in Are Are folklore, believed that it was originally called 'Masina' Rule. 'Masina' was an Are Are word for 'brotherhood' as well as 'the green shoot of a tuber'. The idea of

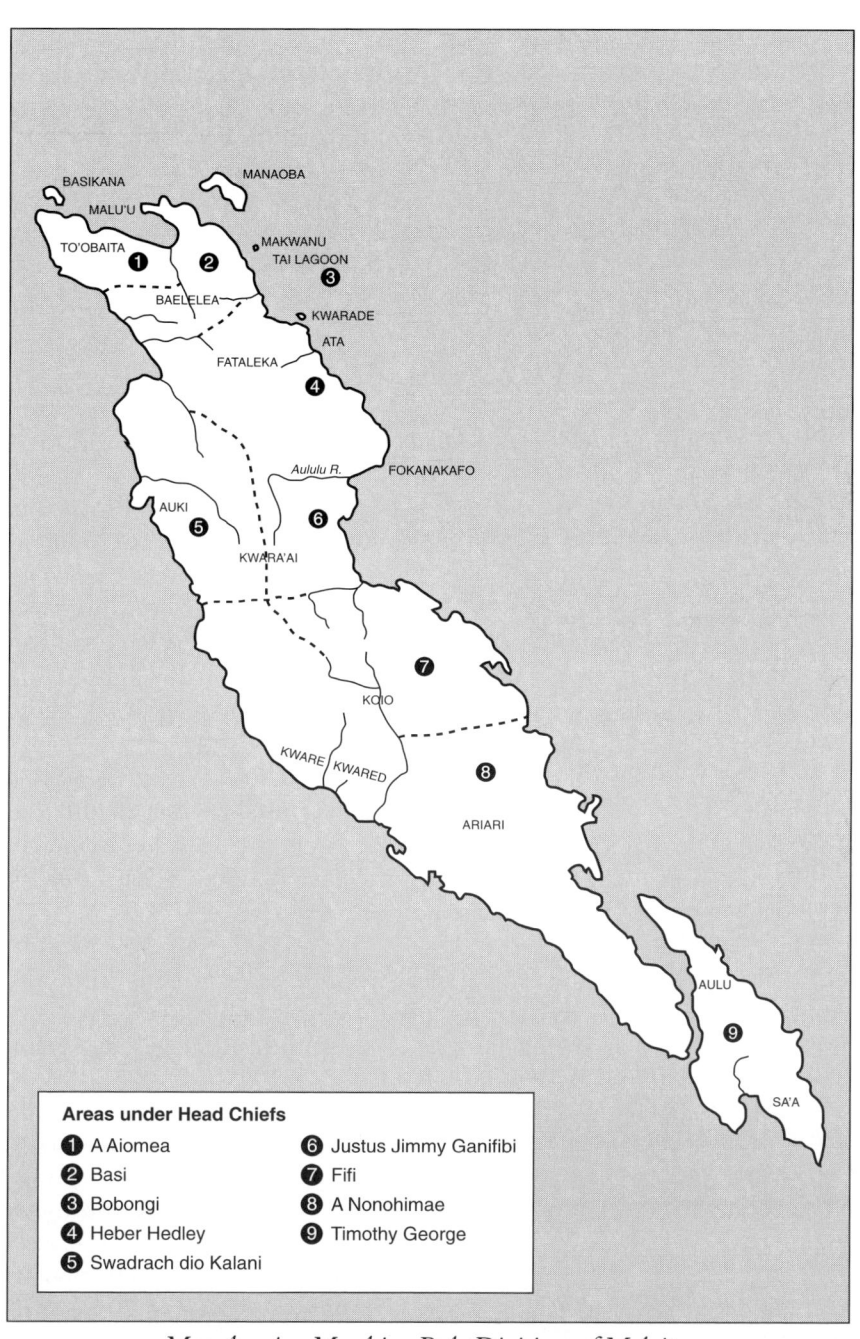

BASIKANA
MANAOBA
MALU'U
TO'OBAITA ❶ ❷ MAKWANU
TAI LAGOON
BAELELEA ❸
KWARADE
ATA
FATALEKA ❹
Aululu R. FOKANAKAFO
AUKI ❻
❺ KWARA'AI
❼
KOIO
KWARE KWARED
❽
ARIARI
AULU
❾
SA'A

Areas under Head Chiefs
❶ A Aiomea   ❻ Justus Jimmy Ganifibi
❷ Basi   ❼ Fifi
❸ Bobongi   ❽ A Nonohimae
❹ Heber Hedley   ❾ Timothy George
❺ Swadrach dio Kalani

Map showing Marching Rule Divisions of Malaita.

something new coming from the old describes the movement accurately.
The Australian press surmised that it might mean 'Marxian Rule'. Large
meetings were held, sometimes 3000 strong, concealed from Government. When these could no longer be hidden, the equivalent of spin
doctors in Marching Rule put out the message that the movement was
not against the administration, missions or plantations. They were only
meeting to discuss improvement of Councils and Courts, better
education, roads and medical services.

Further south the movement had spread to Small Malaita, where the
chief was Timothy George. This leader was born in the sugar-plantations
of Queensland, educated in Australia and spoke good English. Are Are
had a settlement at Marau on Guadalcanal. Small Malaita had contacts
with the Lau Lagoon in North Malaita These links helped the spread of
the movement. A proselytising band, about three hundred strong,
marched through Koio and Eastern Kwara'ae in central Malaita
spreading the message. Soon Ata on the Western coast and Toa' Baita in
the north had been indoctrinated. During the War the few expatriate
missionaries of the South Sea Evangelical Mission (Nonconformist) had
been evacuated to Australia. The indigenous mission preachers had run
the Church during this time. There were churches throughout the
island. In the absence, at that time, of wireless or telephone, these
formed an efficient means of communication.

By the end of 1945 the movement was firmly rooted over the whole
of Malaita. There were pockets of those who refused to have anything to
do with it. The main bulwarks of resistance were two saltwater islands in
the Lau Lagoon, Adagege and Sulafou. These flew the Union flag on
high flagpoles, like warships in a sea of trouble.

Marching Rule had spread to Ulawa, thence to San Cristobal and to
Guadalcanal. It was, however, never strong there. For some time the
Administration seems to have accepted the 'good objectives' story and
followed a policy of laissez-faire as long as nothing illegal was being
done. Doing nothing illegal did not last for long.

During 1946 the official Native Courts began to be by-passed and
offences were referred to illegally constituted bodies. Strong-arm men,
called 'Duties', armed with locally-made police batons and clubs,
escorted chiefs and a hierarchy of lesser chiefs which began to
characterise the movement. This was a sign of rank or importance on
Malaita. In earlier years the Ramo, who was the law enforcer of societies,
had an escort of armed men whenever he went about his business.
'Duties' were used in some instances to coerce doubters into the

movement. Cases were reported of canoes being deliberately holed and houses being burnt. Rumours began to circulate about the return of the Americans. The population was urged to build on the coast large villages named towns (often misspelt as twons), so that it would be ready to receive and welcome them. This showed the grip that the movement had on the population. The people lived in small settlements in the bush or on the salt-water islands in the Lau and Langa Langa Lagoons. Generally the villages were pagan or of one religious denomination, Catholic, South Sea Evangelical Mission (SSEM), Seventh Day Adventist or Melanesian Mission (Anglican). Pagans did not like to associate with Christians. This feeling was so strong that in later years, when villages were being sprayed with DDT to eradicate malaria, specially marked spray canisters had to be used in pagan villages. This showed that they had not been contaminated by previous use in Christian settlements. The process of building larger settlements was not in itself illegal. Administration was made more difficult, however, if it was not known whether villages were inland or on the coast. Although the towns were meant for occasional meetings and to await American landings, some became permanent settlements. The inhabitants became tired of moving between two bases. Young Malaitans, many of whom had served in the Labour Corps, were not coming forward to work outside the island as labourers. Before the War they had served in the capital or on plantations. The message was circulated that the wage should be increased from £2 to £12 per month with accommodation and food. It was difficult to ascertain whether the Movement had forbidden the young men to go to work. Perhaps the hope of a greater wage being offered in future may have deterred the Malaitan from offering his labour.

There were also activities which seemed harmless enough, such as the recording of 'Custom' in the different language areas. As the SSEM pastors usually acted as scribes, the ten commandments were often scattered through the texts. Better education and medical services were part of the platform. The frequently repeated rumour that the Americans were coming seemed bland enough until it took on some of the prophetic elements of the old Kwara'ae 'Bulu' stories. The Americans would bring food and also the same types of wood stoves which Europeans had in their kitchens to cook the food. Therefore the people should cut billets of wood to the requisite size. The effect of the Marching Rule was to divert the population from economic activities yielding income. Instead it engaged in unpaid labour-intensive activities

These included clearing sites for new towns, building new houses there, planting large communal gardens to provide food for meetings, erecting cargo houses for the American food, and cutting large stacks of firewood to cook it. This latter activity brought Marching Rule into the nomenclature of a Cargo Cult, although this was always a peripheral element in the movement.

I referred earlier to the previous history of Secret Societies in Melanesia. I expressed the view that although Marching Rule could not be categorised as a Secret Society, there were some common threads. Within Secret Societies, one writer on the subject identified 'ostensible aims and latent functions'. The ostensible aims of Marching Rule were:

> Better Education and Medical Facilities
> More and better roads
> Basic Labour wage increased from £2 to £12 per month
> Better treatment by Europeans
> Greater involvement in Native Councils and Courts

Had the aim been for improved wages instead of a specific amount of £12, the Government could have agreed with all these objectives.

But the 'latent functions' were not declared. The Government could only express its fears as to the direction in which the Movement was heading. It had to gauge from imperfect intelligence and evidence, as the Movement developed, whether these fears were likely to be realised. During the life of the Movement, the members of the Administration had to base their conclusions mainly on reports from Headmen. They had continually to assess whether latent functions of the movement included:

> Taking over Native Councils and Courts as indigenous institutions
> Refusing to pay government tax of 4/6d per annum
> Demanding Independence before they were capable of running the country

and, in the realm of Public Order,

> Suborning the loyalty of the Police Force
> Clandestine arming with ex-American rifles and sub-machine guns
> Murdering individual government officers and missionaries
> Ambushing government parties engaged on government business
> Sacking government and mission stations

By 1947 the male population was advised by the Movement not to pay tax. Violent coercion to join Marching Rule was increasing. Illegal courts were being held. It was also evident that, if police action had to be taken against the Movement, the loyalty of the Malaitans in the Police Force was questionable. The decision was taken to arrest the nine Marching Rule chiefs. This was done in a meticulous administrative/police operation. Nine government vessels landed Administrative Officers with hand-picked police simultaneously at nine different points on the Malaita coast. The chiefs were taken into custody. They were charged with treason – felony under an old British Law enacted in the reign of Queen Anne, and sentenced to prison for seven years.

Unfortunately this, if anything, had the reverse effect of that intended. Replacement chiefs were put in their place. The mood of the Movement hardened. The population became more truculent. A number of towns were fenced with twelve foot logs sunk into the ground, with heavy wooden gates, and a tall watch-tower. Sometimes there were wooden sentry-boxes at the gate. Passes, such as had been issued to enter American camps during the War, were issued to individual inhabitants. The significance of the watchtower was never truly discovered. It could have derived from the American air traffic control tower on Henderson Airfield. 'Watchtower' was the name of a Church magazine circulated by a Nonconformist Church. 'Watchtower' was also the code name for the American landing on Guadalcanal on the 7th August 1942.

A recruiting campaign took place for police from the Western District, which had remained unaffected by Marching Rule. Many came from the island of Choiseul. The numbers of the Malaita Police Force were strengthened. The Government could not accept that its officers would be prevented from entering villages. Freedom of access was essential for administering many laws, including those on public health, collecting tax and the operations necessary for the taking of a census. Villagers were ordered to remove the fences. In some cases they were removed under police supervision.

Government confrontation with Marching Rule was now stepped up in response to the Movement's instruction to its followers not to pay tax. The public were informed that failure to pay tax would incur, as the law prescribed, imprisonment for up to three months. An additional two months would be given for failure to give names to the census officials. Knowing the limited capacity of prisons on Malaita and elsewhere, the Movement instructed its followers to do neither. The saying at the time was, 'eat Government rice'. Thus all the males in a village or in the larger towns would be assembled with their kit at the ready when an official arrived for tax or census. Courts were strained to keep up. A series of thatched buildings had to be constructed by prison labour as temporary prisons on the road leading north out of Auki, Malaita District headquarters. There were not enough tools to go round for roadmaking. The digging-stick, a sharpened pole used in Melanesian gardens, was called into service. Only one warder was allocated per hundred prisoners. These made no effort to escape. They were carrying out the behest of Marching Rule,

Return from prison did not, however, preclude re-arrest for those who still refused to pay tax or give names for the census. Women now began to play a part. In the five month's absence of the men, gardens had been neglected and houses required repair. The families were now beginning to feel the effects of working without some cash income. Marching Rule met this new challenge by introducing a policy of 'run away'. Government officers entering villages would find them deserted apart from one or two inhabitants too old or frail to move. Government schools and clinics were boycotted.

After a mass meeting at Auki in December 1947, at which Marching Rule leaders told the District Commissioner that they were 'free now', a period of tension followed. There had been a series of dates announced on which the Americans would land, and each one passed like any other. The Marching Rule movement envisaged the possibility that when the Americans landed, the Government would resist them by force of arms. In such a case, should the adherents of Marching Rule hide? As a further measure, a new order went out from Marching Rule to build hidden villages in the bush in case a confrontation should develop between Marching Rule militants and the Government.

In February 1950 a police patrol was attacked with spears in north Malaita, It was obliged to open fire to protect a wounded constable who was being attacked as he lay on the ground. There was one Malaitan fatality. The attackers were arrested and imprisoned and meetings were held around the north explaining what had happened.

The Movement was beginning to crumble. The hardliners in the centre of the island withdrew to a mountain-top south of Auki Government Station. They announced the formation of the Federal Council. This was apparently named after a meeting of Churches in Pennsylvania in the year 1910. Probes by the District Commissioner, Val Andersen, ascertained that the leaders were ready to talk. The High Commissioner, who had by now replaced the Resident Commissioner, came to Auki to meet the leaders. A compromise was hammered out. Instead of having a Marching Rule Council for Malaita, adherents would join the official Malaita Council. Pending elections, they would nominate thirty members and the Government would nominate ten. The Council would be chaired by a chief to be nominated by Marching Rule, provided he took an Oath of Allegiance to the Queen. Marching Rule would agree to suspend operations and support the Malaita Council. But what about the large number of 'Duties', the strong-arm men of the Movement? Val Andersen offered a ready solution. They would all be paid as Malaita Council messengers. Within two years, the Council, confronted like any local authority with a list of projects and a limited budget, gave them low priority and paid most of them off. Malaita was then back on orthodox lines.

How I, personally, fitted into this fascinating period of the history of the Solomon Islands I shall recount in the next chapter.

CHAPTER SIX

Combating Marching Rule

I ARRIVED AT Malu'u in June 1950. I inherited an area of responsibility very different from the Western District, which was a mosaic of large and small islands. The nine chiefs were in prison and, apart from one large settlement near Fokanakafo, fences and watchtowers had been pulled down. Some tax was beginning to trickle in. The introduction of the Census was not expected to begin until November. Some young men were offering their services as plantation workers.

My new charge was the northern part of Malaita, named Bali. This comprised four Subdistricts on the main island, each with a separate language and its own social structure. They were named Toa'baita, Baelilea, Baegu, and Fataleka. A large lagoon, the Lau Lagoon, stretched down the west coast, densely populated, with its own language and culture. The people, known as 'salt-water people' to distinguish them from the 'bush' people' on the main island, also inhabited the Langa Langa Lagoon. This lay on the other side of the island, south of Auki, the District Headquarters. They also had a settlement off Small Malaita, a large island separated from the southern end of Malaita proper by a sound called the Maramasiki passage.

The salt-water people, who had a lighter skin colour, were immigrants of long standing. When they arrived, they were not allowed to settle on the main island. They established themselves on one or two natural islands in the lagoons offshore. But as these soon became too cramped for their numbers, they began to build artificial islands, using coral boulders retrieved from the lagoon floor. These islands were increased in area as populations grew. Today, in the Lau and Langa Langa Lagoons most islands are artificially made. One of them, Sulafou, in the Lau Lagoon, is large enough to have a small football field and a large church. The communities are self-contained, with cage-like pigsties built out over the water. There are gaps in the coral-block walls where a beach extends to haul up their canoes. In places segments of the outside of the wall are marked for male and female latrines. Some individual latrines are also built over the water, like those seen in mediaeval castles in Europe. To extend the artificially created ground, houses are also built on stout wooden piles driven into the lagoon floor around the perimeter. These are clean and fresh, with gaps left between the strips of wood plaited together for flooring. This allows food scraps and detritus to be swept through into the sea below. Although some water comes by catchment from corrugated iron roofs, most houses are thatched with sago-palm leaves. Thus most of the water is ferried from the main island in bamboo containers.

According to folklore, it took many generations for the bush people and the saltwater people to trust each other. The newcomers were adept fishermen. Indeed, I have seen fourteen different fishing methods being used in the lagoon at the same time. They exchanged fish with the bush people for building materials, bamboos, taro, yams, sweet potatoes, vegetables and pigs. There are traditional market-places on the shores of the Lau Lagoon where, it is said, the Lau people would place parcels of fish. This was cooked so that it was still edible after a day's walk back to bush villages. They would then retire to their artificial islands. The bush people would next appear, collect the fish, and place the goods which they had brought in its place. These markets still operated when I arrived, but the commodities were purchased for currency or native money.

Malu'u, the District Station, had only been opened in 1947. Behind an opening in the reef was a small harbour which had been used as an anchorage by missionaries and trading vessels. A small river flowed into the sea, which explained the opening in the reef, as coral does not grow in fresh water. Malaita had many rivers. There were consequently many gaps in the off-shore reef with safe and pleasant anchorages. A flat area on a hill-top behind the coastal flats had been leased by the Government. My predecessor had built a jetty to assist the landing of stores. Steps had been built on the hillside leading to the station and a rudimentary settlement had been established. When I arrived there were no permanent buildings. All were built robustly in local materials, with thatched roofs and walls, but with sawn plank floors in the office building and the District Officer's house. This was a two-roomed house, consisting of a bedroom and living/dining/reception room There were separate ablutions and toilet at the rear, next to a small kitchen. The other buildings on the station were a police barracks, a prison, a store-room and office. These were supplemented by several married quarters for police, clerks and prison warders. The station had a neat appearance. The ground was covered by bright green Japanese clover. There was a parade ground for the police and a recreation area. The oldest church on the island, belonging to the SSEM, was on the station but had fallen into disrepair, and had not been used for many years. However, there was an old well which had supplied the pastor's house. There was no through road, as the main north-and-south 'Government road' followed the coast-line, bypassing the station.

'Government road' was the name by which it was known. It was neither Government maintained nor a road in any real sense. Before the War, under the Native Administration Regulation, male villagers had had to give one day a week in free labour to perform communal duties in their villages under the direction of the Headmen. This edict was now boycotted by Marching Rule. On Malaita it had been interpreted as permitting communal duties to build the 'Government road'. It ran from Auki northwards and round the tip of the island to Fokanako, halfway down the eastern coast. It also extended southwards from Auki Station. There was no wheeled transport pre-war. The existing coastal foot-track was simply widened. Small streams were bridged with logs. Coconut trees and areca palms, which yielded the 'betel nut' for chewing betel, were planted alongside the road. Any traveller was free to take coconuts and the nuts from the areca palm at will. Muddy patches in the road – and there were many – were filled with large stones with crushed rock on top. Unfortunately the road was seen as a very labour-intensive way of preventing Europeans getting their feet wet. Solomon Islanders in the bush did not, and I suspect today do not, wear footwear. It was odd, they thought, to spend days filling wet patches of the road with rocks. Either one could wade through them or make a detour round the side. Besides, widening the track let the sun in. This made it hot to walk. For this reason, under the palm trees alongside the road, planted to yield coconuts, there ran the usual bush-track. It was upon this that the Malaitan traveller preferred to walk.

Whether on the road or the track, I made the journey many times on foot from Malu'u to Auki, a walk of about forty miles. I generally spent the night at a Melanesian Mission Station and Hospital at Fauambu. This was about twenty-four miles south of Malu'u. It marked the south-eastern boundary of my area. A crude track defined the southern boundary of Fataleka. By this one could make a twenty-two mile crossing of the island to Fokanakafo on the other side. The march was usually completed in a day. There was, however, a village about two-thirds of the way across where one could sleep if need be. To complete the circuit of Bali, the coastal track led north as far as Ata at the southern end of the Lau Lagoon. There it was usual, by pre-arrangement with the Headman, to hire a canoe to travel the length of the lagoon as far as

Map of Malaita. Reproduced with the permission of the Public Records Office.

M.V. Mary *on tour off Malaita.*

Author relaxing on board M.V. Mary, *1949.*

Makwanu. Ashore again, one proceeded northwards along the track which cut inland to a Roman Catholic Mission station, leprosarium and hospital at Takwa. From there it was a four-hours' walk to Malu'u. It would be possible to make the journey round the Sub-district in five days On an administrative tour with many daily engagements, however, the circuit would take ten to fourteen days.

The foregoing may give the impression that touring was invariably by foot and canoe. This depended on the reason for the tour. Touring by ship was usually an alternative if there were a vessel on station. I usually had a small vessel, the M.V. *Nancy*, and sometimes one of the M-Class vessels, M.V. *Mary* or M.V. *Margery*, at my disposal. The latter were converted trawler hulls with a small cabin with bunk and desktop, lavatory and shower, spare cabin and crews' quarters. There was a galley with oil stove and refrigerator. Meals were eaten on the top deck or in the cabin if it was raining. There was a thirty-ton hold and the hatch-top and surrounding deckspace were large enough to take up to twenty deck-passengers. Although the ocean is called the Pacific, it does not live up to its name at times. Outside the reef or on open-sea journeys it can be very rough indeed. Usually there were several trolling lines out astern of the ship and on a good day the crew would pull in about ten kingfish, barracuda or tuna. In the evening when the crew were doing their best to eat the whole of the day's catch, less what had been retained for me, I could rely on a calm night at anchor. There were many anchorages behind the reef on the Malaita coast. I was able to type up my tour report or court proceedings before retiring for a comfortable night's sleep, on the upper deck under the stars, if possible.

In some respects one lived better on tour than at base as there was access to fresh food: chickens, vegetables, bananas, plantains and pineapples bought in local markets, fresh fish caught daily; from time to time shellfish, crabs and crayfish, and mangrove oysters in some areas. Malu'u, as a new station, did not have access to these fresh supplies as many of the older and more developed stations had. Even in the capital, Honiara, food supplies were precarious. The routine then was to order tinned foods, flour, sugar, rice and toiletries from Australia at three-monthly intervals. We had no deep-freezes. Kerosene refrigerators were so unreliable that they had to be stood upside down from time to time to recycle the refrigerant. Cooking was on the wood-stoves, much coveted by Marching Rule. Fortunately there were not many house-guests at Malu'u. These were a problem in Honiara and the larger district stations, with food supplies so unreliable.

I hope that this sets the stage for the reader as I describe how I undertook my second assignment.

I would be directly responsible to the District Commissioner, Monty Masterman, at the District Headquarters in Auki. He had one District Officer there, John Bartle, but he tended to be more involved in bureaucratic duties at Auki than in touring. In particular, he had to maintain the station when the District Commissioner went on tour, usually by ship. Before the War Monty Masterman had been a Labour Officer. He had been a member of what was known locally as 'the breathless army', the local force conscripted when Bell, the District Commissioner, was massacred in 1927. A punitive force was formed and sent with local police to apprehend the murderers in Koio, one of the most primitive and mountainous regions of Malaita. They were a motley crew, consisting of junior Government officers, plantation foremen, former police and others. The sobriquet of 'the breathless army' was given to them as they were completely exhausted by the time they reached the top of the first ridge. The regular police had then to continue into the interior to make the arrests.

Monty Masterman was reputed to have built a sea-plane at the old capital of Tulagi and most of the inhabitants were assembled to see the first flight. He taxied it along the harbour but it would not take to the air. He is said to have come ashore in a launch, obtained an axe, and returned to the plane to chop it up. On the outbreak of war, Masterman volunteered. He was said to have been the oldest platoon commander to have landed in Normandy. After the War he returned and was transferred to the Administration. He was Secretary to Government when the first cargo-ship arrived from Australia to take out a load of copra, dried coconut, from Yandina in the Russell Islands. But it could not come alongside the wharf as this was fouled by a mass of bulldozers and heavy trucks, which had been driven into the sea by the Americans before leaving. The Pacific is full of so-called million-dollar points where equipment was driven into the sea instead of being sold for local use. This would have destroyed the market for American manufacturers. Masterman's response to this marine crisis was to pick up an old-fashioned diving-helmet and compressor, dive personally and hook on the various pieces of equipment to a rope towed behind a barge. This then pulled the impediment into deep water where it was disconnected.

He was also reputed to have forced the British Treasury, which monitored Colonial Office subventions to the Solomons, into surrender.

The islands were very short of fuel oil for keeping the electricity generators and its fleet of ships running. There were few cargo ships and these were of small capacity. As Secretary to Government, he received a message from the Government agents in Australia that a ship was leaving shortly for the Solomons and had some cargo space available. Thinking that it was one of the usual small vessels, Masterman telegraphed back: 'Fill her up'. Unfortunately it was a much larger ship than usual and the cost of the oil was several times the amount in the Government Estimates for this service. According to the financial rules of the day, the amount, many thousands of pounds, had to be charged personally to the individual who authorised the transaction – 'Advances: Masterman'. He later made a case to London explaining the circumstances and asking that the sum be transferred back to Government from his advance account. His case was denied. Time had now elapsed. He wrote again to London saying that since the fuel had been purchased the cost had substantially escalated. As the oil now presumably belonged to him, he proposed to sell this to Government at the inflated price. The original decision was swiftly reversed.

He had now been posted as District Commissioner, Malaita. He had two negative attributes, however. He had no political antennae and was about the worst Pidgin English speaker in the service.

My first priority at Malu'u was to get to know all my staff, particularly Sergeant Tamburi from the island of Choiseul, who was in charge of my fifty-strong police detachment. I had to check all arms, ammunition, cash, tax receipts and revenue receipt books, stocks of rations and other stores. I had personally to operate the radio and maintain the batteries. I had to be sure I was familiar with the particular model assigned to the station. I continued morning inspections of the police, including arms inspections, and initiated a training scheme for them. Sergeant Tamburi reported to me each morning. He gave an account of the state of the station, prisoner duties for the day, and any intelligence gathered by the police in the previous twenty-four hours.

In the first six weeks I made a brief tour of the Lau Lagoon by M.V. *Nancy* to meet the coastal headmen and assess their probable reliability. They were under constant pressure from Marching Rule to change their allegiance. The least reliable were almost in the category of double agents, reporting both to Government and the Marching Rule what the other side was planning. I had both good and bad. I also made several short forays into the bush around Malu'u to prospect the villages nearest to the station. I contacted local men of influence in the area. One of these was Shem Irofalu, an SSEM teacher with strong Marching Rule affiliations. When he came to sell me oranges, I knew that I could talk with him. The senior Headman of To'ambaita, Maekali, and Baetalua, his equivalent in Baelilea and Baegu, had a fund of information on the area. I was a ready listener.

At the end of these initial weeks of familiarisation, it was time to get down to serious touring. I set out to walk round the district proceeding in the opposite direction to that described earlier, namely via Takwa to Makwanu and the Lau Lagoon and across the island from Fokanakafo to Fauambu. I planned also to visit Auki for discussions with the District Commissioner. We should be on tour for fifteen days. As there were twelve police, myself and an orderly in the party, it was necessary to have eight carriers for the rations. In my rucksack was a copy of *Stone's Justices' Manual* and a sheaf of Pacific Order-in-Council Court forms, as I should be holding court and adjudicating on disputes en route.

The tour was not as negative as I had feared. I was asked to hold court in various villages. There was no difficulty in conversing with individuals. In the villages in the evenings it was common practice for people to call on neighbours. Without word spoken, they would enter the house and sit in the shadows round the fire in the middle of the floor. Betel nut would be exchanged, pipes would be lit and a buzz of conversation would ensue. When I adjudged that the atmosphere was right, I would enter a house where gossip was taking place, sit down in the shadows, and initially listen. When I felt that I had been accepted I could interject. I teased them about the prophecies of American landings which never took place. I put across the message that when I had been in the Western District, the people were being well paid for their labour. They were, by comparison, much better off.

The following is an extract from my tour report to the District Commissioner:

Native Administration is only possible through close contact between the people and the District Officials. This contact has been severely damaged by the non-cooperative attitude of Marching Rule, and further by the necessity which has driven Administrative Officers to engage in police activities. A common meeting-ground still remains in the bringing of cases for arbitration, in direct relations with touring officers, in the use of government-sponsored facilities, trade stores, recruiter's vessels, dressing stations and hospitals. In the pursuance of a rigorous anti-Marching Rule policy it is important that these links should not be destroyed or further impaired. That children should run screaming from an approaching

Chiefs of the Fokanakafo area.

Government officer on an administrative tour is a serious indication of the present gulf between people and the administration.

Bearing this viewpoint in mind, I therefore made no attempt to implement anti-Marching Rule policy on tour. My primary objective was to make as many contacts as possible, to explain reasons for Government policy, and to make it crystal clear that Government would enforce obedience to the strict letter of the law. The approaching tax and census were mentioned casually in general conversation. An attempt was made to drive a wedge between the petty Marching Rule chiefs who were prodding the Movement along, and the man who simply did what everybody else did.

I enjoyed the walk from Fokanakafo to Fauambu. One follows the Auluta River inland and climbs through dense bamboo forest, with bamboos nine inches in diameter. On one occasion there was a forest fire and trapped air in the segments of bamboo expanded and exploded like bursts of machine gun fire. The route climbs up steeply to the top of a ridge, descending steeply on the other side down to river level. This roller-coaster process is repeated several times on the crossing. On this occasion, one river had to be swum and carriers diverted to a ford much further upstream so as to keep rice and provisions dry. Built-up shoes for my shortened leg, which I had brought with me, had simply disintegrated with this type of treatment. I wore stout leather shoes or army boots, to the detriment of the alignment of my spine and pelvis in later days. We were welcomed at Fauambu, before setting off for Auki, and the hospital establishment was impressive, with capacity for 100 in-patients, x-ray facilities, and a good medical store. A leprosarium was being increased in size from a 26- to a 60-patient facility with the assistance of the New Zealand Leper Trust Board. Leprosy is only transmitted by prolonged physical contact. It was possible to shake hands and converse naturally with the inmates, who were always glad to have visitors. The walk to Auki was accomplished in five hours. After discussions, I led the patrol back to Malu'u the following day.

I learnt to dread the Police Sergeant's morning report on getting back from tour. It invariably began: 'Everything alright along station, Sir.' There then followed a catalogue of catastrophe. Two prisoners had escaped. There had been a mini-hurricane and most of the prison roof and the roofs of the married quarters had been destroyed. There was an epidemic of whooping cough and several deaths in a nearby village. Corporal Agarau's child had been lost at childbirth and the prison rations were getting low.

Meanwhile I was sending out unaccompanied police patrols throughout the district to maintain government contact and to collect intelligence. I never paid for intelligence. This came from Headmen's reports, direct reports from individuals, new prisoners revealing what Marching Rule was plotting, and assessment of the political climate on tour. While most of the police were from Choiseul, the few Malaita police who had been assessed as loyal were superb. Undercover work came to them naturally. Sergeant Tamburi reported to me one morning that an important Marching Rule meeting was to be held in the bush near Kwarade. On asking for the provenance of this report, he told me that Constable Alomai had asked him to open up the prison at ten o'clock at night on the pretext of giving orders for work for the following day. An hour later Sergeant Tamburi returned and basically said, 'I wish this damned District Officer would make his mind up. Orders have been changed and these are the new ones.' The prison barracks was in darkness at that time of day. Constable Alomai had crawled in and out of the door on the two occasions it had been opened, and slithered under a bed. He then listened to all that an influx of new prisoners had been saying to the older ones about the latest plans of the Movement. On a second occasion Constable Alomai asked for a week's leave because of a

Sergeant Tamburi (without rifle) with one of his policemen.

fictitious bereavement. He went home in civilian garb and claimed that he had deserted from the police and was now on the side of Marching Rule. He did his best to ingratiate himself with the community. As a result he was able to crawl under the floor of a house built on piles where a Marching Rule meeting was taking place. He reported back for duty the following morning with a detailed account of what had been said.

Meanwhile efforts to collect tax in the Malu'u area were continuing. Although the policy of 'run-away' had not started, adult males were usually in the gardens or fishing through the day. The most efficient means of confronting them with a demand for tax was to march during the night and enter the villages at dawn. Night marching in single file on dark bush tracks was not easy. Occasionally police copied something which they had seen Fijiian soldiers do during the War. They placed a firefly, a species which was often seen in the bush at night, in the hair at the back of the head to aid the policeman coming behind. The Malaitans considered this nightwork below the belt and representations were made to the District Commissioner to forbid the practice, which proved effective. In conjunction with the District Commissioner, and using the same travel-by-night tactics, I removed the last fences and tower from the large 'town' near the mouth of the Aisato River at Fokanakafo, to the accompaniment of much drum-beating and prancing about with spears.

By November I was satisfied that from Headmen Itea of Fataleka, Tome Wate, Timi Kakalouae and Timi Ramogalo of Lau, Makali in Toambaita, Baetalua in Baelilea and Baegu, I was getting fairly reliable intelligence. Furthermore there were strong links between the north and south of the island. I was relaying to Auki island-wide intelligence which the administration was not obtaining from local sources. One of these reports was that a very large Marching Rule meeting was being planned to confront the District Commissioner at Auki.

This meeting was duly requested of the District Commissioner and took place on the 21st December 1950. I went down for the meeting by ship with a large contingent of Malu'u police to reinforce those at Auki. I stayed with John Bartle and his wife Binnie in the District Officer's house at Auki, on the top of a small hill with a splendid view of Auki Island and the harbour. Throughout the night of the 20th those intending to attend the meeting started to arrive on foot, by canoe, and by cutters made on the island. They were accommodated at the two neighbouring villages of Lilisiana and Ambu. As dusk was falling, large canoes holding up to twenty came up the lagoon from Are Are and Small Malaita. As night fell the whoops coming from the villages would have made a suitable background for the most bloodthirsty of films on the Wild West. Drum-beating went on most of the night.

The meeting was to be held on the station football field. Masterman revealed that he had cunningly placed the table and chairs for the three administrative staff in the shade under the trees on the edge of the field. The crowd would be in the heat of the sun. The police, apart from one unarmed police orderly at the table, would be kept out of sight, ready to respond if necessary.

An hour before the meeting the marchers started to assemble. They marched in twos from Ambu village, adjacent, along the seafront and up the central path to the station. The procession formed a continuous black line, which remained unbroken long after the first marchers had reached the football field. Understanding what had been planned, they placed the table and chairs in the middle of the field and took shelter in the shade under the trees. They bore native weapons, clubs, spears, bows and arrows, and bush-knives. Eventually, when the marching stopped, we sat down at the table with Masterman in the middle. He opened the meeting by saying that they had requested it and he was ready to hear what they had to say.

The speaker was Ariel Bili from Kwai, an ex-SSEM pastor, and they could not have selected a more competent orator. He read out a five-page document, a copy of which I had received from Maekali previously. This was entitled 'THE SETTLEMENT OF BRITISH SOLOMON ISLANDS PROTECTORATE 52 YEARS AGO – NO PLAN MADE FOR NATIVE BENEFIT', with a subtitle, 'EXPECTATION OF NATIVES FOR A FAIR AND BETTER LIVING'.

It gave a long, hysterical, account of wrongs allegedly inflicted in the past by government officials and particularly by overseers on plantations. At times it was almost poetic, one phrase being, 'We groan and moan, sigh and cry with many a tear.'

Ariel Bili knew how to work up his audience. He would pause frequently and say 'Himme true now?' or 'Youme fella wantim?' – 'Is that true?' or 'Is that what we want?' and the crowd would yell 'Eeo' – 'Yes'.

The speech ended with: 'They tries to bound us from our freedom. But we must to be free. Therefore we must free'

A great shout went up, and then the silence of expectation. In the police lines one police sergeant said to the other, 'Our time has come, Bunga' (The sergeant's name). John Bartle and I looked across at each other with the unspoken question, 'What now?'

Masterman courteously thanked them for the speech but asked if they could clarify more particularly what they wanted. This was summarised as four main requests:

> Independence
> A single native leader for Malaita
> Councils
> Release of the nine chiefs.

Masterman said that the first and the last requests were not on. He said that that he would recommend reintroduction of native courts and council. He would also support the appointment of a Malaita member to the Resident Commissioner's Advisory Council. There was a howl of protest. They were, of course, advocating Marching Rule Courts and Councils and few of them had even heard of the Resident Commissioner's Advisory Council. Ariel Bili returned to the charge. Masterman, however, was not prepared to have a public debate on the subject in a situation of what was virtually duress.

He closed the meeting by saying that of course he was only the District Commissioner. He would have to relay what had been said to the Resident Commissioner. He then rose ponderously to his feet and looked at his watch. Turning to John Bartle and myself, he said: 'Well, time for tea'.

We walked towards the crowd, which, during the excitement of the speech, had completely surrounded the table. An opening was made. We walked through, rather as the children of Israel must have done, viewing the walls of water in the Red Sea! We left the crowd, which by this time was forming into ugly groups, shouting and shaking weapons. We returned to the District Commissioner's house which overlooked the football pitch, sat down on the verandah and had morning tea and cucumber sandwiches. After further shouting and movement, the crowd dispersed to Ambu. Later individuals returned to their homes.

Unfortunately, different interpretations were put on Monty Masterman's reply. He carried out a circuminsular tour to explain what had happened. But, as he was aboard ship, he did not contact the bush villagers, many of whom had gone home for Christmas.

It was about this time that Constable Alomai, who was a particularly well-built and hard-headed Malaitan, was detailed to carry the mail to Takwa Mission Station. This service was much appreciated by the Fathers and Sisters on the station. It was a regular duty and the staff were surprised when he did not appear by four o'clock in the afternoon. Before dark someone went out to look for him but failed to locate him. In the morning a search was made further along the path and Alomai was found, ashen-faced and gibbering with fear, hiding behind a fallen log. He was taken back to the station and admitted to hospital. The place where he was found was called a *beu ambu*, literally 'sacred house'. In former days, when a chief died in North Malaita, his body was left in the house where it was allowed to moulder. Eventually the skull was removed and revered. At a later stage a ficus tree was planted on the site of the house. No cutting of shrubs or saplings was allowed in the vicinity. The trees grew very large and over the years vines grew on them and spilled down the branches. Sacred places like this were patently distinguishable, even without someone pointing them out. Alomai claimed that when he was passing one he saw the *akalo* or spirit connected to the tree. Hence he was going to die. Certainly the possibility grew as he refused food and did not respond to any medicines which the Catholic Sisters administered. But someone from the area suggested a solution. The heathen priest, the *fatambu* responsible for this sacred place, lived at a village in the hills. If Alomai could be taken to see him, it was possible that he could be cured. The equivalent of crossing the *fatambu*'s palm with silver, the payment of two strings of native money, was enough to convince Alomai to recover. The old priest pooh-poohed the idea that Alomai could have seen his spirit. If he had, he would be dead. He must only have caught sight of its reflection in a puddle of water. But it took some time for Alomai to regain his former physique.

I myself had a strange experience on New Year's Eve. I was the only European on the station. The political situation was deteriorating since the meeting at Auki. As I did not feel inclined to celebrate the advent of the New Year by myself, I went to bed. At midnight there was a shuffling on the gravel outside my house. On looking out, I found that the Choiseul members of the police had formed themselves into a choir and had come to sing in the New Year. They were of the Methodist faith and were singing in Bambatana language from Choiseul. What they had chosen to sing was a hymn, 'The sands of time are sinking', not, perhaps the most jovial greeting for a New Year. But for me it was an eerie choice. At the end of the family pew in St Aidan's Church in Melrose, thirteen thousand miles distant, was a stained glass window. This was in memory of the wife of an ex-Minister of the church, Anne Cousins, who had written the hymn, 'The sands of time are sinking'.

On the 4th January I set off on an eighteen-day foot patrol heading southwards towards Fokanakafo to gauge more accurately the reactions to the meeting at Auki. The mood of the people seemed to have hardened. The District Commissioner had gained the same impression on his circuminsular tour on M.V. *Biliki*. Deterioration in the situation was already marked by the time I was at Fo'odo, halfway down the Lau coastline. There I received a message in writing from Itea, the Headman at Fokanakafo. This read as follows:

> I received a Marching Rule word last week from my people where I sending them to spy around the Marching Rule Meeting and they came and report some bad news what they want to do for the Government after they meeting with District Commissioner last year... They gave out new meetings to all Marching Rule people in Fataleka. and they sending news

all round Malaita Marching Rule. They said that on 3rd January 1950 they went to ABORAU for their meeting themselves and after that they will come again to Auki and asking again the four questions . . . and if the Government won't let for us these four questions alright, we must show out our power to the Government and all his armed constabulary and all their headmen, we must fight with them on that day. So as I know quite well this report is quite true, I want you to send this report to Auki. They want war, against Government.

I am yours faithfully
District Headman
Itea

Itea was a man I trusted implicitly and I knew that he was not prone to exaggeration. He had been my main informant on the social organisation

District Headman Itea.

of Fataleka, which I later worked up into a monograph. It was published in *Oceania*.

I abandoned the tour to return to Malu'u to contact the District Commissioner by wireless. I proposed setting off immediately by road to Fauambu and across the island to Fokanakafo, from where the report had originated. My enquiries there confirmed that the political mood had deteriorated. On setting off northwards towards Malu'u, I received a report that three thousand men with native arms were waiting for me at Ata. Even allowing for exaggeration, I could assume that a large number of my parishioners expected the pleasure of my company.

I sent the Assistant Headman to Ata. I said that I would like to speak to them. I would expect them on the beach at Feranaso village the next morning, unarmed, at nine o'clock. I had chosen this venue as the village was deserted. There were some houses on high piles at the side of the beach where most of the police could be stationed out of harm's way. From there they could control the situation if matters got out of hand. However, the crowd had shrunk to little more than a hundred and they appeared to be unarmed. I asked them to sit down on the sand, which they did. From that moment onwards I was in control. I explained why the issues raised by Marching Rule leaders at Auki could not be agreed to in full and that increased belligerence by Marching Rule would be pointless. I then continued round the coast to Malu'u, visiting all main villages.

On the 8th February I left Malu'u again, in the late afternoon, accompanied by a police patrol. I intended to march through the night to arrive at a village in the Suaba peninsula at dawn in an endeavour to collect tax. There were rumours at the time of secret villages being constructed in the bush. It was still daytime, but the light was beginning to fade as we heard the noise of chopping timber on one side of the track. Thinking that this might be a hidden village under construction, I detached Sergeant Tamburi and two constables to investigate and carried on with the main patrol along the track. Suddenly there was shouting followed by a burst of sub-machine gun fire. I doubled back with the main patrol, found a small path leading in the direction from which the shots had been heard and came upon a small village. This had a fence about three feet in height, but probably with no more aggressive intention than to keep pigs from straying. Tamburi shouted that it was safe to enter and that the population had fled. As he and the two police, in line abreast, had come towards the village, an old man who had been adzing a tree looked up and saw three armed police advancing towards him. He shouted: 'The army (police) have come to kill me!' The police climbed the fence and entered the village. At this point Sergeant Tamburi with one of the constables was advancing on one side of a house. Constable Naqakesa was on the other. Thus the line of sight between them was temporarily blocked by the building. Suddenly four spears were thrown at Constable Naqakesa. Two grazed his body. The third passed through his wrist and projected about six inches. 'Me die now, Tamburi', he shouted. The Sergeant dashed back, round the house, to find four youths advancing on Naqakesa on the ground. One had an axe upraised and the others rushed in to recover their spears. In his later statement he said that he fired a burst over their heads. Hearing rustling in one of the houses, we took one frightened villager into custody to question later. I ordered immediate return to Malu'u. Not knowing whether the incident was part of, or likely to promote, an insurrection, I had a mobile rearguard follow us back to the station. I gave instructions to fire a warning shot if we were pursued.

On reaching the station, I sent Constable Naqakesa off for medical treatment and arranged for the villager to be fed. I paraded the police and counted rounds to ascertain how many had been fired. I took statements and compiled a telegram to District Headquarters and to the Secretary to Government reporting the incident. I asked the District Commissioner to convene an enquiry. From questioning the villager, Sergeant Tamburi obtained the names of the assailants. I sent off the Assistant District Headman who had accompanied us on patrol to make contact with the four youths. I instructed him to bring them to meet me the next morning at the tax-house at Matakwalao. I went round by ship, and was slightly surprised, and much relieved, to see them there. I arrested them on a charge of malicious wounding and returned to the station. Unfortunately we learnt that there had been a fatality from the police fire.

I was not very pleased to be told by the District Commissioner that he would not conduct an enquiry, as the facts would come out in the Preliminary Enquiry, the procedure preceding trial on a felonious charge. He came to Malu'u personally to hold this. I, of course, was a witness. Some weeks later Monty Masterman proceeded on pre-retirement leave and was replaced as District Commissioner by Colin Allan. The court case was eventually held before the Judicial Commissioner in Honiara. At the end of my testimony I asked, if the accused were found guilty, whether I could speak in mitigation before sentence was passed. This request was granted. I pleaded that the youths, as Malaitans, had, under

HIDDEN VILLAGES
IN THE BUSH
Do not deceive yourselves,

Government knows that some of you are building SECRET VILLAGES in the bush and digging underground places. All these are known and can be seen from the air.

STOP building these Villages they will only bring trouble on you.

Read Luke Chapter 12 Verses 2 and 3.

REPRESENTATION
ON COUNCIL.

You have asked for a Native Representative on the Advisory Council (White man's Parliament).

This will be considered only if you obey the LAW.

To resist Government is WRONG and will bring you nothing but sorrow.

TAX and CENSUS

ALL people in the world pay TAX to their Government and every one submits to CENSUS.

These two things are part of the "Second Living".

PAY your TAX and give your NAME to the Census Officer and live in PEACE.

Propaganda leaflets on hidden villages etc., as dropped by aircraft.

their 'Custom', a duty to come to the defence of their father if they considered his life to be in danger. The cry for assistance was based on the fear that armed police from another island were intent on doing him harm. This plea was taken into account and a light sentence of three years imprisonment was imposed.

After the warning of aggressive action against Auki Station, and with the effects of this incident unknown, it was necessary to make an immediate assessment of the political mood. The threat of violence at Auki was taken seriously and the police detachment there was strengthened. I had recommended that an aerial overflight of the island should be made to see whether hidden villages in the bush were being constructed on a large scale. The Sandringham flying-boat, which brought passengers from Sydney to Tulagi each week, was duly chartered, and a flight over the island was arranged with Monty Masterman on board. He took full advantage of the flight by arranging for a leaflet-drop with simple messages quoting a biblical text against violence. Another was on taxation aimed at South Sea Evangelical Mission followers on the lines of 'Render unto Caesar the things that are Caesar's'. Unfortunately the pamphlets, which were about four inches square, stuck together as the print was not dry. Packed in bundles the size of bricks, they came hurtling down in one piece, bursting through thatched roofs before disintegrating. They were collected as souvenirs and stimulated the thought: 'What on earth is the Government going to do next?' As a dense mist covered Malaita at the time of the flight, it was a fiasco. But we pretended that the modern technology of 1950 allowed us to see through trees and roofs even if the cloud were dense. Having received other intelligence, I had secretly investigated a hidden village in the bush near Fauambu. I was now able to go to the nearest inhabited village and, taking some of the villagers with me, pretend this had been discovered on the flight To their astonishment I was able to say that in a particular house supplies of food and water had been secreted. The paths leading to this village had been carefully blocked and camouflaged with fallen trees and branches.

My patrol on foot round the sub-district had the dual role of providing a show of strength and explaining what had happened in February. In case there was trouble, I dispensed with carriers and we each carried our own rations for the tour. There was a remarkable acceptance of the events in February. The Marching Rule, however, began to circulate rumours of the Americans coming to avenge the death of a Malaitan. Cargo sheds began to be built in three places.

Hidden village in the bush near Fauambu.

On return to the station, I was depressed by the turn of events and by the pressure of producing long detailed reports on touring and intelligence, all laboriously typed by me personally. In an effort to take a more positive line, I compiled four pamphlets in Pidgin English, also translated into Toambaita, giving a simple anti-Marching Rule message. I urged compliance with the law, discounting the rumours of American landings. I said how much better off they would be if they engaged in work for which they would receive pay. The pamphlets were posted in all villages. Some of them were defaced and torn down. I nevertheless believe that they were worth the effort.

Tax gathering was beginning to gain momentum. Gratifyingly, in the Malu'u area where government influence was greatest, the success rate was in excess of 50%, compared with 25% further south. The position appeared to be that the hard core of Marching Rule was getting harder but the power of the Movement was waning. It was time for Government to take the initiative.

Following a meeting between the Resident Commissioner and the nine imprisoned chiefs, a deal was struck. They would be released on licence provided that they publicly renounced Marching Rule on return to Malaita. They should actively recommend the payment of tax and cooperation with the census. The chiefs were duly released on the 6th

June. The four northern chiefs spent a week with me at Malu'u while I assessed their intentions. These seemed genuine. I had slight doubts about Atomea, who came from the Malu'u area. The population took surprisingly little interest. Crowds did not assemble at Malu'u to greet them. The chiefs were, as far as the Movement was concerned, yesterday's men. New chiefs were nominated to succeed them. Those still committed to the Movement regarded them as turncoats. The waverers did not want to show continued loyalty. Among the men nominated to be one of the new chiefs, one did not want to be associated with the hard core He pretended to go along with his selection.

Coupled with the waning popularity of the Movement, the release of the chiefs undoubtedly had an effect on the waverers. But I learnt that the centre of gravity of the Movement had now moved to the centre of the island. There were two Marching Rule Councils, one at Lungunu in Kwara'ae and one other at Kiu in Are Are. They communicated with each other and propagated the Marching Rule instructions. The Kwara'ae Council had also met at other locations including Fokanakafo. It was not long afterwards that the diehards concentrated at Alitsa, on a hill in Kwara'ae south of Auki. The Movement renamed itself the Federal Council.

I left, however, to proceed on leave on the 3rd October, saying farewell to Sergeant Tamburi and the police force with very real regret. On patrol I was very much one of them and accepted as such.

But it was time to go home to get married.

CHAPTER SEVEN

Posting to Fiji and
Return to the Solomons

ANDRÉE, MY FIANCÉE, lived with her French parents in Algeria. I was resident in the Solomon Islands. To conform with marriage regulations, we had both to live in the country where the marriage was to take place for a minimum period. This was longer in Algeria than Scotland. Consequently we arranged to meet in London. After the requisite residence in Scotland, we were married in Melrose and spent our honeymoon in St Andrews. We then stayed a month with her parents in Oran, Algeria, and a further month with my parents, who had returned to Germany. At that time I could see no overt signs of the pre-Independence disorder about to break out in Algeria. Oran was a prosperous town basking in bright sunshine on the shores of the Mediterranean. Rhine-Westphalia, where my father worked, had made remarkable progress since my last visit. I admired the resilience of the German population after the cataclysmic effects of Allied bombing in the area.

We sailed for Australia on an Orient Line passenger ship en route to the Solomons. I expected to resume a District Administration posting there. We were suitably equipped with camp beds and mosquito nets. These would be an unaccustomed luxury on tour. We passed through the Suez Canal to Colombo in what was then Ceylon. We spent a memorable day swimming at the Mount Lavinia Hotel. On the way back to the ship, we visited Buddhist temples in the city, which was bathed in a golden sunset. Thence to Perth, Adelaide and Melbourne, spending a day ashore in each port before debarking in Sydney. We happily enjoyed a week in the Wentworth Hotel, awaiting a flight by Sandringham flying-boat to Tulagi, in the Solomons. This was interrupted by a representative from Burns Philp, the Solomon Islands Agents in Australia. He called with a telegram from the Chief Secretary of the Western Pacific High Commission in Fiji. I learnt that I had been transferred there. Air passages had been booked for us two days later. I immediately telegraphed the Resident Commissioner in the Solomons to query this instruction from someone other than himself. The reality was, however, that I was an officer of the Western Pacific High Commission. I was subject to posting to any part of the jurisdiction. The Resident Commissioner said that he was sorry to lose me. The attachment was expected to be brief. He would keep up the pressure to get me back as soon as possible. All my household goods and my dog, Jock, were in the Solomons. Direct shipping connections between the Solomons and Fiji were few. In those days such a situation was considered a minor service inconvenience.

We duly arrived in Fiji, where I had spent a few weeks previously, awaiting onward travel to the Solomons. We moved into a new bungalow built for Western Pacific High Commission staff. It was inland, not far from Government House. Fortunately, as we were to appreciate later, the house had been built to anti-hurricane standards. Compared with similar housing in the Solomons, it was well-furnished. Another High Commission officer, Bill Marquand and his wife, who lived next door, gave us a good welcome. By coincidence he had also served in the Parachute Regiment. My wife was taken off shopping after I went to work and reported for duty. The office was within walking distance.

At that time the Governor of Fiji was also High Commissioner for the Western Pacific. He was responsible for Fiji, the Solomons, the Gilbert and Ellice Islands, the New Hebrides, Tonga and Pitcairn. He administered Fiji directly, with a Colonial Secretary in charge of a large Secretariat on the coastal strip on the outskirts of Suva. The relationship with the other WPHC Territories was indirect, with Resident Commissioners in the Solomons, the Gilbert and Ellice Islands and the New Hebrides. This Territory had also a French Resident Commissioner, as it was an Anglo-French Condominium. The French Resident Commissioner reported to a French High Commissioner in New Caledonia. The Condominium was jokingly referred to as the 'Pandemonium'. As Tonga was a kingdom, relationship with the United Kingdom was maintained by a British Agent and Consul. He reported to the Western Pacific High Commissioner, who was also directly responsible for Pitcairn. Even in the year 2003, there is no resident British representative there. Such an appointment would not be justified with so small a population. Responsibility for the island now lies with the British High Commissioner to New Zealand.

There was a second mini-secretariat serving the Western Pacific High Commission, about a hundred yards from the office of the Governor of Fiji. This was housed in small wooden buildings in the grounds of Government House. The building subsequently stored the Western Pacific High Commission Archives. Pre-war, it was in charge of a Secretary, Western Pacific High Commission, who was irreverently called by the Resident Commissioners, 'The bottleneck of the Pacific'. The staff in 1951 consisted of a Chief Secretary, a Financial Secretary, a Senior Assistant Secretary and three Assistant Secretaries, of whom I was to be one. There was also an Accountant and supporting clerical staff. When the Governor of Fiji proceeded on leave, the Colonial Secretary, Fiji, acted as Governor, Fiji while the Chief Secretary, Western Pacific High Commission, acted as High Commissioner for the Western Pacific.

I was allocated the duties of Assistant Secretary (Personnel). I was also responsible for dealing with Pitcairn at first instance. I assumed duty on the 31st May 1951. Shortly afterwards I was also asked to take on financial duties for the Financial Secretary. It was very much a nine-to-five job. After the bustle of my first tour in the Western Solomons and in Malu'u, it proved unsatisfying. But I expected to be re-posted to the Solomons in a few months. I knew that most administrative officers would have to spend part of their service in the secretariat. Personnel work, compared with similar duties in the Solomons, was a leisurely occupation. Requests came in from the territories, on standard forms, to fill pensionable Colonial Service vacancies. These could be in administration or in other branches of the Service, Legal, Medical, Education, Audit. The staff indents went forward to London with the Chief Secretary's recommendation. Occasional queries went back to the Territory for additional information, There were also contract posts. Requests to fill Reconstruction or Development and Welfare posts were directed to the Colonial Office. Indents for temporary posts such as secretaries were directed to the Crown Agents in London. The Annual Confidential Reports for all pensionable Colonial Service officers also came through Suva. The Chief Secretary, if he knew the officer concerned personally, would have the opportunity to comment. We were also concerned with promotions for members of the Colonial Service. We were cocooned, however, in that we did not have civil services around us. No Heads of Department thumped our desks complaining about delays. We did not have to arrange leave, housing, passages, admissions to hospital. We were at arm's length from the majority of the civil services in the territories. These gave an extra dimension to the work of the Personnel staff there.

Financial work was more satisfying. At this stage I was merely devilling for the Financial Secretary, who had the budgets of the Territories referred to him for comment. Here again one was removed from the hurly-burly of preparing estimates, arguing for cuts, balancing to tight time-frames. The office was basically advisory. The results of our labours were sometimes difficult to identify.

In February 1952 a telegram was received announcing that King George VI had died and that the Princess Elizabeth was now Queen. We were already aware of this through the radio. There was a series of protocol procedures which flow from the death of the Monarch, such as Messages of Condolence and Affiliations of Loyalty to the new Monarch. I was asked to research the Archives and was able to trace the files dealing with the death of King George V in 1936. It soon became apparent that someone in the Colonial Office had done the same, as we were able to anticipate instructions before they came in. Official despatches and correspondence had to be edged in black. Formal entertainment at Government House or Residency ceased for a certain period. Flags at Government House and public buildings had to be flown at half-mast. One of the interesting conventions applying to Colonies was a formal declaration of fealty to the new Monarch. The Governor or Resident Commissioner identified a list of men and women of standing in the Colony. They were invited to sign a pledge of loyalty to the new Sovereign. This was gazetted in the Colony as well as being sent to the Secretary of State for onward transmission to the Palace. In Fiji, where it was difficult to comprehend someone having a status higher than the Paramount Chief, mourning was real, deep and personal.

Fiji was a very pleasant place in which to live. At that time I could detect none of the racial tensions and disharmony which led in recent times to a coup. The country was still a British Colony. A strong department of Fijian Affairs upheld Fijian rights under the law. The Indian community, originally brought into the country to supply labour for the sugar plantations, was, with certain exceptions, precluded from buying land. Indians were, however, able to cultivate leasehold land, They had also diversified away from agriculture into storekeeping and the professions. Indigenous culture invested Fijians with a natural dignity and good manners. Rudeness was, for them, one of the seven deadly sins. A keen sense of humour was never long out of sight.

Suva, like most of the older established capitals in the Pacific, Port Moresby, Papeete, Honolulu, and Noumea, was developed to an extent which other parts of the country could not enjoy. The main institutions of the country tended to be based in the capital: the main hospital, university, training colleges, port and secondary schools. These attracted substantial wholesale and retail outlets, power, water and drainage in advance of similar developments elsewhere. The capital created a demand for labour and increased population, housing often failing to keep pace with demand. The bright lights could attract unemployed youths. Social problems could develop as in urban communities in more developed countries. Other Pacific capitals have the main airfield as one of these developments. In Fiji topography has dictated the siting of the International airfield at Nadi. This lies on the other side of Viti Levu, the island upon which Suva is sited. Such imbalance of development mirrors the difference between a cash and subsistence economy. It can cause resentment and inter-island factions, as has occurred in recent times in the Solomons.

Socially, our ambit was limited, to some extent, by the nature of the job. I was only in the country temporarily, or so I hoped. But although a civil servant, I was not in the mainstream of the Fiji Civil Service. Nevertheless we moved around and my wife was never consigned to sitting at home while I was at work. There was a squash court at Government House to which we had access at certain times by arrangement with the ADC to the Governor, Sir Brian Freeston. After squash we availed ourselves of the showers and swimming pool. Sometimes we were hailed by the Governor and Lady Freeston to join them for drinks on the terrace. Dinners at Government House were formal affairs, as they were in the Solomons. Ladies wore long dresses and the men either white tuxedoes or white monkey-jackets (bum-freezers), black evening trousers and cummerbunds. After dinner the table was cleared of all dishes. The port decanters were placed in front of the Governor and his wife seated opposite. The decanters were circulated. The Governor then proposed the toast to the Queen. Shortly afterwards the Governor's lady collected eyes. The ladies withdrew. The men who were left slid sideways up the table taking the places vacated by the ladies. The port was again circulated and male conversation, usually shop, took place. When the Governor deemed that it was time to join the ladies, he and the guest opposite placed the stoppers back in the decanters. We filed out. As the ladies were occupying the toilets, the gentlemen then repaired to the lawns of Government house and proceeded to water them. This ritual, for some reason, was always called 'Looking at Africa'.

Nine months passed. It was clear that my recall to the Solomons was not going to take place. As a ship was coming, unusually, from the Solomons direct to Fiji, I sent for my heavy baggage. It was in an interesting condition. Expecting to come back in a few months, I had not taken much care with the packing, I did not, however, expect crates to be turned upside down and subjected to other more destructive activities. My canteen of cutlery had been repacked for shipment together with a 12 volt battery. This was used to provide power for a wireless set purchased for service in outlying district stations without electricity. The state of the cutlery can be imagined. Another crate contained home-brewed ginger beer which, with the passage of time, had exploded and seeped into the crates below.

Now that we were equipped for a long stay, the decision was taken to move the Western Pacific High Commission headquarters to Honiara. This was the capital of the largest of the three territories which were administered by Resident Commissioners. The post of Resident Commissioner in the Solomons would be abolished. As the Governor did in Fiji, the High Commissioner would administer the Solomons directly. The Resident Commissioners in the other two territories would report to him. The Governor of Fiji would retain responsibility for indirect relations with Tonga and continue to administer Pitcairn. The reason for this was self-evident. The area for which the Governor of Fiji was responsible as High Commissioner for the Western Pacific extended over the Pacific for 5,800 miles, more than half the distance from Sydney to London. A former Governor of Fiji, Sir Harry Luke, took nearly two months to tour the countries for which he was responsible in a frigate lent for the purpose by the New Zealand Navy. He recorded his experiences in a fascinating book, *A South Seas Diary*.

Before planning for the move was seriously underway, we were struck by a hurricane. It caused substantial damage and some loss of life in Suva. The warnings had gone out by radio, going through several stages of alert.

I went to the office in the morning as usual. We all assisted in putting up the shutters on the office buildings. The Chief Secretary then sent members of staff to their homes. By the time I reached my house, the wind was already gusting strongly. My diminutive wife, who was struggling to put up hurricane shutters, was in danger of taking off with one of them. The elements were saying, 'I'll huff and I'll puff and I'll blow your house down'.

The noise and the strength of the gusts were frightening. In the study were stable-type doors There were two wooden half doors at the bottom and two glassed doors at the top. My wife called me to see the two wooden doors arcing with the wind pressure. They were on the point of bursting open. Had the wind penetrated the house, the roof would undoubtedly have gone. We obtained spades from the garage. I screwed a row of screw-nails into the floor, bracing the windows with the spade handles placed against the row of nails. The electricity was cut. In the howling of the wind, however, I was able to tune in to the test match in Australia on my battery-operated wireless.

The effects of hurricane damage at Suva, Fiji.

The wind suddenly ceased. The eye of the hurricane was passing over Suva. I dashed along to the Marquands next door to make sure that they were safe. I gave Bill the test score. The wind started plucking again. I returned and battened up. The wind then came from the other side. We were able to peer out. We saw the roof come off a house at the end of the street. It sailed a hundred yards down wind and disintegrated in an explosion of corrugated iron sheets. Sadly, we learnt afterwards that the resident was the architect who had designed our houses to be hurricane-proof.

When the wind abated, we were amazed at the vistas which had opened up. Not a leaf was left on any tree. The following morning we could not understand why the house was so dark. The leaves, shattered into shreds by the wind, had been blown, in heavy rain, against the windows. When the sun came out the next morning, they were pasted on to the glass. It took paint-strippers to clear the panes. I remarked to my wife that some silly fool had left his car standing on the middle of his lawn. She pointed to the wreckage of his garage some distance away.

The Chief Secretary was G.D. Chamberlain, who had been posted from West Africa. He was very much of the old school. He hoped to be promoted as the first independent High Commissioner for the Western Pacific. When the Governor of Fiji went on leave, he was appointed to act temporarily as High Commissioner for the Western Pacific He decided to make a visit to Tonga using a New Zealand Catalina aircraft which had been placed at his disposal for the visit. I was detailed to make the arrangements for his return. We had no formal diplomatic presence in Fiji. Accordingly I had to call upon Fiji Government Customs and Immigration authorities to ask, as a courtesy, that they should accord him VIP status. This would restrict formalities to a minimum. I duly went to meet him. I checked with Customs and Immigration that all would be well. I walked along the wharf where he was to disembark. At the end of the wharf was the car park where his car was parked. The wharf was separated from it by some moveable hurdles. I duly met him and we walked along the wharf, whereupon he pushed one of the hurdles aside, walked straight to his car and was driven off. I was left to go back to Customs and Immigration to explain what had happened and to apologise. Their main concern was my embarrassment. I remarked earlier on Fijian manners. A genial Fijian Immigration Officer said, 'Sir, we get a lot of VIPs coming through here. We expect them to behave as VIPs.' 'Noblesse oblige' in Fijian terms.

The Chief Secretary proceeded on final leave. He was replaced by Robert Stanley as Chief Secretary and High Commissioner designate. He would assume his full responsibility after the move to the Solomons. That injected some degree of urgency into the planning. He arrived by ship with his wife Ursula and their daughter Philada. Philada's sport was archery. She strode down the gangplank like Diana of the Ephesians with a six-foot bow in her hands. She appeared determined to take on Marching Rule on equal terms on arrival in the Solomons. Sir Robert, as he became later, decided to make a reconnaissance visit to the Solomons. He arranged for the M.V. *Betua*, one of the ships in the Solomons, to come to Fiji for the voyage. It was not the most suitable vessel for the purpose. I was the only officer in the office who had had experience in sailing in rough seas in the Solomons on a ship of this size. We believed that his wife had previously had a health problem. I accordingly took it upon myself to express concern that his family would accompany him on what was likely to be a very rough, if not dangerous, voyage. I was rapidly put in my place. His wife had undertaken safaris in the most primitive parts of Africa. She would take anything the Pacific could throw at them. He proved right, as they made the voyage there and back without mishap. My friend, Michael Hamilton, escorted them on the trip. I shall not, however, intrude on his memoirs.

For the move we sent an advance party. This included Adrian Dobbs,

Senior Assistant Secretary, Alasdair Macleod-Smith the Financial
Secretary and Dick Fairlie, an Assistant Secretary. The main party
comprised the Stanley family, myself and my wife, and Philip Dalton, the
Attorney-General. A small rear party would choose when to join us. The
rear party selected which files they would need. These mainly concerned
contracts and supplies in Suva. We established which might be required
immediately we arrived and which might be required on the eight-day
voyage by the High Commissioner. To operate efficiently as soon as we
arrived, we should, additionally, require speedy access to a fully
functioning registry. To achieve this we designed packing crates the exact
dimensions of a file in length and depth, each about six feet long. This
enabled us to duplicate the existing file registry on arrival. Simply by
knocking the tops off the boxes and placing the crates on top of each
other, we replicated the shelves used to store the files originally. In case
we ran into difficulty, we persuaded our Fijian Chief Clerk, Inoke
Lesuma, to come with us for the first six months. His memory was
legendary. You could say 'Inoke, I need a file containing a despatch from
the Secretary of State written about compassionate leave some time
before the War.' Inoke would stand for a moment and tap his temple
twice with his forefinger. 'You want F84/3/7!' He would be right. Close
liaison was maintained with the Secretariat in Honiara, particularly about
our houses on arrival and ceremonies to welcome the new High
Commissioner when he assumed duty in the territory.

For the main move we should be using the RCS *Kurimarau*, the largest
vessel in the Solomon Islands fleet. It had enough cabins for the main
party, a saloon for meals, a lounge, adequate hold capacity and deck space.
The latter was needed as when we did set sail, we looked like the Swiss
Family Robinson. The District Commissioner, Malaita wanted an oxen
cart and two oxen for Auki station. The Chief Agricultural Officer
wanted two Tamworth boars and some planting material for Government
House grounds. The High Commissioner also wanted planting material,
twenty-four Black Australorp, and twenty-four Rhode Island Red poultry.
Not to be outdone, my wife said that we should settle for a dozen of both
kinds of hen. Before we set sail, Philip Dalton, the Attorney General,
looked at the brass plate on the wheel-house which gave the name of the
shipyard which had constructed the ship. 'I'll bet that was a rocky
concern', he said lugubriously.

The worst part of the voyage for me was that coded telegrams kept
coming in addressed to the High Commissioner. He would say 'Russell,
can you bring me the code book?' The code books, together with Secret

and Confidential files, were kept in the High Commissioner's safe, about five feet high. It had been placed on the deck, near the hatch, so that it was under constant observation. Except by the oxen. One of them was tethered with its rear end against the safe door. Not only had I to persuade a reluctant animal of some size to ease over. I had usually to arm myself with a large piece of cardboard and a wet rag to clean off the combination lock. I think that I was revenged, as the two wheels of the ox cart stood at the end of the wharf at Auki for many years, in the style of OK Corral. This led me to believe that the Malaitans probably ate them both.

We called in briefly at Vila in the New Hebrides. Our first sight of the Solomons, en route to San Cristoval, was Anuda Island. We hove to about a mile off shore. Soon, what we had taken to be coconuts floating on the water turned out to be Anudans swimming out to the ship. A net was let down and they swarmed on board, wild looking, with long hair, speaking a Polynesian tongue. A few spoke Pidgin English. They were presented with two cases of tinned meat. A raft was hastily knocked together to enable them to swim it ashore. When the captain sounded the klaxon to indicate that we were leaving, the raft was thrown into the water. Some of them set off with it. Others chattered to each other, surveying the shrinking island as we moved away from it. They finally dived reluctantly off the deck and struck out for an island they could not have seen from sea level. We had no real fears of them getting there as they swam like fish.

We made good progress. It became clear that we would arrive ahead of schedule. This was inappropriate as ceremonies were planned when we reached port. Accordingly we anchored off Nugu Island, about twenty miles east of Honiara. We had a pleasant swim ashore. Before long we were knocking off the tops of the boxes containing our files. It was the 22nd December 1952.

We had been allotted a house half-way up Langakiki Ridge, one of the residential ridges in Honiara. We were invited by another administrative officer, Alex Davidson, and his wife, to have dinner with them that evening. There was a jungle path between the two houses. Night had fallen but it was not too dark to negotiate our way. Suddenly a dark shape rose barking out of the dark. I recognised Jock, my dog, whom I had left in care of the Davidsons when I left twenty-four months before. He was half Alsatian and half Husky, having come originally from the Aleutian Islands aboard an American ship. He had been with me in the Western District and at Malu'u, and recognised me immediately. He sat with his head on my shoe for the rest of the evening. A fine welcome back. But I think, over the years before he died, my wife supplanted me in his affections.

Somehow, despite all our planning, there was a complete misunderstanding about the basic organisation after our arrival. The Solomon Islands Secretariat had envisaged that they would carry on as before. The High Commissioner would have his separate Secretariat responsible for the New Hebrides and the Gilbert and Ellice Colony. This misconception was quickly corrected. I continued with my my previous duties as Assistant Secretary, Personnel and Finance.

But, before I discuss these in further detail, it may be timely to sketch in the environment as it then existed. Henderson field, the main airport for the country, was situated about eight miles to the east of Honiara. The American control tower was still standing as a monument to the battles on Guadalcanal. Driving westwards to Honiara, a visitor would cross the Lunga River by a derelict American bridge, which was later replaced by a more permanent structure. The road wound through coconut palms, reaching another smaller airstrip. This was then derelict but would become a nine-hole golf course and the alternate airfield if, for any reason, the main airport was out of action. Further towards Honiara, on the left, was an American hutted camp which was being used to house single labourers who were working in the capital. To the right was the old American wharf, which was no longer being used. There were new landing facilities which had been installed at Point Cruz in central Honiara. These would ultimately be replaced by a modern port and cargo sheds under the control of a Ports Authority. The land adjacent to the old American wharf would ultimately be developed as a Business Park.

A track to the left led to one of the residential ridges called Kola Ridge. At that time it only had a few houses, The main road continued past the hospital. This was an American wartime institution which had been renovated by the Government. It was known as Number Nine by Solomon Islanders. Further on to the right, before passing over an old American bridge near the mouth of the Matanikau River, lay Chinatown. The small Chinese population chose to live there, servicing a few stores and a restaurant. On the other side of the bridge the road had been named Mendana Avenue after one of the Spanish explorers who first visited the Solomons. A road to the left led on to Vavaya Ridge, where government houses had been built. At that time there were not many buildings along Mendana Avenue. The Public Works Headquarters and the Central District Headquarters building lay to the right, and, further on, the Post Office to the left. After District Headquarters, a road arced to the right going down to the port at Point Cruz. It rejoined Mendana Avenue before running over a small bridge spanning Cruz Creek. Near the coast on the other side of Cruz Creek stood the old Mendana Hotel, built of thatched materials. It later burnt down and was replaced by the present structure. The Secretariat then in use was built of local materials, standing next to the Treasury. Shortly after arrival, we moved to old American buildings further westwards. Government House, then built in the local tradition, had been an Officers Mess for the New Zealand Army during the War. It was close to the beach. Although it posed problems for its occupants, it had an intimacy and charm that was never quite attained by the modern structure which replaced it. Immediately past the old Post Office building, a road ran to the left, skirting the base of a long ridge about five hundred feet high before looping round along the top of Langakiki Ridge. This feature, with several smaller ridges behind, was beginning to provide good building sites. It was to become one of the better residential areas in the capital. From the entry to this road, Mendana Avenue continued through land with few structures on either side to the police barracks at Rove. The road ran on, out of the capital, to the village of Kukumbona and beyond.

The atmosphere was one of a raw frontier town on a development frontier. Common sense had preceded planning, which was soon to come.

We quickly settled down but in 1953 I worked harder than I have ever had to work during my career.

I have mentioned that the WPHC secretariat in Fiji was cocooned and worked in isolation from Departments and the Civil Service. That no longer applied. From the time that we stacked up our files, the administrative minutiae of administering nearly a thousand civil servants and managing a country's budget broke over us like a tidal wave. We had first to marry the files of the two Secretariats. We had to take over all the personal files of the Solomon Islands establishment and the financial files on numerous development projects which were then in hand. We were no longer at arm's length. My work pattern developed into getting to the office about six a.m., breaking for an hour at lunchtime, and working till six p.m. Then, whenever possible and social activities did not intervene, I spread out my files on the dining room table after the evening meal and worked till about two a.m. I found that the only way to make this pattern endurable was to intersperse it with total relaxation at the weekends. We walked up the rivers and on the grassy ridges behind Honiara. We swam at Trench's Beach. We held or attended luncheon and dinner parties both at home and in friends' houses. We danced at the Guadalcanal Club till the small hours. But the work routine was taxing.

During this initial stint in personnel work, I had to give policy formulation lower priority than arranging to get people on leave, filling vacancies, preparing submissions for promotion. I had to attend to postings and confidential reports, get individuals off on training courses, prepare civil lists, seniority lists, and issue amendments to General Orders. These were the Civil Service bible which laid down the procedures to be followed.

The new Chief Secretary, Robert Minnitt, was an excellent personnel manager. He would normally accept my advice on staff matters. However he had had the long experience to know when a case had a sufficient compassionate element to justify ignoring the rules and the precedents. He would then decide what he thought appropriate. I suspected Alasdair Macleod Smith, the Financial Secretary, of working the same hours as myself. Indeed he had a health breakdown when he went on leave, perhaps because the pressure suddenly came off, He was young to have reached the position he then held. Although he did not consciously teach his subordinates, I learnt from his methods of analysis and from his ability to draw verbal conclusions from a tangle of figures. The High Commissioner, Sir Robert Stanley, deliberately gave the impression that he was hard and inflexible. Under the public persona, however, there was a family man with a good sense of humour. He was an officer with a strict sense of fairness and compassion when needed. We realised after he had gone that he had set himself the task of fashioning the status which he ascribed to a post new to the three Western Pacific Territories. He had to appear to be more than a Resident Commissioner, particularly when they were about. I was never sure whether he enjoyed this role or not.

At Christmas, 1953 a few of us decided to get away from Honiara for a brief holiday. The planner-in-chief was Ella Manning, the Fijian wife of Tom Manning, who was in charge of telecommunications. She described herself as a Pacific cocktail, as she had Fijian, Samoan and Tongan blood in her family. She was of ample build. Her life was in superlatives, whether in the fields of entertainment, quantities of food, humour, or humanity. An Australian friend, Norman Wallis, Managing Director of Tenaru Timbers, Ella and my wife were the planning team. Norman chartered one of the government ships, the M.V. *Noula*. We planned to spend the holiday on the island of Nugu, where we had swum on the way to Honiara. We would stay for three nights, 24th 25th and 26th, getting back on the 27th, which was also a holiday. All kudos to the planners. They borrowed tents from the Geological Survey. This was before the days of polystyrene and my wife designed a cool box by finding two boxes, one of which would fit inside the other with about three inches of space to spare. The space around the inner box was packed with sawdust. Champagne and beer was then packed in the inner box amid generous supplies of ice. We took with us decorations for a Christmas Tree, crackers, decorative cloths for the Christmas dinner, candles and pressure lamps, a portable gramophone and records, radio, a cooked ham and a turkey to be roasted on the island. Nor could we survive without Christmas presents, Guinness for Black Velvet on Boxing Day, fishing rods, shotguns and cartridges, bedding and mosquito nets, and evening dress for the Christmas Dinner.

Our servants having opted to come along, we assembled at Point Cruz, Those in the party were Tom Manning, Ella and their daughter Joanna, my wife and myself, Norman, and two bachelors, Chris and Alan. The boat was to be returned after landing us. A second party would arrive on the 26th, when the M.V. *Noula* returned to take us back. We arrived on the island and established camp. Ella ordered some of us on to the reef to collect our supper: clams, lobsters, sea-urchins and various shell-fish. She used these, together with other delicacies from our ample larder, to make a sumptuous evening meal. We all slept well. The following day we went out to shoot and fish. Again we lived off the land and sea for lunch. Meanwhile Ella had been roasting the turkey on a spit. Kotaru, our cook, found a small casuarina, which my wife decorated as a Christmas Tree. The 'table', Pacific fashion, was laid on the sand, and decorated with the crackers and also with hibiscus, which grew wild on the island. I have not spoken about the numerous swims which we had at various times of the day. We had decided to dress for dinner, the men in black evening trousers, black ties and monkey-jackets, the ladies in long evening dresses. Neither sex wore shoes. We sat cross-legged round the table and had a traditional Christmas dinner with all the trimmings, with ice-cold champagne as an accompaniment to the sweet. The gramophone was turned on with suitable songs from *South Pacific* while we sipped brandy and coffee. It was self-service for the evening. A separate repast had been prepared for the servants, who had their own party going on elsewhere on the beach. It could have been an anti-climax the following day, but the party carried on, enlivened by shrieks from Ella, 'A crocodile! A crocodile!' We rapidly reached for our shotguns The reptile, however, turned out to be a harmless iguana. It climbed a tree and vanished. We duly drank our Black Velvet when the second party arrived. We set out the following morning for Point Cruz, where a reception party awaited us to hear how we had fared. A friend discreetly suggested that we had been shooting edible birds and not pigeons, which were out of season. We hastily agreed. Distant memories tell me that the party still went on that evening.

In the office the next morning, shortly before midday, the Financial Secretary sent for me and said 'Do you know anything about this?' I did. Prior to leaving the office before lunch on Christmas Eve, Macleod-Smith handed me a telegram and said 'Please get this off this afternoon. It's important'. The Solomons was then in receipt of Grant-in-Aid from the United Kingdom, a sum which varied each year to balance the local budget. We were due to receive the last tranche of this sum for the first quarter of the new year. Macleod-Smith's telegram read: 'May we please have final instalment of Grant-in-Aid amounting to £XXX before 31st December'. It was addressed to the Secretary of State for the Colonies and signed 'High Commissioner for the Western Pacific'. In these days all official mail sent to the Colonial Office was sent over the signature of the Governor or High Commissioner. When Macleod-Smith handed me the telegram, the staff had already left for lunch. I was heading for Point Cruz to board the M.V. *Noula*. I therefore pinned a note to the telegram which I left on my secretary's desk reading: 'Can you please get this off first thing this afternoon? And a Merry Christmas to you all. TR'

Each morning when he came to his desk, the High Commissioner read through a folder of any correspondence which had issued from the Secretariat in the last twenty-four hours. He came to one which read:

'May we please have the final instalment of Grant-in-Aid amounting to £XXX before 31st December, and a Merry Christmas to you all.

High Commissioner for the Western Pacific'

Knowing that it had emanated from the Financial Secretary's Office Sir Robert had taken him to task for such frivolity. Macleod-Smith subsequently explained matters, but I think that he too was surprised when a copy of a formal despatch from the High Commissioner to The Secretary of State came down to us. The tenor of it was that Sir Robert referred to telegram reference XYZ of the 24th December to the Secretary of State, in which Christmas wishes had been inappropriately conveyed. While he did not wish to disassociate himself from the sentiments expressed, he regretted that in the exuberance of the Christmas season this had occurred. He proffered his sincere apologies. By coincidence, a few years later, when I was seconded to the Finance

Department of the Colonial Office, the file bearing the correspondence came across my desk. I was able to establish that the High Commissioner need not have been so concerned.

But concerned he was, before I went on leave, expressing his dissatisfaction to the Chief Secretary about 'the inordinate delay on file F23/6/2 by the Assistant Secretary, Personnel and Finance,' He asked that his displeasure be conveyed to Mr Russell. In carrying out this instruction, Robert Minnitt said that he was obliged to inform me of the High Commissioner's displeasure but knew that I was under severe pressure. I said that I should like my side of the occurrence to be understood, and that I should let him have my response within forty-eight hours. I duly asked for a personal interview with the High Commissioner. In the meantime I prepared my ground. Each file bore a file ladder on the front showing the date it came to an officer from the Registry or other source, and the date, and to whom, it had been passed on. I had been keeping a record of the files landing on my desk each day, the number processed in a day, my hours of work, and the numbers of files left on my desk each day. I knew that I was a relatively fast worker, could not put in any more hours of work in a normal week, and was being overtaken at the rate of about forty files a week. Nearly a hundred files required attention. At the beginning of each day, I had to assign to each file the priority that I considered appropriate. The file to which the High Commissioner had referred would not have been accorded priority treatment unless I had been directed to deal with it immediately. Senior officers were fully entitled to demand this. My request for an interview with the High Commissioner was granted. I said that the delay to which he had taken exception had to be seen in a context of which he might not be familiar. I said that I had willingly faced the hours of work which had been demanded this tour but was not prepared to put either my health or marriage at risk indefinitely. While I did not expect a retraction, he said that he was completely unaware of the pressures under which I had been working. He would be posting me as District Commissioner, Malaita, when I returned from leave, and hoped this would be less demanding. He said that I had been selected or this because of my knowledge of the island and for commendable service at Malu'u. I should not assume that this was in any way a negative comment on my performance in the Secretariat. He had cleared the air. When I returned from leave, I found that two additional posts had been created. There were three officers dealing with the work load with which I had been coping.

We proceeded on leave on the 16th February 1954.

CHAPTER EIGHT

Return to Malaita

ON RETURN FROM LEAVE, we recovered our household effects from the Public Works Department stores, where they had been kept during our absence. We had them loaded on the M.V. *Margery* and set out for Auki. Our house was a pre-war bungalow, four hundred yards from Auki harbour. A broad verandah had originally run all round the house with the rooms in the middle. Alterations through the years to add extra rooms had reduced the verandah to that running along the front of the house. As usual, the kitchen premises and servants' quarters were at the rear. The house stood on the site of the original District Commissioner's house occupied by Mr Bell. This had been on high piles. It was entered through a trapdoor by a ladder which was drawn up at night.

I took over as District Commissioner from Val Andersen, who had made a remarkable change in the political climate since the rapprochement with Marching Rule. Later in his career he was to become Resident Commissioner of the Gilbert and Ellice Islands Colony. He had a basic philosophy that if one could get the economy right, other problems would fade. Thus the main Secondary school, King George V School, had been rebuilt at Auki, about three miles to the north of the station. The new Council premises for the Malaita Council at Aimela were nearby. An Agricultural station had been built at Dala, about fifteen miles north of Auki. A campaign had started to encourage peasant farmers to grow cocoa under shade, to diversify and to supplement income from copra, dried coconut. This was also produced as a peasant crop. The methodology of drying the copra was also being improved, using hot-air drying instead of smoking. A higher price was obtained from better quality produce. The 'Government Road' leading both north and south from the station was being converted into a motorable road by the Public Works Department. A bridge over the river at Fiu was now passable for a landrover. The Auki hospital had been improved and staff increased. Moreover the Armed Constabulary was being phased out, to be replaced by a police force run on more modern lines, without arms. In the absence of a military presence, however, some of them would have to be trained as an armed reserve which could be called out in emergency. Inspectors of Police had been recruited from England. One had been posted to Auki in charge of the Malaita police establishment. This corrected the previous unsustainable situation in which the person responsible for the police who approved criminal charges was also the magistrate.

My first task was to check the cash, accounts, stores and the documentation with the outgoing District Commissioner. After handover, I had to make familiarisation visits to the various institutions in or near Auki, and have meetings with key staff. Importantly, I had to get to know the President of the Malaita Council, Salana Gaa, the 'Big Man' nominated by Marching Rule to be its head. I then set off on a circum-insular tour by ship to visit the coastal villages, the mission stations and the one substantial plantation at Baunani towards the south of Malaita. I endeavoured to meet as many ex-Marching Rule protagonists as I could, as well as the Headmen and Assistant Headmen. I was greeted by many of my old police detachment at Malu'u. Guy Wallington was the District Officer, with his wife gracing the large thatched house which I had built there and briefly occupied before my departure.

Having been immersed in intelligence work during my stint at Malu'u, I had still to satisfy myself that Marching Rule had finished as a movement when the Malaita Council was set up. What I feared might happen was that the Marching Rule Councils might continue underground. Although the officially sponsored Malaita Council was ostensibly in charge of local government, the Marching Rule bodies could still be making the important decisions. They could possibly be undermining the official body. Fortunately this did not happen, although some of the former Marching Rule leaders did not put their shoulders to the wheel. On the contrary, I found that the energies of the movement were channelled into the Malaita Council. This proved at that time to be a power-house. By comparison with other local government councils elsewhere, it was dynamic, imaginative, and relatively efficient in getting things done.

On this initial tour I reviewed Native Court cases decisions, which could not be put into effect until a review had been carried out by an Administrative Officer. It was clear that instruction in procedures was merited. There were in effect three possible courses of action when someone was wronged or a criminal act took place. The Administrative Officer could adjudicate under the Pacific Order in Council, or hear the case as a criminal matter. If it was a misdemeanour he could deal with it. If it was a felony he could hold a Preliminary Enquiry and refer the case for trial before a Judicial Commissioner. But most misdemeanours could

View from the District Officer's house at Malu'u.

The new District Officer's house at Malu'u, completed in 1950.

be held before a Native Court as a customary matter. Usually they were settled by an order to the person in the wrong to pay compensation in native money to the aggrieved party. Such were the cases that had to be reviewed. In one case I found that several persons had been accused of affray in a village. Someone had given evidence as a witness. The accused had been acquitted and the luckless witness found guilty. One of the less educated Headmen asked if customary methods for finding out whether someone was telling the truth could be used in cases involving custom. These included holding stones heated in a fire or swimming across the Maramasiki passage, where crocodiles were common. Consequently when I returned, I started work on preparing a week's course on Native Court procedure. I brought in the Native Court justices to Auki. There they could also be taken to Malaita Council headquarters to see what was being done and spread the word when they returned to their communities.

It was also apparent on this first tour that relations between the bush people and the salt-water people were worsening. The bush people were demanding the right to fish in waters which they still considered their property. The salt-water people had enjoyed the fishing rights for generations. They saw their traditional markets disappearing if the bush people caught the fish directly. I consulted the legal authorities in Honiara. It was decided that the Judicial Commissioner should come across to hold one important case in Small Malaita. I could then take the remaining outstanding cases having regard to the decision made by the Judicial Commissioner. The Judicial Commissioner duly arrived. We travelled down to Small Malaita. A meeting-house was requisitioned as a court building. The bench was created out of a large packing-crate covered by a Protectorate flag. Jeoffrey Horsfall, the Judicial Commissioner, appeared in full Judge's robes. These so overawed the first witness that he keeled over in a faint. Jeoffrey merely observed, 'Next witness'. The second witness, having been asked his name and place of residence, suddenly sprinted out of the door. Finally a verdict was given. It was hot as we walked back to the boat. There was no one to observe one of Her Majesty's Judiciary in a pair of swimming trunks, which is all that he had been wearing, with his robes over his arm. He was followed by a policeman carrying his wig He also heard outstanding cases when we returned to Auki. By coincidence, he was subsequently transferred to the Cayman Islands. He had retired before I arrived there.

Visits to Honiara were not infrequent for various meetings or to replenish stores. On one of these visits Michael Hamilton, who was

District Commissioner, Central District, said that the labourers on one of the plantations in the Russell Islands, which were part of his District, had refused to work. They came from Koio in Malaita. He suggested that we made a joint visit to endeavour to put matters right. It was the first, and probably the only, time that District Commissioners had worked in tandem. The plantation overseer was genuinely puzzled and angry. The workers had formerly bathed in the sea and had carried water for cooking from a source some four hundred yards from their sleeping quarters. He had installed showers next to their dormitory, with a tap from which they could draw water for cooking. They refused to use this and demanded that the water came from another source at a much greater distance than the present one. Exasperated, the foreman dug in his heels and considered the workers ungrateful and unmanageable. They were pagan. When we persuaded them to talk, it transpired that the water-pipe bringing the water to the tap to be used for cooking passed under a public road. This was used by women on a regular basis. If one of these happened to be menstruating, the water would consequently be unclean. This should have been patently obvious to the management of the plantation. There was no argument. The water for cooking would have to be brought in from another source. The overseer agreed to do so. The labourers went back to work and Michael and I returned to Honiara.

When I arrived back in Auki, there were about two hundred men sitting on the grass near the office. There also seemed to be many yards of washing-line stretching out near them. Guy Wallington had been bringing back a remittance of money from the Treasury in Honiara on the M.V. *Nancy*, a small vessel without a hold. The locked wooden chest containing the money was secured on the small deck at the stern. He ran into very heavy weather on the way back from Honiara. The chest was soaked with sea water. On arrival, he found bundles of sodden banknotes and wet bags of coins awash with salt water. His response to this situation was to make a quick visit to the Chinese store. He purchased some rolls of fishing line and as many clothes pegs as he could obtain. Returning to the office he had some poles erected, and rigged his washing line. Under a police guard, he hung out the banknotes individually to dry. It was the custom on some parts of Malaita that when a chief died his strings of native money were hung up on display to show his importance. The practice also proved that he had not squandered the money he had inherited. This made him 'high' or important. The rumour went out that the Government was doing something similar. A small crowd had gathered to see this new phenomenon. Guy did not do things by halves. When the notes were dry, he dusted them with talcum powder. He counted them into bundles and secured them with elastic bands. One of my end-of-the-month duties was to count the cash to reconcile it with the book figure. When I opened my safe, it smelled of medicated talcum powder, which was all that he had been able to purchase. The notes were so slippery that they tended to fly off the table as they were counted. This was one of the routine duties at the end of the month both at District and Malaita Council headquarters. One tried to arrange tours so as to be on the station at the month's end. Court cases could also be taken at the same time.

I varied the touring pattern between tours by ship and on foot. There were more cross-island tracks in the south of the island. One from Auki led up the Fiu River valley to arrive on the far coast south of Fokanakafo. Another followed the boundary between Are Are and Koio. This was particularly arduous. A third crossed Are Are where the island narrowed. It was less taxing than the others. On one occasion we entered moss-forest only found at high altitudes, and more common on Guadalcanal than Malaita. Trees are stunted and covered with lichen and moss. The track wound its way across spongy moss residue, and the plant and bird life was noticeably different from that at lower altitudes. Eerily, on one occasion we were shrouded in dense mist and, without a guide, would have been completely lost. Even a half a mile from the coast on high ground, where one would expect a view of the sea, the height of the trees and density of the vegetation totally blocks the line of sight. On all the crossings, descent was made into one or more of the river valleys. A swim in pellucid water flowing over flat pebbles was a stimulus for the remainder of the crossing. In certain places in Koio the only clothing for both sexes, if this was worn at all, was a small apron covering the genitals. Women did not like to be seen by strangers. They would dash giggling into the bushes if they saw a patrol coming towards them. The men were muscled and sturdy. They were capable of walking prodigious distances with heavy loads. Yet it was the women who carried loads of vegetables down to the coast to market. The man preceded his wife and daughters, carrying only a machete to slash protruding vegetation. In former days it was also to defend them from attack. Unlike the airy houses of the saltwater people, the bush-dwellers' houses were little more than a shelter from the elements. They had a compressed mud floor, with a fire in the middle. There was a bunk-type bed made of wooden slats crudely fashioned by a machete. One or two cooking pots and weapons were in evidence. A few bamboo water containers leant against the wall, filled each morning by the women from a spring three hundred feet below. Oil for lighting was too expensive and inaccessible. The working day finished at sunset, although there was some conversation in the smoke and glow of the fire after the evening meal. Entering one of these shelters and sitting on a log by the fire, tired from a day's march and soaked by rain, I felt the sanctity of the place. Here were the elements of life itself: man, woman, child, shelter, fire, water, food. I reflected upon our own consumer society and the paraphernalia with which we surround ourselves in the pursuit of comfort and happiness. I recalled the camaraderie we had shared as prisoners-of-war with our total possessions in a cardboard box.

The Polynesian island of Sikaiana, or Stewart Island was part of my district, lying about ninety miles to the east of Malaita. But that is an approximation as the Admiralty charts record that 'This group is reported to lie 13 miles to the eastward of the position shown'. I made several visits there. The easiest way to land was to go ashore in a canoe, as there was no entrance through the reef which surrounded the islands. The ship had to place kedge anchors on to the reef at a place where there was an outflow of water which held the ship off the rocks. Going over the reef on the canoe was always exciting. The paddlers would line up the canoe and wait for the seventh wave. This was said to be much larger than the others. A shout would go up. The paddlers would make long deep strokes, sending the canoe charging towards the maelstrom ahead. And over we would go. Their life was as arduous as that on the larger Melanesian islands. Yet they gave the impression that for them life was there to be enjoyed. Laughter and shrieks of merriment are part of the dance. In Melanesia, dances are often serious rituals with clubs, spears and shields. Sikaiana was an atoll. The only stones were relatively soft coral boulders. Consequently the old adzes were made of clamshell. Agriculture was difficult as the soil was sandy. As was to be expected, fish was a staple in the diet. Coconuts were dried in the sun for export and sale. A cash income was also earned by sending young men out to work. Remittances sent back to the island were one of the few sources of cash. Men did the heavy work in house building and repairs, fishing, and bush-clearing for agriculture. There had therefore to be a limit to the number who left the island at any given time. It was noticeable that if thirty men returned from work on a ship, approximately the same number sought passages to go to work in their place. The islanders appeared to have arrived an a formula where labour for fishing, agriculture and building, or on work outside the island, was related to maximising cash income from the sale of coconuts and remittances. If too many men left the island, living conditions and income from coconuts declined. Houses went into disrepair and there was insufficient food from the gardens.

There were two forms of welcome for the visitor on Sikaiana, The first was to be thrown from the deck of the ship into the sea by the women. In the second, the men brewed up large quantities of coconut toddy, which was presented to the guest. This was to be consumed communally on the night of arrival. On three visits I always received the men's welcome. I was assured, however, by Alfred Hill, Bishop of Melanesia, that he was allowed to take his watch off before he was thrown into the sea, After my first visit I learnt to make my departure from the toddy-party early. I left the doctor from Auki, who always accompanied me, to deputise for me. This was an instance either of pulling rank or delegation of duties.

There was no radio receiver on the island. Communication was by ships infrequently visiting the island. There was a school and a clinic, but no resident doctor. On one occasion we took a cinema projector driven by twelve-volt batteries, spools of film and rolled up screen. This had to come ashore by canoe over the reef. It proved very popular. Court cases were few, but I was able to conduct a census to compare the population with previous head-counts which had been done from time to time. There was a Council and a Native Court, although the latter seemed to have little to do. I suspected that disputes were quietly resolved by the chiefs, who held greater sway in a Polynesian society than in parts of Melanesia, where the hereditary principle did not always apply.

Sir Robert Stanley had been replaced as High Commissioner by Sir John Gutch with his wife Diana. They had three boys, all being educated in England, who came out for school holidays. Sir John's style was very different from that of his predecessor. He expected others to have the same level of dedication as himself. He was not a general who sited slit trenches. He was respected throughout the service. He and his wife made an official visit to the District on a difficult assignment. There had been a savage murder at one of the Melanesian Mission schools on Guadalcanal. A European priest who was teaching at the school had called one of the boys to his house after having Sunday lunch with the headmaster. As the boy entered the porch, the teacher drove a pick-axe through the boy's head and killed him. He was subsequently tried for murder, found guilty and sentenced to death, a sentence widely approved by the Melanesian community. The case went on appeal to the Court of Appeal in Fiji. There the Court's finding was set aside. One of 'Guilty but Insane' was substituted. The death sentence was commuted to one of life imprisonment to be served in a suitable institution in the United Kingdom. Consequently he was sent to Broadmoor.

The murdered boy had come from the island of Sulafou in the Lau Lagoon of Malaita. It was one of the two islands steadfastly loyal to Government during Marching Rule. It still flew the Union Jack on its flagpole. We could not, however, know how this news would be received on the island, or indeed on Malaita as a whole. A Melanesian boy had been murdered by a European. The last murderer, who had come from the island of Adagege, a quarter of a mile from Sulafou, had been hanged. A European murderer was now to be spared hanging and sent out of the jurisdiction to England. Sir John considered this of such importance that he should go to the island, accompanied by me as District Commissioner, to inform the people of the Fijian Court of Appeal decision. This would be done in the course of a High Commissioner's tour of the island. The Commissioner of Police, however, apprehensive for the High Commissioner's safety, decreed that a detachment of armed police should accompany Sir John. It would be on stand-by when he went ashore. The result was that Sir John and Lady Gutch were on one vessel. My wife and I were on another. A third came along astern with a detachment of about twenty police. When we anchored off Sulafou, I went ashore unaccompanied. I knew well the Chief, Tome Wate, and many of the population. I had previously advised them of the visit by the High Commissioner. There were the usual decorations for the occasion. I could not inform Tome Wate of what Sir John was going to say. I said, however, that the High Commissioner had some serious news for them. I hoped that they would take it quietly. I am sure that Tome Wate surmised it was something to do with the murder. I nevertheless remained fairly certain that there would be no trouble following the news that had to be broken. My wife had joined the Gutches on their ship. When I reported to the High Commissioner, both wives decided to come ashore with us as they did on a normal High Commissioner's visit. Sir John addressed the crowd and broke the news. There was silence. Then one of the elders spoke.

He said that Sulafou had always been a loyal island. Even if his people did not like what they had been told, they would accept it quietly. What hurt the people was the fact that the Government had seen fit to bring a detachment of police which they could see aboard ship. They considered this a breach of the trust which had existed between Sulafou and the Government. This was a quiet reproach, but I was sure that I could patch things up later. The Court of Appeal could not, of course, take into account, where a man's life was at stake, the racial overtones that their decision would create. Had the murdered boy come from one of the more primitive parts of the island, the ending to the story might have been different.

We carried on with the tour, and I had arranged to visit Sinerango, where Mr Bell had been massacred before the War. I had asked the Headman to assemble the people there so that the High Commissioner could address them. They were from Koio, one of the areas least enthusiastic about the Malaita Council. Sir John told the listeners about the Fiji Court of Appeal decision. He then spoke on the theme: 'The Malaita Council is there for you to use; if you don't use it, it will collapse and will not be able to look after you.' This was the site where Bell had been battered to death and his cadet, Lillies, chopped to pieces within living memory. Sir John used a metaphor which might have been risky. 'If you have a knife, use it, or it will get blunt and useless.' Most of his audience were carrying, as usual, the machetes they brought with them to clear the bush tracks as they walked along.

Sinerango is a most impressive place, with densely forested mountains rising up in folds, usually into cloud. The harbour is large enough to anchor a fleet of ships. The landing place where the tax-house once stood, and where the massacre took place, is dwarfed by the scale of the anchorage. Behind lies a spring of ice-cold water flowing from the base of the mountains. Like Glencoe, it has its memories.

Before leaving on tour, I had put in train the installation of a telephone system on the station. In Honiara I had managed to acquire four ex-American Army field telephones. I planned to link up my house, my office, the Police Station, and the Hospital. It is difficult to comprehend in today's world of mobiles that in 1954 there were no telephones on the island. There were wireless links with headquarters and with some mission stations and plantations. When I returned, the system had been installed. Each of the four units had a call signal such as two long rings and a short, two long, three short. This was signalled using a crank handle on the box holding the telephone proper. When I returned home, I went to test the installation by telephoning the doctor. I transmitted the call sign. There was a click as the telephone came off the hook at the other end, followed by heavy breathing. I said, 'Can I talk to Dr Bevin please?' A Malaitan spoke, obviously not to me: 'This something hime talk!' I said again, 'Can you please get Dr Bevin to come to the telephone.' The voice at the other end went up an octave: 'Himme talk moa'. Beginning to lose my patience I talked more sternly this time. I could almost visualise the Malaitan at the other end coming to attention. There was a loud clatter as he dropped the telephone. I reverted to previous practice. I sent a runner to tell Dr Bevin what had happened. Once the system was running, primitive although it was, it contributed greatly to the smooth running of the District station.

There was a visit to Malaita by a fisheries expert from the South Pacific Commission. Dick Fairlie the District Officer at Auki, took him first down the Langa Langa Lagoon and to Small Malaita. This would show him the fishing methods of the saltwater people in the southern half of the island. We then set off for the Lau Lagoon in the north. I had something to show him. Diversifying the economy was one of our aims. The local traditional markets were held on only three days per week. On the other four days per week no fishing took place. There was plenty of fish to catch. There was a dearth of fish in Honiara the capital. We had, however, no deep-freezes. The answer appeared to be to smoke the fish. I obtained the design of a kipper-stack from a fisherman in Eyemouth in Scotland, and duly erected this on Adagege in the Lau lagoon. We did not have oak chips for the smoking process but there were always abundant supplies of coconut husks. After the fish was caught, it had to be gutted and opened out. It was then soaked in brine for twenty-four hours. My fisherman friend had advised me that to test the degree of salinity, salt had to be added to sea water until a raw potato floated to the surface. Whether a sweet potato had the same specific gravity as an Irish potato I never found out. The fish were then threaded across the shoulders on poles sharpened at each end. Starting six feet above the fire, grooves were cut in the sides of the stack at twelve inch intervals until the top one was about six feet from the top of the stack. The poles containing the fish were then placed across the stack with the ends in the grooves about a foot apart. The set of poles on the next tier were so arranged that the rows of fish on the top tier were suspended between the rows of fish below.

After experimenting with the optimum time for smoking, the islanders were producing a marketable product. We also experimented with sun-dried fish broken into meal-like consistency, which could be reconstituted by adding water. The Fisheries expert, a Dutchman, was suitably impressed, but I was to learn a basic rule of marketing. Firstly the Solomon Islanders did not eat smoked fish. But more importantly, there was a ready market for fresh fish in the local markets. After a great deal of work to produce the smoked product, there was a substantial weight-loss. It might have been possible in the initial stages to waive the freight charges to Honiara on government ships. Even so, I had to accept that the fish could not be sold at a cost attractive to the buyer, and which yielded a price acceptable to the producer.

But the derelict smoke-stack stood as a monument to my endeavour for some years to come.

Another experiment failed. Encouraged by one of the Agricultural staff at Dala, I persuaded a Malaitan who lived at a high altitude to grow a crop of Irish potatoes, which were successfully grown in the highlands of Papua New Guinea. I received some small new potatoes of good quality but on the basis of one, possibly two, potatoes for each one that had been planted. Not an economic proposition. Bob Meadows, the Public Works Foreman at Auki, on the other hand, had green fingers. He was popular with the Auki housewives for the supplies of fresh vegetables which he grew on the station. After the grant of Independence to Indonesia, we had recruited a number of Dutch agriculturists highly qualified in tropical agriculture. One of these, Orly Torling, designed a project with overhead sprinklers irrigating a small plot. He used an abandoned motor cycle engine to drive a pump alongside a stream. The plot was covered with sheets of mosquito netting to break up the tropical rain, which could blast young seedlings out of the ground. On this plot he grew copious supplies of all vegetables in use. His aim was to show local farmers that by a small investment and low recurrent costs, they could vastly improve on traditional methods. But peasant farmers are notoriously slow to change. In Melanesia the egalitarian element in society was strong. One acre of cacao was sufficient to give a family an income. This was the size advocated by the Agricultural Department. One farmer had the enterprise to plant ten acres of cacao His reward was to have the young trees on a large area chopped down. This would make him the same as his less industrious neighbours.

We were now about to spend our second Christmas period in Auki, which would involve entertainment in the various homes on the station. That would be spontaneous and enjoyable. There was, however, no rest-house or hotel on Auki at that time. Most visitors to the station had to be accommodated by the District Commissioner. At the end of our first twelve months, my wife and I realised that we had averaged guests staying with us for five nights out of seven for the whole year. Guests were other administrative officers, visiting Heads of Department from Honiara who might be accompanied by their wives, advisers, and occasionally visitors from London. The pressure was so constant that on one or two especially fraught occasions we had difficulty in retaining our staff. They loyally stayed with us for most of the time we were in the Solomons. Their efficiency reflected the training given to them by those wives for whom they worked, and also single men and women employed by the Government. By far the majority of house staff were men. It was an honourable occupation. There was usually a bond between the employer and the employed which went far beyond a mere master/servant relationship.

The main social event in the year was the Queen's Birthday, when, traditionally, islanders flocked to Auki station They came from as far away as Small Malaita by large canoes. The pre-War pattern had been re-established with the demise of Marching Rule. Neighbouring villages supplied accommodation as far as they could. But gifts of sacks of rice and cases of meat strained the official entertainment vote to the limit. In addition the District Commissioner's bank balance usually declined. The main celebration took place on the football field, with displays of dancing and pan-pipe orchestras keeping the crowds amused until dusk intervened. There was usually an afternoon function at the District Commissioner's house. Tea was followed by drinks. The ladies of the station gave invaluable support.

During the year there were informal drinks parties and dinner parties. Formal wear was reserved for occasions such as High Commissioner's visits. I remember many happy occasions. One of them ended up with a game of skittles on the verandah. Croquet balls and the papier mâché covers for champagne bottles were brought into use.

We were dependent on the goodwill of the Malaitan in charge of the electricity supplies at such times. The generator was turned off at eleven o'clock each night. There was an unspoken agreement that if the lights in the District Commissioner's house were still on, switch-off was delayed until the lights went out there. I recall noting that the light from a dim kerosene pressure lamp in a particular house always remained lit after the station lights were switched off. On enquiry, I ascertained that the house belonged to Fred Osifelo, a junior clerk in my office and the son of a Headman in north Malaita. He was initially employed as a messenger. He only had basic education in the vernacular of the area from which he came. I noted one day that he was using his spare time in the office to record the ins and outs of the correspondence register. He was then promoted to Assistant Clerical Officer. At nights he was studying assiduously to improve his English and Mathematics. He had reached the rank of Assistant Administrative Officer by the time that I reached Honiara. He subsequently accompanied me on a visit to Papua New Guinea. After I left the Solomons, he was elevated to Speaker of the Solomon Islands Parliament and subsequently knighted.

Melanesian functions to which the District Commissioner was invited were infrequent. Weddings were family affairs. I attended a number of feasts, which were an anti-climax after attending feasts in Fiji. There the display of food was mouth-watering. The social ingredient was also as important as the quality of the food. On Malaita the feasting conventions were based on pagan times, when one ate in the security of one's family and lineage. Sorcerers from the world outside might poison the food. Consequently once the food had been cooked – pigs in earth ovens, baked fish, sweet potatoes, pudding made from mashed nuts and taro, the host would call out the names of the chiefs of the various lineages in turn. They would come forward with their escorts to collect the share of the food allocated for their 'line' (lineage). They would take this away. In some cases they would take it home to eat there rather than eat it in the vicinity of the feast.

As District Commissioner, I had sometimes to do what I should have preferred not to do. On one of those occasions I was invited to the funerary feast to be given a year after the death of a prominent chief in the Lau Lagoon. I knew that the status of the chief would be measured by the number of pigs to be ritually killed and eaten at the ceremony. When I arrived, I was shown the pigs to be slaughtered, laid in neat rows with feet tied and the muzzle bound by vines so that the wretched animal could only breathe through its nostrils. The pagan priest, the *fatambu*, was to officiate in front of a large expectant crowd. He called for the first pig which was laid in front of him. After a short invocation he raised his hand dramatically and plunged two fingers into the pig's nostrils. It threshed violently for a very short time and lay dead, suffocated. He pulled his fingers out. If there were any sign of blood from nostrils, ears or mouth, the pig was discarded as unfit to eat. The others were taken away to be cooked. Worse than the killing itself was the mounting hysteria of the crowd. This went back to the Colosseum or the knitting-women of the French Revolution. A great shout went up each time the priest raised his hand. This seemed to grow in intensity. I did not stay until the pigs were cooked.

It would not be long before we were due to leave, and a Malaitan who was genuinely sorry to see us go was, in reality, a Melanesian Spiv, Siru Luluakalo. He ingratiated himself shamelessly with authority. He kept my wife well supplied with vegetables at inflated prices. He bubbled with good humour. He was a Headman. He grew cacao on a larger scale than his neighbours, despite the incident which I have recounted. He also ran a successful contracting business by supplying panels of made-up thatch to the Public Works Department in Honiara. This was used for maintenance of the thatched buildings in the capital. There sago-palm leaf for thatch was scarce. I found out that as a Government ship was on the point of sailing for Honiara, Siru would turn up at the wharf. He had loads of thatch. He would say to the ship's captain, 'The District Commissioner wants this taken to Honiara immediately.' If he could avoid paying for the freight, his profitability substantially increased. I still do not know how many times he had successfully played this game before I became aware of it. On one occasion he was drunk. He was involved in an affray with four policemen. They had great difficulty in taking him into custody. I had to sentence him to six months imprisonment and to revoke his appointment as a Headman. After the six months had expired, my office orderly reported that a man called Saevavia wished to see me. I said, 'I know no-one of that name, but show him in nevertheless.' In walked Siru. When I remarked upon the different name, Siru said cheerfully. 'Oh, you are cross with the other name so I have changed it to that of my grandfather.'

I have mentioned his propensity for ingratiating himself with authority. This must have gone on for some time as he called his male children, not without some embarrassment to the persons concerned, by the surnames of the various District Commissioners. During Sir John Gutch's visit, we had called in at Siru's village. He had lined up his children and wife to present to the High Commissioner. His wife was heavily pregnant. He introduced the boys first, Bentley, Foster, and Allan (all former District Commissioners). Then patting his wife on the belly, he said 'And this, Sir, if it's a boy, is Russell'. Russell Luluakalo subsequently appeared.

Although this final episode involving Siru is out of sequence, it illustrates the relationship which he had with me. I paid a visit to the Solomons in 1992, eighteen years after my working life there had concluded. I arranged to visit Malaita again. I sent Siru a letter saying when I would arrive. I asked him to meet me at Auki for a meal. When I arrived I was met by one of the sons. He said that Siru had died earlier in the year. He had asked his son to tell me that he was sorry he could not wait for me. He was sure, however, that I should wish to visit his grave. I was duly taken southwards by Landrover and escorted into the bush for about three miles. Siru's extended family awaited me. He had left about thirty grandchildren. I was escorted to a large thatched house on a small eminence where refreshments had been prepared. Some twenty yards in front of the house, probably in contravention of whatever Sanitation Laws existed, was Siru's grave It was decorated with hibiscus. In accordance with local practice, it was being allowed to settle for a year before cement capping was added.

As I was about to leave, Russell Luluakalo looked at me earnestly and said. 'You can do Siru a last favour. Can you send him a gravestone?' They were not available locally. He then handed me an inscription, drafted by the family. It must have been modelled on the 25th Chapter of Genesis. Looking at the length of it, I promised to send the family a gravestone if the inscription was left to my discretion. I returned to my home in Farnham and commissioned the gravestone from a monumental mason. He must have thought he was qualifying for the Queen's Prize for Industry in fulfilling his first overseas order. I had it engraved and shipped to Honiara to the manageress of a local shipping company, Joan Gordon, who kindly had it delivered to the family in Auki. A year later I had a reminder from an insurance company that the complimentary insurance of the gravestone ran out at the end of twelve months. I declined to renew the policy. I wondered if they had any concept of what they had purported to cover for the past year.

Towards the end of July 1954 we left Malaita by M.V. *Margery* to go on leave. Goodbyes are a sad feature of life. But departure by ship is perhaps the saddest of all, as the ship, very slowly, draws away from the wharf for the last time. The separation between land and sea symbolises that between friends. We were due to leave Honiara by plane via Sydney for London, where I was to be seconded to the Colonial Office for a year. We had some anxieties about the flight as my wife was well advanced into her first pregnancy. She could have been denied an air passage. The planes in use at this time were Super-Constellations. The flight from Australia involved five legs, each of nine to eleven hours. It was the time of the Suez crisis. Our plane was diverted to Karachi to allow the pilot to have a face-to-face discussion with the pilot of the plane coming in the opposite direction. He had to assess the safety of landing in Egypt. All went well, but we were the last commercial plane into Egypt until the war situation stabilised. We had about ten days to find rented accommodation before I was due to start work in the Colonial Office and found an acceptable apartment in Stanley Gardens in the Notting Hill area. I reconnoitred bus and underground routes and was ready for my next assignment.

CHAPTER NINE

A Spell of Duty in England

I HAD THE GOOD FORTUNE to be seconded to the Colonial Office at a time when substantial changes were taking place. These concerned, firstly, the system of staffing in the Colonies and secondly the responsibility in Whitehall for progress to Independence and, until then, for Good Governance. 1954 was a fateful year. The speed at which Colonies became Independent was likely to preclude Colonial Service officers recruited on pensionable terms from completing their careers. Furthermore it would be necessary to compensate them for loss of career or offer them career security when a Colony became Independent. The decision was taken the year I joined the office to wind up the Colonial Service and replace it by Her Majesty's Overseas Civil Service. (HMOCS). Pensionable officers of the Colonial Service would transfer with their pension rights intact. New entrants would be recruited on contract terms. It was hoped that many would still intend to follow an overseas career in the Colonies. Due to problems with the very large Colonies, such as Nigeria, the conversion of the Colonial Service to HMOCS took some years. Pensionable recruitment, on a diminishing scale, continued until 1957.[3]

A decade later, the pre-war Ministerial responsibility for relations with foreign countries was reviewed. The Foreign Service and Foreign Office were responsible for representation in, and relations with, foreign countries which were neither members of the Commonwealth nor Colonies. The Commonwealth Office had the same responsibility for Commonwealth countries. The Colonial Office was responsible for stimulating the advance of Colonies to Independence at their request and at a time of their choosing. Until that time was reached, the Colonial Secretary had to ensure that each Colony was properly administered.

To streamline the system, the Colonial Office was absorbed into the Commonwealth Office in 1965, but continued for some time to operate as an independent unit. By that time seventeen former Colonies had been granted Independence. In 1966 the Commonwealth Office had

---

3. Anthony Kirk-Greene, *On Crown Service*, I.B. Tauris, 1999.

been absorbed into the Foreign Office, which later became the Foreign and Commonwealth Office. The Foreign Service became The Diplomatic Service, which would supply Ambassadors to non-Commonwealth countries and High Commissioners to Commonwealth countries. Since the demise of HMOCS in 1997, Diplomatic Service officers have increasingly been appointed Governors of the remaining Colonies, now styled United Kingdom Overseas Territories.

In advance of these latter changes, yet to be made, a ferment of policy review was taking place. Although India and Pakistan had become Independent countries in 1947 and Ceylon in 1948, the spate of countries gaining Independence in the 1960's had not yet started. While mission statements were not yet in vogue, the theme of Independence for the Colonies dominated the approach to problems in all Departments. This was also the period when the Colonial Service was at its peak. The officers in all branches of the Service were selected and offered appointment by the Colonial Office. Hence the Department of the Office dealing with Colonial Service matters was one of the largest. Reports on all officers in the Colonial Service were submitted annually. Promotions and transfers between Colonies were made in the name of the Colonial Secretary, who was regarded as one of the senior Ministers of State.

In 1954 the Colonial Office was housed in Church House in Great Smith Street, near Westminster Abbey, and in the Whitehall area of the main Government Departments. Space was at a premium. Pressure to move to other premises was mounting. Eventually a site was selected which is now occupied by the Queen Elizabeth Conference Centre. By that time, however, the decision had been made to merge the Colonial Office with the Commonwealth Office.

When I reported for duty to the Finance Department, I was informed that I should have an induction period of a fortnight before being assigned to duties. An hour later I had been told to report as a matter of urgency to Patrick Dodd, who was managing the section responsible for the administration of Colonial Development and Welfare Aid to the Colonies. One of his two desk officers had been ill for some time and my desk was heaped with files requiring attention. Just like Honiara! It was a pressure job, but varied and interesting. Each Colony was allocated a tranche of British aid, made available under the Colonial and Development Acts. Within that sum, the individual Colony applied for funds for specific projects: hospitals, schools, dams, roads, forestry, geological survey, agriculture, fisheries. There was a small pamphlet, which had to be kept up to date, setting out the form applications must take. In later years this process was refined so that each Colony drew up a Development Plan. This was approved in London. The individual development schemes had to conform to the Plan. There was a small team of accounting staff back-stage, who kept details of the expenditure on each scheme as submitted by the Territory. It was also possible to have supplementary grants when expenditure was going to overrun approved provision. We were very stern about applying for this in advance. If and when a Colony overspent without previous approval, it had to make up the overspent amount from its own funds.

The Colonial Office maintained a staff of advisers for each technical branch of the Colonial Service. To name but a few: Education, Medical Services, Co-operatives, Agriculture, Fisheries, Forestry, Engineering. In addition there was an Auditor General, who inspected the Audit staff, and an Inspector-General of Colonial Police, who inspected Colonial Police Forces. The advisers were all men or women with long and distinguished experience in their particular fields. Any scheme which affected their discipline was referred to them for advice. Often this required further reference to the Colony concerned.

The Colonial Development and Welfare Act required that expenditure under the Act would be approved by the Colonial Secretary in consultation with Their Lordships of the Treasury. In Civil Service terms, this meant that every fortnight the three of us in the Section took the schemes which we were endorsing across to the Treasury. We had a meeting with members of staff there. Advance copies had been sent to them for study. Most of the smaller schemes were generally agreed. But on what were then large schemes, such as road-building in Nigeria, further technical advice might be required. Once a year formal documents were submitted to Ministers containing details of the schemes provisionally approved by their officials. This procedure conformed with the niceties of the Act.

There were several schemes, particularly for scholarships or training in the United Kingdom, which were centrally administered by us, and the application procedures differed. Difference in currency values between then and today comes into focus when I recall that we talked in hushed tones about the One Million Pounds Scholarship Scheme.

The need to develop the economies of the colonies before they could aspire to self-government led to a greater development input by the British Government. By 1961, as part of the redesign of overseas responsibilities, a new Department was established, the Department of

Technical Cooperation. This took over the work that we had been doing and also responsibility for much of the recruitment formerly undertaken by the Colonial Office. In 1964 it became a Ministry in its own right, developing regional offices overseas, each with its own staff of economists and advisers. In 1975 that, in turn, was renamed the Overseas Development Administration.

Secondment to the Colonial Office earned the sobriquet of 'beach-combing' from those in the field. The supposition was that in working in the office which was responsible for promotions and postings, one might pick something up. Fortunately that betrayed ignorance of how the system worked.

There were two other Colonial Service Administrators seconded to the Colonial Office at the time.

One was Walter Wallace (CVO, CBE, DSC), who, after War service in the Royal Marines, had been posted to Sierra Leone, to which he returned after secondment. Following the Grant of Independence to Sierra Leone, he served in the Bahamas, Bermuda, and Anguilla before being appointed Governor of the British Virgin Islands. He subsequently served as Adviser on Dependent Territories in the Foreign and Commonwealth Office and advised on the Constitutions for a number of the British Overseas Territories which still remain. Our careers have overlapped during our secondments to the Colonial Office, when we were both Governors in the West Indies, and subsequently when we were both working in London.

The second was (Sir) Ian Turbott (Kt., AO, CMG, CVO) a New Zealander with War Service in the Pacific, who had been an Administrative Officer in the Gilbert and Ellice Islands. We had both travelled on the M.V. *Matua* in 1948 en route to our respective High Commission territories. Our berths on the ship were identified on our tickets as M.O.F. I jokingly remarked that it must mean mattress-on-floor. I was percipient. The pressure on passages to Suva was such that a number of us slept in the ship's lounge. Worse was to come for Ian. He left Suva for Tarawa in the Gilbert Islands on a tiny vessel. There was what looked like a dog kennel on the top deck This was his cabin for the voyage. He was later appointed Administrator of Antigua and afterwards Governor of Grenada. He returned to the Antipodes in 1968. He has had a distinguished career in business and academia. He has been Chancellor of the University of Western Sydney since 1989.

A task which came my way several times was to sit on the interview board for the selection of Administrative Officers. They were still being recruited by the Colonial Office. There was no written examination for the Colonial Service and candidates were selected on the information which they provided, and after a series of interviews.

I remember my own final interview vividly. It was held in a long room in Whitehall with an elegant painted ceiling. The Board sat at a table at the far end. My name was called. I started to walk the length of the room, feeling that I was getting smaller with every step. I was being analysed by seven pairs of eyes. What I looked like? How I walked? Was I composed? I thought that I was fairly composed until I neared the table and read the notice in front of the Chairman: 'SPEAK UP'. I was, however, given a very fair hearing.

I sat on these distinguished Boards as an Assessor. The convention was that a serving officer should always be present. The Board was imaginatively constructed, usually with a retired Governor of one of the large African Colonies as Chairman. The members might include a senior officer from the Colonial Office Personnel Department, a university don from Oxford or Cambridge, the head of establishments of a large commercial firm such as ICI or Unilever, and the Inspector-General of Colonial Police. After the candidate had retired, the Chairman turned to the Service assessor and said, 'Now, Mr Russell, would you be happy serving with Mr X?' Your reasons for the reply would then be sought.

I learnt a great deal about interviewing from this experience. The main lesson was never to regard the process as merely one to confirm a preliminary judgement made from the Curriculum Vitae. This was demonstrated by two candidates who appeared one day in sequence.

The first had the ball at his feet. He was the son of an ex-Governor of a large Colony. He had been exposed to colonial life. He had been to one of the better public schools and one of the more illustrious Oxford Colleges. He had a Blue in a major sport. He was, however, lack-lustre at interview. He gave the impression that he had applied because his father had pressed him to do so. I would have said that I would be prepared, rather than happy, to serve with him. He walked as far as the door, paused, and came back in front of the table. 'Could I ask a question, Sir?' he said to the Chairman. 'I have a year's trip to Europe planned. I feel that during this time I would have the opportunity to reflect whether I am doing the right thing in committing myself to this career. May I ask whether, if I am offered appointment, I can delay reply for some months?' The Chairman said 'The Board will consider your question.' The candidate left. Without asking any member of the Board for an opinion, the Chairman looked along the table in both directions, slowly shaking his head. No-one dissented.

The second candidate, on paper, seemed almost a waste of time. After secondary education he had stayed in three separate jobs for no longer than six months. He had then decided to enter the priesthood. He had attended a seminary in Italy for three-and-a-half years. On the eve of ordination, he had decided that the priesthood was not for him. He had held one executive-level job since his return for about a year. He had now applied for the Colonial Administrative Service. The unspoken concern of every member of the Board was: 'If you have, at your age, been through so many jobs and apparently cannot make your mind up about what you want to do, what guarantee have we that you will commit yourself to the Service?' At interview he shone. Pressed about the Board's major concern, he revealed considerable knowledge of what he would be expected to do both in the Secretariat or in District administration. He persuaded the Board that his experience strengthened his resolve to get into the job he had chosen as a career and to stay there. He dealt with other questions intelligently and thoughtfully. It was one interview which stimulated considerable discussion after he had left, but he won through.

On occasions, even the most august of Boards could dissolve into laughter. One of the text-books on colonial administration was a long treatise by Lord Hailey. A candidate is said to have been asked whether he had read anything on the subject. He looked up wearily at the Board and said, 'Well, I've ploughed through Hailey.' Lord Hailey was the Chairman that day.

On the personal side, we were now proud parents of our only son, Malcolm, who was born in University College Hospital on the 28th September 1956. I am not sure whether it is within the sound of Bow Bells when the wind is blowing in the right direction. He may be able to claim to be not only half French and half Scots, but a Cockney as well.

Although our social life was constrained by an infant child, we saw something of Ian Turbott and his wife Nancy, an American whom he had met on Canton Island in the Gilbert and Ellice Islands. They lived near Smithfield Market and we were surprised at the vast amounts of meat that they were able to buy at give-away prices. The discount was always in sausages, great strings of them, which were heaped into their basket before they left.

Alex Davidson, a colleague from the Solomons, and his wife Margaret (Bunny) were also on leave in London at the time. Theirs was a romantic story. Alex was in the Merchant Navy and torpedoed during the War. He was adrift on a raft in the Atlantic for many days. Some sailors slid off in exhaustion. Others were attacked by sharks. Eventually he came into Madeira more dead than alive. Margaret was a nursing auxiliary who helped him to recover. She later became his wife. His health was badly affected by his wartime experiences. He had several operations for abdominal problems. Because of these, he was transferred to Malawi, where the climate was expected to be more favourable. In his place an officer was transferred in who had a history of abdominal problems. In Malawi Alex and his wife divorced and remarried. He returned with Anne, his second wife, to the Solomons, from which he retired. He has since died. Alex was one of the most translucently honest persons I was privileged to know. He did not earn promotion to senior posts or medals; I do not think that he wanted these. He was one of the rock-solid officers who epitomised the Overseas Service.

We visited Germany, Scotland and Algeria during our spell in Europe. The unrest which precluded Algerian Independence in 1962 was beginning to affect normal life in Oran. Buses were grilled against bomb-throwing. Entrants to a supermarket were submitted to body searches. My father-in law, a retired railway engineer, had been responsible for the rail network over a third of the country. He had pronounced views on the ability of the Arab politicians to govern it. On entering a supermarket one day, he was searched. The security guard paused when he came to a bulge in his hip pocket. 'What is that, Sir?' 'What do you think it is?' was the reply. He continued with his shopping and his Luger. Of greater concern was the day on which my wife visited a bank with steep steps leading to the door. She left Malcolm in his push-chair, with the wheels locked, beside a pillar. She duly cashed her cheque. She had moved away with the pram, when there was a loud explosion. There was a rubbish-receptacle near the pillar and a bomb had been placed in it. No-one was injured. Eventually, however, the main towns in Algeria were as dangerous as parts of Israel are to-day.

In Germany my father had been invited to run an occasional English class. On one of our visits he asked me if I would give a talk on the Solomon Islands. The Germans had formerly colonised the islands of Bougainville and Choiseul. They were still interested in the area. In Herford, in Rhine Westphalia, where my father was now stationed, some of the houses had Pacific names, such as 'Nukualofa'. To our mutual surprise, the attendance was three times the usual number. When I finished my talk, I opened up the meeting for discussion. I was astounded both at the interest expressed and the nature of the questions. 'What is the treatment you are using for yaws?' was one. This was a disease few people in Britain knew about. I was able to say that their colonial presence was remembered, as the Pidgin English for a shilling was a 'Mark.' We were still using German charts in the extreme west of the Solomons. One of the badges of rank for the older men in Malaita was a German Kriegsmarine hat. I did not tell them that I sometimes went on parole walks as a prisoner of war. When I handed in the necessary paper promising not to escape during the walk, the German guard would say. 'Wir haben ein gentleman's agreement gemacht'. This seemed to indicate that there was no word in German for either 'agreement' or 'gentleman' Perhaps he was merely showing off his knowledge of English.

During visits to Europe by air with a child in a carrycot, we found that it was just the right length for carrying baguettes underneath the mattress.

But it was soon time to go back to the Solomons.

CHAPTER TEN

Honiara in the Late Fifties

O N RETURNING from my assignment in London, we were allotted a house on a spur behind Langakiki Ridge. The houses of the Chief Secretary and the Financial Secretary, Sandy Wilkie, were not far away. The offices of the Geological Survey were further along the spur. John Grover, the Chief Geologist, later to be joined by his new wife, Caroline, was a neighbour.

The houses were perched on cement piles about three feet high, each capped with zinc as a protection against termites. They were wooden-framed with ply-wood panels forming the walls and originally painted a dark khaki colour with paint inherited from the U.S. Marine Corps. Roofs were of corrugated iron. They were not air-conditioned. There were no glass windows. Window apertures had 'push-outs', rectangles of ply-wood hinged at the top. These were held open in daytime with wooden battens chocked against the window-sill. A bolt secured them at night. Some houses had metal mosquito screening instead of 'push-outs' The kitchen was built separately and connected to the main house by a short covered passage-way. There was also a two-roomed servants' quarter at some distance from the house.

Our house had a pleasant view over Iron Bottom Sound. It had two small double bedrooms and a single bedroom, lounge, dining-room and bathroom. The government only supplied hard furnishings. These varied in quantity according to an officer's grade. We were sufficiently high up the ladder to merit a standard lamp. Carpeting or floor coverings, pictures, ornaments, crockery, cutlery, were the officer's responsibility. As houses had to be vacated each time an officer proceeded on leave, these effects had to be packed for storage every two years Important items of equipment were mosquito nets, as malaria was rife. Houses had electricity, water and sewerage, with individual septic tanks. Telephones could be installed by the officer. There was no hot water, however, even when I left the Solomons in 1974. Electric showers were sometimes installed by officers at their own expense. Cooking was by wood stoves but refrigerators had graduated from kerosene to electricity. The house stood in an area of bare soil and rock. There had

The House on Langakiki Ridge which we occupied on return from London.

been no landscaping, apart from an unpaved driveway leading to the house. On the ridges, gardening was a challenge even to the most fervent horticulturist. With our young son we were very happy there.

My wife was startled one day to hear the clanging of bells of the one fire-engine in the capital. They grew louder and louder as it approached the house. Rushing out to find out what the crisis was, she found Malcolm given pride of place by the firemen. He had decorated himself with his mother's lipstick. He was stark naked with a pair of high-heeled lady's shoes in one hand, his nappy held over his shoulder with the other. On the way to a bush fire, the fire-crew had found him walking down the road heading for Honiara. They had identified him and brought him home. This was in the best tradition of the French pompiers, who are prepared to deal with emergencies of any kind.

The house in which we lived was typical of that occupied by Overseas Civil Service officers. Some were more run down. Others were less well sited. Economists would later criticise the generous spacing between houses on the three residential ridges, Langakiki, Vavaya and Kola'a. They would advocate infilling the spaces between houses to make use of services already there. We did our own infilling as the spaces were eradicated by the warmth of social contact. We had a relaxed lifestyle, dropping into houses informally. Sometimes there would be a call by telephone: 'Why don't you come over for coffee, drinks or supper – so-and-so has just looked in.' The men were in contact with each other by day. A minority of the women worked. The others would arrange to meet in the mornings or afternoons. Sport was usually assigned to the evening, when the temperature was cooler. Children had to be taken to, and collected from, kindergarten or school. Casual social occasions might ensue from the daily meeting of parents.

Although most of the expatriates were birds of passage, Honiara had a sense of stability which smaller outstations, such as Gizo and Auki, had not. There were a few settlers who had made their home there. The senior officers of Government held posts tied to central administration in the capital. These included the High Commissioner, the Chief Secretary, Judge, (later the Chief Justice), the Attorney General and Secretariat officers at Deputy level. Although all of these could be transferred elsewhere, the average tenure of office was about five years. Heads of Department tended to be at post for longer. John Grover, the Chief Geologist, Gordon Cox, Director of Public Works, Jimmy Macgregor, the Chief Medical Officer, Keith Trenaman, the Conservator of Forests, Chris Taylor of the Marine Department, Geoffrey Bovey, the Director of Education, Roger Burrow-Wilkes, Collector of Customs – these were a part of the scenery when District Commissioners paid visits to Headquarters. In addition, many of the subordinate officers in these Honiara-based Departments spent long careers there. Among these were Jock Elliott and Russ Richardson of the Public Works Department, Tony Child and Jean Heseltine of the Department of Education, Tony Cross the surgeon, and Christine Woods the Matron, in the Medical Department. Officers in the administration tended to move around more. They could be transferred from the Secretariat to a District, or from Central District Headquarters in Honiara to another District. Mike Allen, John Hunter, Derek Cudmore and Douglas Freegard moved from the Solomons to the Gilbert and Ellice Islands. Mike Townsend, Alex Mitchell and Guy Wallington went to the New Hebrides. Dick Turpin and John Yaxley came to the Solomons from other Western Pacific High Commission Territories. When other colonies became Independent, Overseas Service officers were often given the choice of continuing their careers elsewhere. Among these, Bim Davies, John Smith, and Trevor Clark all spent their Protectorate careers in Honiara. Others, including John Pepys-Cockerell, Bill Wright and Bob Finnimore, spent a substantial period of their Protectorate service there.

Friendships between families inevitably matured through the years. In the religious sphere there were some churchmen such as Bishop Steyvenberg, Bishop Hill, Father Wall, Brian Macdonald Milne and Edgar Wood who were semi-permanent residents of Honiara. 'Johnno' the butcher was someone with whom the housewives had to be friendly. Eric Lawson, the manager of the Trade Scheme, Ewalt Tischler, the builder, Jock Stevenson, the architect, Daisy Dethridge of the Book Shop, had all put their roots down in the capital.

Ken Hay, as Kenneth Dalrymple-Hay was known, presided over the only hotel in Honiara, the Hotel Mendana. He was an Australian, of medium height. He had a massive belly. He was very proud of his Scottish connection. He had become something of a loner, possibly because of failing health.

He had prospected for gold on Guadalcanal, high up in the foothills south of Honiara. The area is known as Gold Ridge to this day. Until recent public unrest in the Solomons stopped production, it was being mined for gold, justifying Ken Hay's original activities. During the War he became a Coastwatcher. He was said to have given sanctuary up in the mountains to a Catholic nun. Falling sick, he sent a message to the Americans to rendezvous with him on the coast where he could receive treatment. On reaching the rendezvous, he said to the American patrol leader: 'I'm all knocked up', meaning 'I'm sick'. The phrase is American slang for being pregnant. The patrol commander looked at his expansive belly and said: 'Yeah, I believe you are!'

He was an astute businessman and re-established himself after the War by collecting abandoned American equipment or purchasing it cheaply and on-selling it at a profit. He believed, however, that a few Solomon Islanders resident on Guadalcanal had betrayed his whereabouts to the Japanese. The Mendana Hotel, of which he was proprietor, had replaced an old thatched building. This had stood on the same site near Cruz Creek. The hotel had a public bar, which, under the terms of his liquor licence, had to be open to all members of the public. It was certainly open to Australians on ANZAC Day, when large sums exchanged hands in 'two-up' sessions. But he debarred entrance to the main hotel to Solomon Islanders. This was not on racial grounds, as Fijians and visitors from Papua New Guinea were admitted. Despite this public antipathy to Solomon Islanders, he secretly paid for the education of children of his employees. He supported local charities. He had a habit of sitting facing the entrance to the hotel where he could survey the guests who entered. Occasionally he would imperiously pat the empty chair next to him as an invitation to talk. If he was in the right mood, he would recount tales of the Solomons before the War.

He eventually died after returning to Australia for hospital treatment. I was then Chief Secretary. I received a message from his executors that his ashes were to be scattered from a plane over Gold Ridge. He had asked that I participate in the ceremony. Both planes of Solair, the local airline, had been chartered. We circled to gain height on taking off from Henderson Field. I was sitting in one of the rear seats in a small aircraft. The pilot and the executor were in front. When the time came, Ken's ashes were shaken out of the window from a plastic bag. At least some of them were. Those of us in the rear seats were removing specks of Ken's remains from our eyes. The pilots then did a wing-tip to wing-tip flight over Honiara before we landed.

A few days later a small delegation of villagers from the vicinity of Gold Ridge came to see me in the Chief Secretary's office. The spokesman said that their taro gardens had been polluted by the remains of a foreigner dropping from the sky. He suggested that a compensatory payment might assuage their concern. However, he did not press the point.

Ken would have been perturbed to know that after his death the Mendana Hotel was sold to a Japanese hotelier.

Apart from the hotel, there was one Chinese restaurant in Chinatown. The Guadalcanal Club was a popular venue. It had a bar and a large area for functions or for dancing. Tennis courts, a swimming-pool, and latterly a restaurant, were added. A golf course had been constructed by a few enthusiasts, with Government approval, on the relief landing-strip beyond Kukum. The number of holes was gradually increased until it was a nine-hole course It boasted a small thatched clubhouse. A Yacht Club near the mouth of the Cruz Creek had the amenities improved through the years.

In addition to informal and semi-formal meals in each other's homes, there were receptions and dinners given by senior government officials, businessmen and societies. On Queen's Birthday, following the traditional parade, there was a reception at Government House. On Old Year's night, the New Year's Honours were traditionally announced at midnight at the Guadalcanal Club. This was a fancy dress occasion and a group of us arranged to precede the main festivities with a progressive dinner party. This started with pre-dinner drinks and savouries at the first port of call. After a series of courses in different houses, brandy and coffee were served in one which was conveniently near the club.

Visiting warships were popular. Royal Navy. Royal Australian Navy and French Navy ships made official calls several times each year. In addition to a reception at Government House, the programme included lunch or dinner on board for a selected few. There would also be a reception on board for a number of guests, dictated by the size of the ship. The various sporting clubs, tennis, golf, football, and rugby would arrange fixtures with ships' crews and individual houses would offer hospitality. Friendships made on these visits were often renewed in the United Kingdom.

Solomon Islanders have not featured prominently in these paragraphs dealing with social activities. There is a reason for this. At this time Solomon Islanders were not permitted to purchase or consume alcohol. This was an uncomfortable situation. At large functions with a bar, where guests ordered what they wanted, the embargo was less noticeable. In the home, or on less formal occasions, the discrimination was more embarrassing. The number of Solomon Islanders in senior positions in the civil service or in business was then relatively small. The majority were Assistant Medical Practitioners who had qualified in Fiji. There were a few in administration and in the teaching profession. Expatriate administrators were, I believe, more concerned about the situation than Melanesian Civil Servants.

One of the reasons for declaring the Solomons a Protectorate was to stop the widespread distribution of arms and liquor in the recruitment of Pacific Islanders. A law to prohibit Solomon Islanders from drinking alcohol was accordingly made. This had strong support from the Churches and at this time a move to repeal the law would not have commanded popular support. Lurid tales were related of drinking habits in other Pacific territories where the ban had been lifted. Indeed, a few years later, I saw competitive drinking in Papua New Guinea. The empty beer bottles were placed at the drinker's feet. These were counted before the bar closed. The winner was then declared. Break-ins to steal beer and spirits were common. The bar had barred windows. The tables and benches were bolted to the floor. There were no decorations and the walls and ceilings were dark brown with cigarette smoke. A prisoner in such a cell would have complained of the conditions.

Even harder for the newcomer to the Pacific to understand was the Native Adultery Regulation which made it a criminal offence for a Solomon Islander to commit adultery. This was qualified by the need for the aggrieved spouse to lodge a complaint. For his European neighbour adultery was a social or civil matter. There was a reason for this situation too. In most Solomon Island societies, where brideprice was traditional, adultery, before there was a Government, was punishable by death. When this sanction was forbidden by Government, the plea was made to introduce a lesser punishment and to enshrine this in legislation. These two prohibitions were discriminative and ultimately removed.

As elsewhere, sporting activities embraced all races. Football and rugby, team sports, had an advantage over tennis and golf, which required purchase of equipment. In societies such as the Red Cross, there was a good racial mix. As Solomon Islanders and their wives showed that they were at ease in different social environments, they were welcomed. The apparent discrimination of the late fifties gradually dissipated.

As Honiara was on the coast, the reader would expect watersports to feature strongly among sporting activities. Swimming in the sea was dangerous, however, because of sharks. Swimming in the river-mouths was dangerous because of crocodiles. *Crocodilus estuarius* was a formidable reptile, which swam in open sea between river mouths. I have seen one miles out to sea swimming between islands. It was believed that the sharks gained a taste for human flesh from the thousands of drowned mariners during the War. In the 1950's, they were considered a real danger. Casualties were sometimes not recovered, as the corpse was secreted by the crocodile under river banks or rocks. It was allowed to rot before it was devoured. Solomon Islanders living near the coast defecate in the sea. There were four or five fatalities a year on Guadalcanal. I saw one lucky man in hospital who looked as though he was wearing the crown of thorns. He had a ring of shark-tooth marks around his forehead. He had been taken by a shark head-on. He had the presence of mind to remove a knife from his belt. He stabbed the shark in the belly. It then spat him out. He lived to tell the tale. The son and daughter of a Secretariat Registry officer had come out for the Christmas holidays. The family went swimming at Trench's beach outside Honiara. There was a scream from the daughter. There was a patch of blood on the water. The son had vanished. The daughter believed that a fish had grazed her thigh as it turned towards her brother. A week later, however, I saw two large crocodiles swimming past the beach. They had a habit of lying in the surf parallel to the shore and could be mistaken for floating logs.

The residents of longstanding took these dangers in their stride. The Palmer family had joined their father Ernie Palmer on his lovely schooner on a recruiting trip to Malaita. I was walking along the beach at

Fokanakafu where the ship was anchored. The children were swimming near the ship about a hundred yards from the shore. On going out to the ship, I told the mother, Inge Palmer, that a large crocodile was basking in the surf about seventy yards from the swimming children. She walked calmly to the rail and called to the children: 'Boys, I think that you had better come on board. There's a crocodile there today.' Thus swimming was at swimmer's risk. Although yachting and canoeing were common, watersports were considered too dangerous. Whether because the next generations of shark have changed their habits, or we exaggerated the danger, water-skiing, scuba-diving and jet-skiing are now common sports.

Although the range of activities did not match those at Oflag VA, there were many interest-groups in the community. The Red Cross and the Women's Corona Club were active. The Freemasons had a club-house, known to Melanesians as the 'Tambu-house'. This was very much in their own tradition, as a place of secrets. The Boy Scouts and Girl Guides were active. A botanic garden was opened, although those in the know would go to Geoff Dennis's garden to see the best display of orchids in the Protectorate. Fishing trips could be organised. At weekends, walking expeditions were infinitely varied. Wartime battlefields had their peculiar fascination, although children had to be cautioned not to pick up munitions, including shells, grenades and cartridges. A headmaster in England wrote a stern letter to the parents of a boy who had successfully walked through English Customs with his suitcase. It contained his holiday souvenirs: unprimed grenades, a very rusty submachine gun, an American helmet and several bayonets. Apart from the battlefields, the foothills near Mount Austin and behind Rove had their own charm. There were several river-courses, some with dry river-beds in the summer. The walk to Tenaru Falls, where one could swim in the pool below the waterfall, was a favourite. As there was only one road passing through Honiara, motoring in either direction soon lost its novelty. It provided access, however, to countless destinations both on the seacoast and inland. One of the Chief Secretaries, Michael Gass, was a keen birdwatcher and there was a good variety. In 1948, when I first arrived, great flocks of white cockatoos used to wheel above Honiara, with their habitat in the trees fringing the town. As houses were built in the gullies, and the trees were cut down both for house sites and firewood, the birds disappeared. They had moved their habitat inland where trees were still standing.

We worked hard and there was a remarkable degree of interaction between our Secretariat desks and Departments, and between Departments themselves. Many jobs in England are undertaken away from the place of residence. Our jobs, our homes, and our families were in the same small area, Most of the expatriate community was there for the same purpose. There was a surprisingly small amount of backbiting or denigration of others. If this did take place, the offender could very rapidly feel the cold draught of ostracism. But even that would be a warning to come back on board rather than a lasting social punishment.

CHAPTER ELEVEN

Learning the Ropes

I HAD BEEN PROMOTED to Administrative Officer Class A when I took over Malaita. The post was the equivalent in grade to Senior Assistant Secretary. Promotion took my salary out of what was called 'the long scale'. This seems to have been designed to cover one's whole service. Class 'A' was on what was euphemistically called Superscale. It was marginally above the breadline.

For the next seven years following return from England in November 1957, I served in the posts of Senior Assistant Secretary (Finance), Acting Secretary for Protectorate Affairs and Senior Assistant Secretary (Personnel). These were all demanding posts. In retrospect, however, their main value was to give broad experience in central administration.

The Financial Secretary was now Sandy Wilkie, an honours graduate in modern languages of Glasgow University. He was short of stature. He was later transferred as British Resident Commissioner, New Hebrides. He had to stand, on ceremonial parades, next to a very tall French Resident Commissioner. The British Resident Commissioner wore tropical white uniform with white Wolsley helmet, like that worn by the Marines. A Governor wears the same helmet with a plume of white and red feathers on the top. This small figure appeared in white uniform with a large-brimmed white helmet on the parade for the 14th July. Whereupon a Frenchman was heard to utter: 'Oh regardez! Un petit champignon!' But a very efficient Financial Secretary and good friend he was. I learnt much from him, as I did from Macleod-Smith. Unfortunately, while he was on a visit to Honiara from the New Hebrides, he suffered a heart attack. While he underwent medical treatment, his wife Margaret had to return to Vila as she had left twin children there. Sandy stayed part of the time as our guest until he was fit to travel home. Sadly, he had a further attack on board ship and died.

Financial

As Senior Assistant Secretary (Finance), my task was to relieve the Financial Secretary from as much routine financial work as possible. He required the latitude to concentrate on financial and economic policy.

Financial policy was reflected in the annual Estimates for the country. Economic policy was pursued through the framing and implementation of Development Plans and individual Development Schemes. The degree to which the Financial Secretary was involved in the preparation of the Estimates and Development Plans depended upon his style and how far he was prepared to delegate. In cases of urgent financial problems, whoever was under least pressure picked up the ball.

As in the United Kingdom, budgets were produced in an annual cycle. These were approved in the Legislative Council by an Appropriation Law. We altered that cycle from a year commencing on 1st April to one beginning on 1st January. Statistics for the country followed the calendar year. As soon as a budget was approved, warrants were issued. These authorised vote controllers to incur expenditure up to the statutory limit in the approved Estimates. By liaison with the local Treasury, we monitored this expenditure. If necessary we issued warrants authorising supplementary funds. These had to be found from savings elsewhere in the budget. Alternatively, additional funds could be approved by the Finance Committee of the Legislative Council, or incorporated in a supplementary Appropriation Law. The system was complicated by the inability of the country to raise enough local revenue to cover essential expenditure. The difference was made up annually by the United Kingdom in the form of what was known as Grant-in-Aid. This amount had to be agreed by the Colonial Office, which negotiated the amount with the British Treasury. Any application for additional Grant-in-Aid during the year caused difficulties. The original amount allocated to the Solomon Islands was included in the Colonial Office budget. Hence the problems of the Solomons were replicated in London.

Financial control and its mechanisms permeated the system of government. The 'bible' for administration in the colonies was drawn up in London. It was known as Colonial Regulations. It was in two parts. One was on Staffing and Discipline. The second, on Finance, laid down how Colonial Estimates were to be constructed. Recurrent Expenditure, comprising Personal Emoluments and Other Charges, was to be kept separate from Capital Expenditure. Annual Returns to be made to the Secretary of State were listed. Limits of writing off missing stores or money were laid down. Audit Reports were to be made to the Governor, debated in the Legislature, and forwarded with his comments to the Secretary of State. These broad procedures came to be amplified by local Finance and Control Laws, and by specific Financial Instructions. These had to be in conformity with Colonial Regulations. A uniform financial system throughout the colonies made it easier for Accountants-General, Auditors-General or Financial Secretaries to adjust to a new colony on arrival. It also aided researchers seeking financial information on individual colonies. Returns and basic financial documents were in standard form.

In addition to monitoring expenditure throughout the calendar year, we began the preparation of the following year's Estimates as early as March. Vote Controllers were asked to list any New Services they recommended for the following year. Examination at official level of possible revenue increases would be put in hand. About mid-year, Vote Controllers were asked to submit estimates for the following year. By this time the funds required for New Services had been determined. After examination of submissions, we would call in the individual Vote Controllers to agree their final estimates. The Financial Secretary would then indicate to the Colonial Office what the total expenditure figure was likely to be for the next year. He would, in all likelihood, at the same time, ask whether an increase in Grant-in-Aid of £X000 was likely to be approved. After the Colonial Office had consulted with the British Treasury, he would be authorised to prepare the Appropriation Law within certain limits. At the end of the 1950's there was not much political input into the annual budget.

In 1958 the Protectorate received a Grant-in-Aid of £502,000 from the United Kingdom. Total expenditure amounted to £1,910,000.[4]

In parallel with the budgetary expenditure, ran the development programme. If colonies were to be moved forward to Independence, money would have to be allocated for the development of their economies. For that reason the United Kingdom Development and Welfare Act was passed. Individual schemes would be approved, such as those with which I had been involved in the Colonial Office. These would be subject to prior inclusion in a Development Plan agreed between the colony and London. Proposals for an initial plan were first put forward by Alasdair Macleod-Smith in descriptive terms without detailed estimates. From this emerged the First Development Plan, covering the period 1954-1960. It was revised in 1957. The Second Development Plan, which I assisted in preparing, ran from 1960-64. It too was revised. The Third Development Plan ran from 1963-1966.

Part of my duties was the preparation of individual development

---

4. See PRO File CO 1036/403.

schemes for which provision had been made in the Plan. The scheme had to conform to precise guidelines. We were dealing with nearly sixty individual schemes at that time, including supplementary schemes, which were not uncommon. If, for example, the salaries of government officers were increased, all schemes had to be revised. Each had to be accounted for separately and individually audited. Figures kept by the administering Department, the local Treasury, the Financial Secretary's office, and the Colonial Office had to be reconciled when schemes were wound up. There appeared to be more interest in London in accounting for the pennies than in whether the Protectorate had a new airfield or the building of a school had been completed.

However, post-War development was surging ahead. In 1957 there were schemes for improving medical services, including a Tuberculosis Survey. Provision was made for a Geological Survey and Meteorological Services. To improve agriculture, money was set aside for cattle improvement and a Government Farm on Guadalcanal Plains. This led indirectly to commercial production of rice and soya bean. Extensive planting of oil palms followed. A large oil extraction mill was subsequently constructed by the Commonwealth Development Corporation. Attention was given to rural areas by provision for community development. Honiara benefited by a grant for a water supply. We had also to prepare an individual scheme for provision of a gramophone record library for Honiara Radio for as little as £200.

The contribution made to the development of the Protectorate by Colonial and Welfare Schemes cannot be overstated. The money had been voted by the British Parliament, and, subject to approved Plans and Schemes, was released without question. The annual level of Grant-in-Aid, on the other hand, was a constant battleground between the Colonial Office and the Treasury.

The job also included keeping Financial Instructions up to date and issuing circulars drawing attention to defaults in financial administration. I chivvied Heads of Departments who were being slow in answering Audit Queries. I served as a member of, and later chaired, the Copra Board. This purchased most of the copra from farmers and middlemen, set the price and arranged grading. Along with other Pacific producer-countries, it also negotiated a shipping contract with the Bank Shipping Line, which freighted the copra to Europe. I was give sundry isolated assignments. These included reporting upon the Government Unallocated Stores, the Marine Fleet and Housing in Honiara.

Keeping in close touch with other members of the Secretariat staff was critically important. A later Financial Secretary was described as 'an inverted Micawber, waiting for something to turn down'. I tried to convey that the financial portfolio had a dual responsibility. One aim was to find the money for deserving propositions. This was of equal importance to husbanding the public purse and ensuring that the monies were properly disbursed.

A Royal Visit

In 1959 Prince Philip visited the Solomon Islands. He travelled on H.M.Y. *Britannia*. The visit was part of a gruelling tour in which he called on India and Pakistan, Singapore, Hong Kong, Borneo, Brunei, the Solomon Islands and Gilbert and Ellice Islands. The Bahamas and Bermuda were later added to the itinerary.

I was not personally involved with planning for the Visit. I was, however, placed in charge of the arrangements for the Press for a day spent on Honiara. I understand that visits to Gizo, on arrival on the 18th March, to Malaita on the 20th March, and to Graciosa Bay in Eastern District on 21st March went well.

In Honiara visits to Government Departments and two small factories were part of the programme. One of the factories made biscuits; the second processed tobacco. The latter, today, would probably be politically incorrect on a Royal programme. Stick tobacco was, however, almost an item of currency in Melanesia. It was smoked in pipes by men and women. It was also shaved into shreds which were rolled in whatever paper came to hand and smoked as cigarettes. Almost in disbelief, Prince Philip looked at tobacco being marinated in large cast-iron pots. The brew contained molasses, spirits and flavouring. Eventually it was pressed into longitudinal cakes known locally as sticks. Prince Philip said to one of the labourers, 'Do you really smoke this stuff?' 'Oh, yes,' was the cheerful reply. 'Show me,' said Prince Philip. The labourer shaved a stick of tobacco into shreds. He next tore off a quarter of a page of newspaper. He then rolled the tobacco into a long tube. He lit this with obvious enjoyment. He had, however, in the excitement of the occasion, distributed the tobacco irregularly. There was a large gap in the centre. Suddenly the cigarette was cast urgently to the floor as it burst spectacularly into flames. The would-be smoker joined the laughter of the onlookers.

In the evening, before H.M.Y. *Britannia* left Honiara, there was a dinner on board. My wife and I were privileged to be among the guests. After dinner, guests were invited on deck to watch a fireworks display

My wife Andrée.

ashore. The Visit organisers had been slightly shamefaced at the meagre display of bunting in Honiara. We were working on a tight budget. Our revenue had to be topped up with British funds. A low-cost idea proved very successful. At three-foot intervals along the coast schoolchildren awaited a signal. They were delighted to be part of the welcome. On signal each one lit a candle. This stood in a brown paper bag containing sand to hold the candle erect. The flames were protected from the evening breeze. They were strong enough to be seen as a chain of winking lights edging the shore. This preceded a modest fireworks display organised by the Public Works Department. Some very loud bangs indicated that salvaged wartime explosives had been used to prolong the display.

H.M.Y. *Britannia* sailed for Bina Harbour, on Malaita, overnight. The morning's programme included a visit to the salt-water island of Laulasi in the Langa Langa Lagoon. Native shell money is made on the island. How it is manufactured was on display. Malaitans would be delighted to show their 'custom' in its home setting.

The District Commissioner, St J. Andersen, was holding a reception in honour of the Duke of Edinburgh that night. He had ordered canapes from the Hotel Mendana in Honiara and had arranged for them to be shipped over the previous evening. Hotel staff duly arrived with the order at the wharf at Point Cruz in Honiara. They asked if a ship were sailing for Auki that night. H.M.Y. *Britannia* was pointed out. The officers aboard believed the canapes to be a generous gift to the wardroom. They had made some inroads into the consignment before the destination was explained.

Part of the final day of the Visit was spent at Graciosa Bay, where Prince Philip took the unscheduled opportunity to sail in one of the large ocean-going outrigger canoes unique to that region of the Solomons. He was to repeat this experience in the Gilbert Islands in a different type of outrigger canoe. Dick Turpin, his sailing companion on that occasion, was an ex-Navy District Commissioner who later sailed round the world. Sir John and Lady Gutch were invited on board H.M.Y. *Britannia* so that Sir John, as High Commissioner, could be in Tarawa to welcome Prince Philip on arrival. Our own ships were too slow to allow him to use one of our vessels.

Prince Philip's visit may give the reader some idea of the immensity of the Pacific. Four days were spent in the Solomon Islands. The voyage to Tarawa took four more days. Calls on Bairiki and Betio islands in the Tarawa Atoll on Ocean Island, the Ellice Islands and Christmas Island took a further seven days.

The days following a Royal Visit have a peculiar emptiness. Planning, preparations and rehearsals precede the Visit. The Visit itself creates great excitement in the community. It then has to adjust to normality.

Home Affairs

I acted as Secretary for Protectorate Affairs for the year 1960. The post had previously been called Senior Assistant Secretary (Native Affairs). It had been upgraded to a level between that of Chief Secretary and Financial Secretary. The substantive holder of the post was Val Andersen. A shrewd New Zealander, he had been District Commissioner, Malaita at the time of rapprochement with Marching Rule. He thus brought a full knowledge of District administration to his duties.

It was clear that in the plans to develop the economy of the country, rural development would play a major part. Peasant production of copra, peasant farming, development of a cocoa industry and increased livestock production were rural activities. District Commissioners supervised government policies in the four areas for which they were responsible. Their enthusiasm and the co-ordination of their efforts were critical.

The political development of the Solomon Islands was elementary. There had been an Advisory Council, which the Resident Commissioner could consult, since 1921. The few members, none of whom were Solomon Islanders, were nominated, not elected. In 1960 a Legislative Council was created with twenty-one members. There was also an Executive Council comprising the top civil servants and four others nominated from the membership of the Legislative Council. Eleven of the Council members were officials and ten non-officials. All of these were appointed by the High Commissioner. At the time there had been no elections either for Local Government Councils in the Districts or for the central legislative body.

The Secretary for Protectorate Affairs was also heavily engaged in reorganising the Local Government structure. This was controlled by the Native Administration Regulation, 1953. Councils could be established, but Councillors were nominated by their communities and not elected. There was power to pass resolutions but these did not have the force of bye-laws. Moreover the Native Tax Regulation prescribed that a small head tax would be credited to the General Revenue of the country. It was collected by the Councils. It was then credited to Government Revenue and transferred back to the Councils. It required reference to London to allow the Councils to retain the tax which they had collected. Paying tax, said the Treasury, was an act of fealty to the Crown. An important matter of principle was a stake. For us, what was important was the book-keeping. A few years later a Local Councils Regulation was enacted. Councils were authorised to keep the tax. The new law would give them power to make bye-laws and take over a raft of powers formerly exercised by Central Government. One of these was registration of births, deaths and marriages. These powers could be given by warrant and increased as Councils demonstrated their administrative ability. Moreover, Councils were to be elected.

Planning ahead for this required many meetings with legal draftsmen. Electoral regulations had to be framed. As we were dealing with an electorate which was largely illiterate, we could not rely simply on names on a ballot paper. Candidates were authorised to choose symbols: a canoe, a house, a bird, a fish, a club. There would be one ballot-box for each individual candidate, each prominently marked with a symbol. The system worked but on the second occasion the ballot-boxes were nailed to the shelf on which they stood. Voters were entering the polling-booth, picking up the boxes one by one and shaking them. The heaviest one with most votes attracted most voters as that most nearly indicating consensus. It paid to be on the winning side.

Council elections were the training slope for general elections to the Legislative Council. These would not take place on a Protectorate-wide basis until 1967, and then only in thirteen out of the fourteen constituencies. Independence would follow only eleven years later.

I was responsible for internal security. The Commissioner of Police consequently kept me informed of crime and of matters likely to affect public order. The Police Head of Estimates was discussed at the preparation stage. If necessary, I consulted the Senior Assistant Secretary (Finance) to stress the need for more transport, better communications equipment, or simply more policemen.

Of substantial importance for rural development was the Co-operative movement, with Mike Hamilton, formerly District Commissioner, Central District, in charge. His title was Registrar of Co-operatives, but the least part of his duties was sitting behind a Register. Some members of the administration discounted the concept of a co-operative move-ment. Running small businesses in Melanesia was difficult. Relatives could not be refused purchases by a storekeeper simply because they had no money. Credit was limitless. Perhaps the gift of a pig would be made, without any reference to the credit given. Yet once the co-operative philosophy had been implanted, the virtues of joint ownership became apparent. Initially the movement concentrated on consumers but spread to producers as well. There was scope for this in copra production and the infant cocoa industry, which were peasant-based. The success of the venture depended upon meticulous records and regular inspections. Officers concerned were regularly on tour to all major islands in the Solomons.

A promotional film, *Daybreak at Udi*, extolled the virtues of Community Development. For a short time it became Pandora's box for rural development. Without doubt the technique worked. One deployed a variety of staff. They were given a bag of money and sent to a village. They set up a committee to agree with what they were going to do. After a year they left. They reported on what they had achieved. It was not, however, a generic solution to rural development. It was lavish in the allocation of staff to one place. It denied other villages the services of the officers involved. Nevertheless the theory was adopted as policy at this time.

Those of us in the Secretariat helped to assemble Development Plans and construct schemes. Those in the field had a greater sense of urgency. Mike Hamilton in Co-operatives, David Meadows in Agriculture, and a few others from different Departments, decided to use Honiara Radio. They invented a fictional village, Boralour, with local characters. They wrote the script and put on a weekly programme. This had a different theme each time, based on what Departments were promoting in the districts. Most villages possessed a radio. This was a most effective tool, which proved popular and cost the government little.

When the new Legislative Council and Executive Council were established, I was appointed an official member of both. I was to continue serving in both bodies for fourteen years. As an official politician, I was something of a hybrid. The phrase 'learning the ropes', which forms the title to this chapter, accurately describes this aspect of my career. Over a period, the procedures of the House of Commons were introduced. I had to learn how to move and reply to motions, answer questions and supplementary questions, introduce Bills and sum up the debate. Later I had to chair Select Committees and introduce Budgets and Development Plans. Each of us had to learn from watching his seniors. A few were natural orators. Over the course of years, Bim Davies and John Smith stood out as masters of their craft. A great advantage was being brought into close contact with Solomon Islands politicians. They were also learning parliamentary procedures. When should they use a rapier instead of a bludgeon? When I left the Solomon Islands for the Cayman Islands on appointment as Governor, I had to preside over the Legislative Assembly as Speaker. Many times I was grateful for what I had learnt on the floor of the House. I could also appreciate how to defuse a heated debate by adjourning at the right time. I could use the coffee break to advantage.

During this period in Protectorate Affairs, I was able to pay a visit to Kira Kira. This was the headquarters of Eastern District on the island of San Cristoval. The District Commissioner there was also responsible for the islands of Ugi and Ulawa, the Santa Cruz Islands, Tikopia, Anuda and Mitre Islands. Sea journeys to the outer islands were notoriously rough.

Kira Kira was known to have a ghost. This resided in the District Commissioner's old house. A new one had been built. The old one was now used as a guest house. It was said that a woman had hanged herself on the site of the old house. The ghost, a poltergeist, only made itself known to bachelors. Roy Davies, before he took over Western District, had been District Commissioner there. He was then unmarried. He talked of taps opened throughout the night; doors banged open; the air suddenly became cold; mysteriously, furniture was moved. Married District Commissioners, Guy Wallington and Robin Low, were immune.

The station had another memory for me. I escorted two Members of the House of Commons to Kira Kira. They wished to see an out-station. A Northwest storm was brewing. We took off in a small aircraft piloted by Willy Jenkins, an Australian pilot who had to give up commercial flying at the age of sixty. Willy had been fifty-nine as long as I had known him. I would have flown anywhere with him. He was, however, a joker. On a previous flight a lady tourist had to be placed in the co-pilot's seat as the few seats in the cabin were occupied. There was no co-pilot. She was obviously nervous. Willy pretended to be reading a book after take-off. Slowly the port wing went down and was rapidly restored to the horizontal. This happened several times until the lady glanced over and read the title of the book: *Learn how to fly*. The joke was over. The book was put away. The flight continued on an even keel.

I had to ask him on this trip if he still had the book. We ran into appalling weather. He had difficulty in discerning Kira Kira airstrip, which was some way from the station. We landed in one piece. We were met by the District Commissioner. The river between the airfield and the station was in flood. He hoped that the small bridge would be passable. We crossed safely on the station landrover. The pilot wanted to get back to Honiara as quickly as possible because of the weather. We had an abbreviated programme after lunch. We headed back to the airfield. Henderson Field, the airport for Honiara, had been closed for lack of visibility. Although we waited almost until dusk, there was no change. We returned, disconsolately to Kira Kira. I was sorry for both the District Commissioner and his wife. They had expected us only for lunch. She was now faced with putting up four guests for the night. Unexpectedly she had to provide dinner for us. I happily stayed in the haunted house. It was dry.

We rose early in the hope of taking off. The bridge had by now been swept away. The rain was descending in torrents. The only way to the airfield was by a small boat with an outboard motor. We had to cross a bay in which there was a heavy swell. Waves crashed on the beach. The pilot, the three visitors, the District Commissioner and a boatman crammed on to the small boat. We crossed the bay, admiring the skill of the boatman. He eased the prow obliquely up the incoming waves and down the other side. We should have to disembark on a rocky shoreline near the airfield. Slowly this approached. But before we could congratulate ourselves on a safe arrival, one of the MP's stood up. Over we went. We all scrambled ashore. I recall an arm above the waves holding the Royal Mailbag, like Excalibur. A head, shoulders, and the body of the pilot slowly emerged. One of the MP's was wearing shorts and grazed a leg on the rocks. We thus arrived at the plane drenched and ready for take-off. The news from Honiara was that the airfield, at that time, was open. The forecast was bad. Visibility was poor and variable. Willy decided 'to have a go'. We lurched into the air and headed for Guadalcanal. By the time we reached it, the visibility was so poor that Willy descended to several hundred feet. He followed the white line of the waves breaking on the shore. I was conscious of the mountains off to port, which were totally invisible. It was vital not to lose sight of the coastline. We even flew along one side of a promontory and back towards the main shoreline on the other side. Dramatically a hole opened in the dense clouds ahead of us, and, dimly visible, Henderson Field lay ahead. The hole had closed up again five minutes after we had landed. The flight had been too exciting for us to notice that we were still dripping with sea-water. We were amused to receive press clippings from home with a headline: 'MPs shipwrecked in the Solomons'. Getting tipped out of a boat or a canoe in getting ashore was almost a routine occurrence.

An Australian, John Bergelin, who had worked in the Solomons before the War, had been appointed an Administrative Officer. He usually served in Honiara as a District Officer in Central District. He was now serving in the Secretariat. He was a bachelor, very earnest, sometimes monosyllabic. Yet he was likeable and a hard worker. One year he had been given the task of editing, and partly writing, the Annual Report on the Solomons. He came to the chapter on the ecology, and to the paragraphs dealing with flora and fauna. In the Solomons mammals were scarce. There were opossums, wild pig and, reputedly, a large rat on Guadalcanal called *mus rex*. I have never met anyone who has seen one. The draft Annual Report was duly submitted. In this section of the Report one could imagine John sucking his pencil. How could he pad out the section on fauna? He wrote: 'Mammals are scarce in the Solomon Islands. There are opossums and wild pig. Reptiles include crocodiles and iguana. The anthropoid ape is entirely absent.' – together with lions, tigers, elephants and giraffes. The offending ape was consigned to greater absence by deletion from the text.

When Val Andersen returned to duty, I resumed my financial duties. Following leave, I was assigned to the duties of Senior Assistant Secretary (Personnel). This dealt with the staffing of the Protectorate. I would also have some responsibility for staff in the other two Western Pacific High Commission Territories.

Personnel administration

As Senior Assistant Secretary (Personnel), I was responsible to the Chief Secretary for the staff administration of the Solomon Islands Civil Service. I also bore responsibility for recommending Administrative staff placements throughout the three Western Pacific High Commission (WPHC) territories. Administrative staff were appointed to the WPHC and not to any particular territory.

1962 was a fateful year for the decolonisation process. The Gold coast, Malaya, Cyprus, Nigeria, British Somaliland, Tanganyika and Sierra Leone had become Independent in the last five years. The West Indies Federation was now breaking up. Jamaica, and Trinidad and Tobago, as well as Uganda, became Independent in that year. Another nineteen colonies would follow suit in the next decade.

Pensionable recruitment had now ceased. With the demise of the Colonial Service, the mechanics of staffing the new Service, Her Majesty's Overseas Civil Service (HMOCS), came into sharper focus. Under the Overseas Service Aid Scheme, (OSAS), HMOCS officers would receive an inducement allowance, paid by the United Kingdom, in addition to their local salary, paid by the territory. They would also receive education allowances to educate their children outside the territory, and education passages for their children to visit them in the school holidays. Incoming officers, however, could not receive more beneficial terms than officers already serving. Converting these to the new terms engendered a considerable amount of work.

Popular as this was with expatriate officers, it drove a wedge between them and local officers. Two persons doing the same job, with the same job title, were remunerated differently. This was seen as racial discrimination. There was no alternative. Salaries in the Colony reflected the state of the local economy. It was becoming increasingly difficult, and sometimes impossible, to attract staff from the United Kingdom on local salary rates. These were substantially lower than English salaries. At least the equivalent of the English salary had to be offered. There was a good

argument for paying more. Recruits had to be induced to take a job in a
strange country. The differential should be sufficient to make them want
to stay. Continuity was important. Recruitment was slow and expensive.

Making recommendations to the Chief Secretary for postings within
the WPHC was not an easy task. Ideally the officer should be willing, if
not keen, to go. Was it a Secretariat or a District posting? What was the
officer's skill or experience in either role? If the New Hebrides, was he a
French speaker? If the more remote Gilbert and Ellice Islands Colony,
would there be family difficulties? Did the post offer promotion
prospects? Before the WPHC split into separate jurisdictions, there were
about eighty administrative staff in the three territories. In 1962 there
were thirty-two administrative staff in the Solomons, including five leave
reliefs. Officers were absent on leave for about five months every two
and a half years. A leave roster for officers had to be maintained. The
ideal time for posting to other territories was at conclusion of leave.

The Personnel portfolio was regarded by many officers as mundane.
Work was under high pressure. It is true that many of the tasks were
routine and bureaucratic. I was responsible for keeping up to date the
Civil List, issued annually, the Precedence List and Seniority Rolls for
each grade of officer. I had to find time for amendments to General
Orders, the local rule book for the Civil Service, recruitment, retirements, promotions. I arranged for annual reports on all officers and
preparation of cases for disciplinary procedure. Some of these duties
would later pass to the Public Service Commission. The Solomon
Islands Civil Service numbered 178 expatriates and 709 local officers in
1960.[5] These were managed centrally for terms of appointment, leave,
complaints, and the minutiae of staff administration.

Within the Civil Service was a group known as the 'Common-User'
staff. These were primarily Executive and Clerical officers who were
posted to different Departments. There were priority needs, particularly
in the Treasury and for revenue collection. If necessary, staff could be
transferred to meet a crisis. 'Common-User' staff could be withdrawn
for training. Their promotion was safeguarded. This was important for
staff assigned to smaller Departments, where there were few staff in the
higher grades. The 'Common-User' system was not popular with Heads
of Departments. An Executive Officer who had developed a particular
skill might suddenly be promoted to a higher post in another
Department. To counter this, a Head of Department would try to

---

5. See PRO File CO 1036/712.

redesignate a post occupied by an Executive or Clerical Officer in the next Annual Estimates. They would be termed Assistant Auditor or Accountancy Assistant. If this ploy was not spotted, the post dropped out of the 'Common-User' category.

The last two paragraphs may convey the routine nature of the job. Staff matters had to be addressed. Time had to be found, however, to consider staff policy. Localisation, that is, replacing expatriate staff by Solomon Islanders, was an integral part of advancing towards Independence. We had to be ready to promote Solomon Islanders quicker than we had expatriate officers in the past. Manpower surveys had to identify what posts would be required in future. Scholarship schemes were drawn up to make sure that local candidates came through the system. For many expatriate posts, understudies had to be identified and put in place. This usually proved difficult.

Tied in with the introduction of the Overseas Service Aid Scheme, a revision of salaries had been approved. The Commissioner duly arrived. I was appointed Clerk to the Commission. I had to arrange for submissions from Departments and from the Civil Service Association to be available. We debated the merits of a fundamental scale for salaries with all posts fitting on to it. The alternative was to have special scales for professions, nurses, teachers and seamen. After initial work in the Solomons, we set out for the Gilbert and Ellice Islands and the New Hebrides.

We flew to Fiji in a Heron aircraft which had a glass bubble on the roof. Periodically the co-pilot would come into the cabin with a sextant. Taking a sight through the glass bubble, he assured himself that he was in the right ocean. After spending a night at Nadi, we flew on to Tarawa in the Gilbert Islands. We landed briefly at Funafuti, the capital of the Ellice Islands. The flight from there was undertaken at low altitude, in bright sunlight, over countless atolls and reefs. In the lagoons the low coral walls marking out the fish-pens or turtle-crawls were clearly visible. Children waved happily to the plane. All too soon we were touching down on Tarawa Atoll. This had been the scene of an American landing against the Japanese not many years before. There had been many casualties. A massive Japanese pill-box remained. It had been adapted to house an electric generator. The roof was the highest point on the island. There was also a British gun which had been captured at the fall of Singapore. The Japanese had brought it with them.

The Secretary to Government met us and took us to a new thatched house. Elaine Bernacchi, the wife of the Resident Commissioner, had stocked it with food. She had also allotted us a cook. On opening the refrigerator, we found a bunch of grapes. We learnt afterwards that these were part of the first consignment ever to arrive on Tarawa. There had, we heard, been solemn debate as to whether we should have any. We might gain the impression that Civil Servants could afford such luxuries.

We were invited to the Residency for dinner that night. Black tie was expected. We were the first guests to arrive. Suddenly, straight out of Somerset Maugham, a figure bounced in. It was the Chief of Police with white tunic and medals. Close-fitting navy blue tights moulded a tubby stomach. He wore mess Wellingtons and spurs. He bowed deeply as he entered, like a new peer being admitted to the House of Lords. We hoped that the stitching of his trousers would take the strain.

The next morning we got down to work. It was not, however, the kind of place where appointments were easy to arrange. Government Headquarters was spread over several islands. Although a road joined them, it was impassable when the tide was in. The tide tables had to be consulted before a meeting was arranged with a Department on a different island. This had to be completed in time to travel home. The later construction of causeways changed these unusual circumstances. We visited the islands of Bikenebeu and Betio. We held meetings with all the major Departments and the staff association. Views were sought from the Resident Commissioner, the Secretary to Government and the officer dealing with personnel matters. These meetings allowed us to probe more deeply into written submissions. We were impressed by the calibre of local officers.

It was soon time to leave. From our house we could look out to sea in both directions. The island was only a few hundred yards wide. Coconut and pandanus trees grew indiscriminately between the houses. Rooted in sand, with a meagre supply of water, they survived and produced fruit. Beyond them, in the shallow waters of the lagoon, stood a line of children. A look-out watched for a sudden squall of wind rippling the surface. A cry rang out. A flurry of colour dotted the lagoon, quickly to disappear. Each child had a model canoe with an outrigger. Each outrigger canoe had a brightly-coloured sail about three feet high. When the cry went up, the children released the canoes into the wind. If the model was properly balanced, the outrigger came out of the water. The tiny craft then shot down wind for up to a hundred yards. Its voyage was done when there was a sudden change of wind. Over it went. Recovery, repair, if necessary, and return to the start took time. There were not many races in a morning. We were fortunate to see one. We had time to inspect one of the small models. They were exact replicas of the full-scale racing canoes still in use. They were exquisitely made. The gaily-coloured sails were off-cuts of material used to make skirts and lava-lavas. Has this activity been replaced by computer games in 2003?

We enjoyed the flight back to Funafuti. We returned to Honiara via Vila in the New Hebrides. Unlike Honiara or Tarawa, Vila had not suffered from Japanese occupation. The Americans had used it as a base. There were no scars of war. It had a settled orderliness absent in the capitals of the other two WPHC territories. It had a French ambience. There were French advertisements in evidence. The tricolour flew from the French Residency and from some other buildings. There were one or two French restaurants. In the market place the radishes were in bouquets. There was a surprising variety of good quality vegetables. As regards development, one could almost visualise the French shrug of the shoulders. Demain. Peut être.

We carried out a programme very similar to that arranged in Tarawa. We had some problems with the salary of the British judge. He considered himself the poor relation of the French judge. There were three sets of law in the New Hebrides: French Law, British law and Condominium law. The Protocol which established the New Hebrides provided for a French court. This administered French law for French citizens or New Hebrideans opting to be French ressortissants. There was a British court for the British equivalents. The joint court to administer Condominium law was to be presided over by a neutral judge appointed by the King of Spain. As there was then no King of Spain, the post was vacant.

Even compared with the Gilbert and Ellice establishment, the British Civil Service in the New Hebrides was small. It numbered less than thirty expatriates and about one hundred and twenty local officers.

Shortly afterwards the Commissioner submitted his report, He recommended modest increases and some adjustment of salary scales. He endeavoured to satisfy many complaints about conditions of service.

About this time the Colonial Office addressed Governors about the fate of the smaller colonies. Where economic self-sufficiency was unlikely, Independence might not be the best solution. Close association with the United Kingdom or integration were suggested as alternatives which might have to be considered. Views were sought. Sir David Trench, who had replaced Sir John Gutch as High Commissioner, consulted his senior staff. His view was that the Solomon Islands were large enough to plan for Independence. It would take time, however, to reach economic maturity. Consequently, in a letter to Sir Hilary Poynton in 1962, he advocated the Independence option. He wrote:

> An optimistic estimate has been made in this paper that by common-sense estimates it would take the Protectorate some fifteen years at best to overcome the present main obstacles to Independence.[6]

The Solomons became Independent in 1978. His forecast was wrong by one year. This was the time-scale that dominated our thinking. Staffing was a problem both for the WPHC and for London. Contract officers were employed on contract for two-year contracts. Administration demanded continuity. It would be patently unfair to the community to have a succession of strangers unfamiliar with the local scene dealing with their problems. Accordingly we corresponded with the Colonial Office on offering long-term contracts for agreed posts. Retention of existing officers also came into sharper focus. When administrative officers were recruited in the years immediately following the War, they were informed of the 'Seven Year Rule'. Conditions in the Western Pacific were considered more arduous than elsewhere. Malaria was rife. Isolation and climate were unattractive features of life. Hence, after seven years, officers could expect to be transferred to more attractive colonies. The 'Rule' was quietly placed in abeyance. High Commissioners, responsible for the administration of the territories, were faced with losing experienced officers. It was at the time when most of them could expect local promotion. No announcement was made. We knew, however, that the 'Rule' was a dead duck.

As another incentive to keep officers at post, the Pension Laws of the three WPHC territories were amended in the 1950's. The normal minimum retiring age was fifty-five. At this age it might be difficult to embark on a second career. Managers of the Service believed that in the Pacific officers might resign prematurely through disillusionment. By legally reducing the minimum retiring age to forty-five, officers would be induced to stay long enough in the Service to retire on pension. At this age they would be able to start a second career at home. Officers were not obliged to elect whether they wished to take advantage of this concession. They simply gave six months notice when the time came.

Many post-war officers joined the Service about the age of thirty. The time was fast approaching when they might retire. The new staffing arrangement required a review of this policy, by which the core of pensionable officers could quickly be eroded. The solution was the

6. See PRO File CO 1036/1291.

introduction of a Benefit Scheme for the Western Pacific. Officers could agree to waive their right to retire at forty-five. They would be paid ten thousand pounds over five years, in instalments. In return they would agree not to retire before reaching the age of fifty. There was a certain degree of panic in these arrangements, as many of us did not have early retirement in mind.

Apart from policy, personnel administration meant dealing with people on a daily basis. Compassionate cases were difficult. Occasionally the Chief Secretary's sanction had to be obtained when the rule book was not appropriate for the problem. On such occasions Michael Gass, who was Chief Secretary from 1959 to 1965, invariably leant towards the compassionate solution.

I raised his eyebrows on one occasion. One of my ex-headmen from Malaita was told by the District Commissioner that he did not merit a pension on retirement. He would be paid a lump-sum gratuity. He did not understand the difference between the two terms. He sought an interview with me for clarification. He sat, ill at ease, on his chair. I was behind my desk. He jumped off his chair, and, in Pidgin English, said 'This is no good. Come outside with me, and I shall tell you.' We went outside the Secretariat. He motioned to me to sit down beside him on the gravel. He scooped a handful of stones into his basket. Then, to establish dates, he put down a stone to mark when 'Mr Bell gettim kill' – 1927. 'Go, go fifteen year.' He laid out fifteen stones on the ground. At this point a voice said: 'Tom, what on earth are you doing down there?' It was Michael Gass, the Chief Secretary. I indicated that I was performing my duties 'custom-fashion'. He entered the Secretariat slowly shaking his head. I had to tell my friend that the District Commissioner was correct. He only merited a gratuity. He thanked me and said that he accepted my advice. He replaced the gravel and left.

It was useful discharging personnel and financial duties in turn. One of the responsibilities of the financial portfolio was to safeguard the public purse. Nevertheless the labourer is worthy of his hire. An officer is entitled to payment of salary, payments for subsistence, costs of official travel, when due. The resources to meet such debts on time should always be in place. Later in my career I was able to insist, on occasion, that this policy was followed.

Although I cannot recall the circumstances why both the Chief Secretary and the Financial Secretary were absent at the same time, for six weeks during this tour of duty, I acted as Chief Secretary. I was promoted to Financial Secretary in September 1965.

CHAPTER TWELVE

Financial Secretary

I WAS PROMOTED Deputy Financial Secretary, working to Bim Davies as Financial Secretary, in October 1962. In September 1965, Michael Gass, the Chief Secretary, was transferred to Hong Kong as Colonial Secretary. Bim was promoted Chief Secretary. I inherited the Financial Secretary's post. I was supported for part of the time when I was Deputy Financial Secretary by Dick Turpin, who had transferred from the Gilbert and Ellice Islands Colony. He left the portfolio to be District Commissioner, Malaita. He held that stimulating post for longer than any officer after the War. I was fortunate to be supported by John Yaxley for much of the time that I was Financial Secretary.

John had served previously in the New Hebrides and had we had a fast-track scheme, he would definitely have been in it. He conformed to the old definition of a gentleman in that he behaved towards senior officers exactly as he behaved towards his juniors. On one occasion I was asked if he showed enough aggression to secure his objectives. I responded by saying that he nearly always attained his objectives. Perhaps his technique was better than that of the questioner. In 1975 he was seconded to the Foreign and Commonwealth Office and transferred to Hong Kong in 1977. He held various senior posts: Deputy Financial Secretary, Secretary for Economic Services, Director of Industry. He completed his career as Hong Kong Commissioner in London at a time I was the Cayman Islands Government Representative there. In the years leading to the agreement with China on the future of the Colony, John Yaxley's new post was a high-profile job. He was still securing his objectives as he had in the Pacific. He was awarded the CBE in 1990.

I shall not attempt to separate the periods in which I was Deputy Financial Secretary and Financial Secretary. The duties of the two posts were closely intertwined. Moreover we had long periods of leave every two years. Consequently officers acted in the post above them for substantial periods. I acted as Financial Secretary and as Chief Secretary for one third of the time that I occupied the post below. For a quarter of the time that I was Chief Secretary, I acted as High Commissioner. Not only was this excellent training, but it also enabled the officer to appreciate what was required of his own post.

In describing the duties of the post of Senior Assistant Secretary Finance (now Deputy Financial Secretary), I said that the main aim was to relieve the Financial Secretary of routine, so as to enable him to concentrate on policy. The policy was to develop the infrastructure and economy of the Protectorate to the stage where it would float free of aid from United Kingdom. It would then be in a position to contemplate internal self-government and Independence thereafter. Development of the economy was often synonymous with creation. Without burdening the reader with the exact timings of events, let me depict the scope of the Financial Secretary's objectives.

I shall describe these under 'infrastructure' and 'economic develop-ments'.

First, infrastructure. We started almost with a clean slate. The War had destroyed the few assets which existed. The main ports of Tulagi and Gizo had been destroyed. There were no airfields; there were no motorable road systems. Education, which had been the sole prerogative of the missions, had been disrupted. School buildings, of fragile local construction, were derelict. Hospital buildings and clinics had been destroyed or were in disrepair. There were no piped water supplies in District stations. The supply in the capital, Honiara, was rudimentary. Power supplies were provided from ex-American generators of dubious ancestry. Telecommunications and communication with the outside world were hit-and-miss. Accommodation for provision of essential government services and for the officers involved was mostly con-structed of temporary materials.

Our Development Plans, which were incremental, a series of building blocks, addressed this situation. Cargo sheds and a Queen's Warehouse, managed by the Customs Department, were constructed at Point Cruz. This was within the perimeter of Honiara and allowed us to close the old American Jetty at Kukum, which had become dangerous from the depredations of north-west storms. The next phase was construction of a port facility with berths for two cargo ships at the same time. Development Plans provided the money first for mooring bollards, and then for piling, to allow ships to come alongside. A Ports Authority was established to manage this. I was chairman for several years. Gizo was opened as a port of entry for ships arriving from overseas as soon as I reestablished the Government station there in 1949. A bond shed was one of the buildings erected prior to the station re-opening.

The American forces had left wartime airstrips at Henderson Field near Honiara, Munda in New Georgia, Bilua on Vella Lavella, Segi in the Marovo Lagoon, and on Stirling Island in the Shortland Islands. This was a welcome legacy. They had crushed coral surfaces, sometimes covered by steel matting. The matting had been removed and sold as scrap. Before commercial flights could be permitted, the airfields had to be brought up to civilian standards. Dramatically improving communications between islands would assist in fostering a feeling of nationhood. The history of inter-island rivalry, headhunting and fighting did not make this easy. Airfields on each island would also assist administration to a marked degree. Eddie Nielsen, Director of Civil Aviation, set himself the task of resuscitating the American airstrips and reconnoitring sites for airfields at Kira Kira, Auki, and Gizo. Construction was not always with heavy machinery. Richard Feachem who had volunteered for Voluntary Service Overseas was told on arrival on Guadalcanal that his assignment was to build an airfield at Avu Avu on the weather coast. He had to persuade the villagers of the advantages. He had then to mobilise them to clear a site and roughly level it, all without payment. At this stage a small bulldozer and a grader were sent round by sea – we had obtained landing-craft from Colonial Development and Welfare funds for such operations – and the airfield was completed. I had the pleasure of officiating as Financial Secretary at the opening, followed by a feast. What an achievement for a young man at the end of his secondary education!

Initially we limited road development to the coastal roads on the western side of Malaita and the eastern side of Guadalcanal. This ran from Vissale, through Honiara, to the Guadalcanal plains. Later, Bob Finnimore, when he was District Commissioner, Malaita, drove a road across Malaita to the far coast. Except in Honiara, roads did not have tarred surfaces. Consequently they had to be graded regularly to keep them open. Machinery was expensive. Provision for its purchase had to be made in the Road Schemes. Both Malaita and Guadalcanal are well furnished with rivers and bridging added greatly to the cost of road construction. Bailey bridging was used with success. One of the early bridges on Malaita was over the river Fiu. Of stout wooden construction, it could well have been the main prop for the film, *Bridge Over the River Kwai*. The District Officer in charge had carefully noted the mark of the highest flood ever known and built the bridge four feet higher. An announcement was made on Radio Honiara: 'The Fiu bridge is now open for traffic'. The only traffic on the island was the District

Commissioner's landrover. It had broken down. Rain had been falling for two days and the night following the announcement there were thunderstorms and a tropical deluge. The bridge was struck by the butt end of a huge tree washed down the river and disintegrated. The virgin Fiu bridge was no longer open for traffic. The destruction of bridges was not uncommon on Guadalcanal, which was subject to heavy flooding in the rainy season. The other six months of the year were jokingly referred to as the wet season.

In many Colonies the Churches had been responsible for education before the War. This was so in the Protectorate. But education at an enhanced rate and to a higher standard was an imperative for Government.

With a fifteen-year target for Independence, civil servants and future politicians had to have their natural skills honed in the classroom. Both the quantity and the quality of schools were improved. Government primary schools were established in main centres. The Woodford School in Honiara was opened for the children of expatriates. To the credit of the school management, it also encouraged admission of Melanesian children. The King George VI secondary school was moved from Auki to Honiara and the facilities vastly improved. A teacher's training college was established. A technical training college was built at Kukum, featuring marine training, secretarial training and practical instruction of mechanics, electricians and carpenters. Subsidies were given to the Church schools of the Melanesian Mission, the Catholic Church, the Methodists, the Seventh Day Adventists, and the South Sea Evangelical Mission on Malaita. I recall, as Financial Secretary, chairing meetings at which the the Roman Catholic Bishop, Bishop Steyvenberg, and the Anglican Bishop, Bishop Hill were present. The government representatives included the Director of Education, Geoffrey Bovey, or Dennis Hibbert, who succeeded him. Although money was scarce, there was a remarkable degree of agreement on objectives. The government was also generous with scholarships abroad to the extent that funds allowed.

Public health required a massive injection of such development funds as were available. Schemes were drawn up for the renovation of the main hospital in Honiara, in Central District, and for hospitals at Gizo, Auki and Kira Kira. Funds were approved to upgrade rural clinics. The most significant medical project was a bold initiative to eradicate malaria. This was endemic. Before the War blackwater fever – also mosquito-borne, and often fatal – was not uncommon. Approval was given for a pilot project financed jointly by the World Health Organisation and Colonial Development and Welfare funds. A Protectorate-wide scheme was then launched. This challenged the logistic capacity of the Department of Health. It involved spraying with a DDT solution the interior wall of every building in the Solomons twice a year. This included garden sheds. The project was based on a simple proposition. The anopheles mosquito, which transmits malaria, flies to rest on a vertical surface after a blood meal. It transmits malaria by feeding on infected blood. When it feeds on the next victim, it passes on the disease. If it can be poisoned before this stage, the disease will gradually disappear. To spray the wall of every building in the country would be a formidable proposition in Europe. Often houses in the Solomons were unmapped. Many people lived in hamlets of two or three houses. Some were perched on mountain tops. Pagan communities were inimical to visits by strangers. The campaign owed much of its success to the leader, Doctor Tross, appointed by the World Health Organisation. He was a German who had been a member of the Hitler Jugend. He was a brilliant organiser and was popular with his team. I suspected, however, that the mosquitoes sprang to attention when he was in their vicinity. After some years it was announced that malaria had been eradicated except for two limited areas. One of these was the island of Savo. A cheaper way to complete the campaign would be to give anti-malarial pills to all the members of the population in both places. Alas, it was impossible to guarantee that all inhabitants complied. Malaria revived and today it is of a more malevolent strain than in the past.

Water and electricity were problems. Supplies of water were insufficient. Electricity supplies were expensive. Monetary provision was made for improving water supplies in Honiara, Auki and Gizo. Electricity, however, was generated by black oil generators. An extra one was ordered if demand increased. The possibility of hydro-electric power being used by damming the river Lunga was mooted. The Department of Overseas Development was not prepared to finance the project, which was estimated to cost about three million pounds. William Halcrow and Partners carried out a feasibility study. I visited Washington to talk to the World Bank. I was accompanied by a diplomat from the British Embassy. Two hurdles were erected. As the Protectorate was, in effect, a British Colony, why did it not approach the British Government for funding? Secondly the scheme would only benefit those living in the capital, Honiara. If the World Bank lent the same amount of money to India, it would benefit millions. Alternate sources of finance were not readily available. The scheme would not be viable at full commercial lending rates and it was doubtful if the Treasury would approve a loan of this kind. The Commonwealth Development Corporation was reluctant to lend directly to Governments. Hence no Lunga Dam.

We were, however, successful in arranging for Cable and Wireless to take over our communications and in installing what, in those days, were state-of-the-art telephone exchanges. We also upgraded various government buildings and had several Colonial and Welfare schemes for building staff housing in the capital and on outstations.

Meanwhile, Brian Twomey, the Commissioner of Lands, was modernising the Land Registry. He was also systematically mapping the Protectorate and setting the stage for development.

To include these activities in Development plans, and later in specific schemes, took a great deal of liaison with Heads of Departments, Permanent Secretaries and politicians. It was always satisfying to see plans implemented upon the ground.

In the development of the economy one played a greater personal part.

Before the war copra, the dried flesh of the coconut, had been the main export. It was produced as a plantation crop and also by peasant farmers. Levers Pacific Plantations had substantial acreages in the Russell Islands. Some plantations had been damaged during the War. A replanting programme was being promoted. To the layman this should not be difficult. Unharvested coconuts sprout where they fall. Replanting should simply be a matter of putting sprouting coconuts in rows. Not so. Research on coconuts at Yandina, Levers' headquarters, must have been as sophisticated as anywhere else in the tropics. The Government was closely involved. Different types of palm produce different sized nuts. Some trees come into bearing after three or four years, others take longer. Spacing between trees and between rows affects the yield. Should one plant a smaller number of trees producing more nuts or a greater number of trees? Which method gave a better yield? Cross pollination produced hybrids. The Malayan Dwarf fruited well and came into bearing quickly. The Rennell Tall bore fewer nuts of a greater size. Hybrids and the yield of individual trees were studied. There was talk of cloning from good parent trees. Coconut pests were identified and control measures introduced. One of the pests was the stick insect. Good detective work by an entomologist identified small tick-like predators on dead specimens in the British Museum. Fiji was known to harbour the predators. They were then captured. They were released in the Russell Island plantations.

At the same time as scientific replanting was going on, the quality of copra was being monitored. The Copra Board, of which I was Chairman for a number of years, determined different grades and employed inspectors. Higher prices were paid for the better grades.

Cocoa was being actively promoted as a peasant crop, grown under specially planted shade trees. Cattle were being imported from Australia to increase the meagre numbers which survived the War. Experimentation by Levers expanded. Could cattle be successfully grazed in the coconut plantations? Would coconut trees provide enough shade for cocoa? 'Yes' was the answer to both questions.

Of critical importance to development of agriculture was the exploitation of the Guadalcanal plains, the only significant area of arable land in the Protectorate. Ken Hay, the proprietor of the Mendana Hotel, had opened a farm there. The Government also had a small experimental farm. The majority of the land area, however, was under dispute by a number of landowners and the government. The chances of reaching a quick decision in the Courts were slim, as each claim would have to be considered separately. The District Commissioner succeeded in bringing the various landowners together. A meeting was arranged including myself and the Commissioner of Lands. We solved the impasse by conceding that the land belonged to the various landowners. In return for this admission, they would enter into long-term leases. This permitted the Commonwealth Development Corporation to go ahead with trials in oil-palm. The Corporation also conducted trials in Fiji and Papua New Guinea. The Solomons were selected. The sunlight conditions, important for oil-palm propagation, were the best. Eventually sufficient palms were planted to justify the construction of a mill to extract the oil on the spot. David Kausimae, the Solomon Islands Minister responsible for Agriculture, and I, as Financial Secretary, jointly planted the first tree. Elsewhere on the plains, as a separate venture, rice was being grown on a commercial scale. The area involved was large enough to justify the use of crop-dusting planes.

Two economists had been sent out by the Department of Overseas Development to assist in drawing up Development Plans. I remarked to one that I found something odd. We were planting a large area of palm trees on the only treeless arable land in the Solomons. He looked at me as if I came from another planet. 'A question of cash return per acre,' was his response.

Forestry was obviously an industry which could be developed in a country with huge acreages of primary forest. There was a small export of *kauri* timber from Vanikoro in the Santa Cruz islands. There was also Japanese interest in the stands of timber on Kolombangara and New Georgia in the Western Solomons. I chaired a Select Committee of the Legislative Assembly to recommend the policy which we should adopt. Keith Trenaman, the Conservator of Forests, with advice from the Secretary of State's Forestry adviser, was quite clear what we should do. Our main conclusion was that there must be reafforestation of any cleared areas. The agreement between Government and the contractor would specify whether an increased royalty would be paid. If so, the Conservator of Forests would perform the replanting. Alternatively a lesser royalty would be written into the agreement. The contractor would then have the responsibility of reafforesting to the satisfaction of the Conservator of Forests. I do not believe that this policy has survived Independence. The temptation for the Government has been to accept the higher royalty and forgo the expense of reafforestation. Negotiations with Japanese contractors followed. On the first occasion, immediately the agreement was signed, a fleet of ships came over the horizon. They were loaded with a prefabricated hutted camp, electricity generators, bulldozers and heavy logging equipment. They were in operation within seventy-two hours.

One had the feeling that the Japanese aim of having a co-prosperity zone in the Pacific in wartime was being achieved after peace had been declared. They had purchased the Government Trade Scheme. They were later to purchase the Mendana Hotel. They were now interested in Forestry, Fisheries and Mining.

Negotiations also took place over fishing for tuna in Solomon Island waters. The company representatives quickly realised that permission would hinge on their operating a cannery ashore. We secured this. We also stipulated that they would carry Solomon Islander inspectors on each vessel. These would monitor fish size and record catches. They would be obliged to purchase bait fish from local villages. The bait fish are small whitebait-size fish. They are stored live in tanks aboard the fishing vessel. The shoal of tuna is identified by radar and buckets of baitfish are thrown over the side.

The tuna go into a feeding frenzy. During this they will snap at anything that moves. The Korean fishermen who crew the boats line up along the side. They have fishing poles with a gorge, which has no barb, at the end of twelve feet of line. They lower the gorge into the water. The fish snaps at it. It is then pulled forcibly out of the water and, at the end of the line, flies over the fisherman's head. As it reaches the top of its trajectory the gorge disengages and the fish drops into the hold. The gorge is immediately dropped into the water again and the operation continues while the bait fish last.

We also wrote into the agreement that the company would endeavour to replace the Korean crew by Solomon Islanders within a specified time.

For more than a decade the Geological Survey had been in operation. There were about six geologists under the dynamic leadership of John Grover, the Chief Geologist. He was an Australian who had fought in debilitating jungle conditions in Papua New Guinea during the War. He was also a keen vulcanologist. He had his own theories as to the connection between earthquakes and volcanic eruptions. He closely monitored the island of Savo, about twelve miles from Honiara, with thermometers and tilt-meters. Although Savo was extinct, it had fumeroles. It was of the Mount Pelean type of volcano. If it did erupt, the blast would be lateral. Honiara would be in the danger area.

On one occasion he came into the office of Wyn Jones. Wyn was then the Permanent Secretary for the Natural Resources Ministry. 'Wyn,' said John, impressively, 'Savo has tilted .09 of a degree.' Wyn rose slowly from his seat and sought a window overlooking Savo. 'John,' he said, 'I think I liked it better as it was.'

Apart from his vulcanologist interests, John Grover was an indefatigable Head of Department. He led from the front. He and his fellow geologists undertook the most exhausting tours into the mountains of Guadalcanal and other islands. These could be dangerous. Coming through one of the gorges on Guadalcanal, he was caught by a flash flood. Within seconds the gorge was filled by flood waters several metres deep, rushing down the river bed. The party had seconds to climb on to a ledge to wait until the waters subsided.

One of the mountains on Guadalcanal, Mount Tatuve, was a sacred mountain and it was *tambu* (forbidden) to climb it. John regarded this embargo as an impediment to science. He and a geological party disembarked from a ship and made their way up the mountain. When they reached the upper slopes, they were confronted by a line of Guadalcanal villagers. There was a distinct air of menace. 'Nobody is allowed to climb our mountain,' they said. John accepted this with what grace he could muster. He returned to the boat and proceeded south round the tip of Guadalcanal. He disembarked opposite Mount Tatuve on the weather coast.

Up they went again. On reaching the same level as previously they were confronted by the same line of villagers. 'We told you, Mr Grover,' (he was well known), 'Nobody is allowed to climb our mountain.' He returned to the ship. He used to tell this story as demonstrating the impossible. Someone had deterred him from reaching his objective.

He had, over the years, produced a geological map of the Protectorate. The map of Guadalcanal had been enhanced by a geodetic survey by aircraft. These flew at low altitude in parallel lines across the island. They towed 'the bird', a metal cylinder full of gadgetry, behind the aircraft. This picked up anomalies in the earth beneath which could then be investigated by ground parties. The Protectorate had deposits of nickel, copper, gold, bauxite and phosphate.

Again, the Japanese were the first to show interest and we had tangled discussions with them on rights to mine for bauxite on Rennell Island. As these would be highly technical, we had in our team experts in mining negotiations and in the revenue aspects of the proposal. The Japanese had brought sophisticated calculators with them. We might suggest that the Government would take its revenue from the mine in the shape of royalties at a certain level. They would ask for a suspension. On resumption, they would lay out the expected revenue and expenditure for twenty years of mining and show that our proposal was unacceptable. It was an interesting negotiation. We finally reached agreement. In the next few months the price of bauxite fell dramatically and mining did not eventuate.

I was also Chairman of the Agricultural and Industrial Loans Board, from which developers could borrow for small business ventures. We had laid out an industrial estate at Kukum and introduced Pioneer Tax Concessions to attract entrepreneurs. Kukum, however, where the Technical College was sited, had a problem area. Labourers were required in increasing numbers by the Public Works Department, by the Town Council and other employers. These workers inhabited the 'labour lines', dormitory-type huts erected by American Forces during the War. Not only was accommodation sub-standard and insanitary, but the occupants were either single males or married young men who had left their families behind. Two visiting MP's were so concerned that they put down a Parliamentary Question. As a result, an experienced Commonwealth Development Corporation housing expert came out. He made a report recommending the appointment of a Housing Officer to deal with the problem. I had previously submitted a report on the situation recommending that sites for low-cost housing which were identified should be furnished with services. Supply of roads, electricity and sewerage would be a start. Nothing however was done at the time. If we proceeded on these lines, I argued, we could achieve quicker results than waiting for an expert. He would also require time to familiarise himself with the local situation.

I obtained approval to chair a committee in-spanning all officers concerned with housing in the capital. These included the Director of Public Works, the Chairman of Honiara Town Council, the Welfare Officer, an Architect, the Deputy Financial Secretary, the Director of Medical Services, the District Commissioner and Tony Hughes, Lands Officer. I have never served on a more enthusiastic or effective committee. I set aside funds for installing essential services on the first site. Low cost designs were produced on a modular basis, with two sizes of house. A local fibre-glass factory which made dinghies was induced to produce units with a wash-basin, a shower and a lavatory. These stood behind the houses and required two connections to bring into service. All frills were cut out. Corrugated iron was ordered in rolls. Instead of using standard six feet sheets, we could cut one sheet for each side of the roof. In the estates we provided for primary school buildings and shops, using the same modular approach. As gardens were important to Melanesians sociologically, we purchased land for allotments not too far from each development. We set rents and established a scheme in which the inhabitant could purchase by instalments. Alternatively he could pay monthly rentals, or convert the rental payments into purchase instalments. The Honiara Town Council took over the scheme once the buildings were completed. Revenue went into a revolving fund which funded more houses. When the scheme was running at peak efficiency, we were averaging completion at the rate of two houses per day.

Installation of essential services for the sites was considered a fair charge to Colonial Development and Welfare funds. The two economists, however, persuaded the Department of Technical Cooperation that we were spending too great a proportion of available funds on welfare instead of revenue-earning projects. We thereupon established a Housing Authority. The momentum, however, had been lost.

My son came back with us on leave in 1964 to enter a preparatory school in England. On our way home we travelled from Hawaii to Mexico City, Lima in Peru, Rio de Janeiro in Brazil and from there to Madrid. We spent a few days in each place. The most memorable visit was to Huancayo. This was a village at ten thousand feet in the Andes, behind Lima. We tacked up the mountain by train. The train went forward into a siding. It then went backwards into another, angling up the mountain. This process was repeated until we reached the summit.

In one of the pastures there were circles of stone wall with an aperture to admit animals, such as are common on Scottish moors. When there is a blizzard, the sheep go inside while the snow drifts against the outside wall. The railway had been built by Scottish engineers and construction staff. The stone circles were used by the llama in the winter.

Huancayo was the market for craftwork produced in neighbouring villages. There was the village of the silversmiths, the village of the weavers, the village of the potters. The women wore a black flower-pot hat and ran, rather than walked, with a shuffling movement. At that altitude we were content to walk . . . slowly.

On one of my son's school holidays in the Solomons, we walked up the Poha River valley. In a relatively small cave opening he found a carving on the cave wall. Part of it was covered by the earth floor. This indicated that the cave floor had been lower when the carving was made. Possibly it had been occupied over a period. Professor Bill Davenport, Professor of Anthropology at Santa Cruz University in California, was later in Honiara. He had done some archaeological work in the Eastern Solomons. He had a week in hand before returning to America. I assisted him in a trial excavation of the cave. There had been fighting there during the War and we first found bullets, human remains and a decaying wallet with photographs of two Japanese children. There were sufficient artifacts and evidence of human habitation to merit continuance of the dig. I arranged with Bill to send any carbon to Santa Cruz for carbon dating. Over a two-year period I continued the excavation at week-ends, sometimes with the help of Jim Tedder and Lindsay Wall. Jim was District Commissioner, Central District. Lindsay's husband, David, was a soil scientist engaged in a Land Resources survey of the Protectorate. She had previously worked at the Borneo Museum with Tom Harrison.

The cave was twelve yards deep and twelve yards wide at the back. We took the floor level down about twelve feet until we reached sterile soil. The material was sieved into the river-bed below the cave. Of greatest interest were the rock-carvings, petroglyphs, which appeared on the rock wall as the floor-level descended. Although crude, a fish, a hornbill, a snake and several human faces, were discernible. The outlines had been chiselled into the rock. We were able to take perfect impressions by painting the rock face with liquid latex, vulcanising it, and peeling the rubber off like a mask. Once we had perfected the technique, we enlisted the assistance of the sixth form at King George VI School. The rubber masks were placed face up on a bed of wet sand and concrete or plaster of Paris was poured over them. When this set, there was an exact impression of the cave wall and the carving. These reproductions were placed in the Honiara Museum, together with all artifacts, shells and bone material which we unearthed. Apart from a few adzes and a nut hammer and anvil, there were many sea-shells, showing that these had been brought from the coast for food. The nut anvils showed that the *gnali* nut, canarium almond, was a staple food. It still is today. According to carbon dating, the inhabitants of the cave had been there three thousand years before. But deposits at the front of the cave, excavated subsequently, took habitation back six thousand years.

I have been guilty of a digression.

As well as carrying out the work which I have described earlier, I was busy with the weekly meetings of the Executive Council and the quarterly meetings of the Legislative Council. We now had a Solomon Islander as Speaker and Lily Poznanski as Clerk to the Council. Sir Robert Foster had succeeded Sir David Trench as High Commissioner.

I was a Director of Air Pacific, formerly Fiji Airways. The major shareholders were BOAC, Qantas, Air New Zealand and Fiji Government. Each of the other Pacific countries which the airline served had a token shareholding and a seat on the Board. Meetings were held in Fiji. It was interesting to see how thoroughly the company prepared the documentation for its board meetings. Management was supplied by Qantas.

As Chairman of the Copra Board, I attended annual meetings of representatives of Pacific Boards to agree the freight contract with the Bank Shipping line. This picked up the copra at designated ports in each territory and freighted it to England. Port Moresby, where the meetings took place, was more populous than other Pacific capitals. It was obvious that many were unemployed, attracted by the bright lights, and they constituted a potential social problem.

A visit of a different kind was one to Bangkok to attend an economic conference organised by ECAFE, an organ of the United Nations. In one discussion I described the difficulties we had in raising funds for the Lunga Dam. I said that even if we were allocated as little as 1% of international funds provided for large countries, this would help. They, on the other hand, would scarcely notice the shortfall. To my amazement I was supported by the delegate for India. As guests of the Thai Government, we were taken by coach up-river to visit the old capital of Ayuthaya. It had been sacked by the Burmese many years before and huge statues of the Buddha lay in the grass. One of these, which looked unusually well featured, had been transported to Bangkok and offloaded on to a wharf. There it lay for a long time awaiting a decision where to put it. One day someone noticed a bright golden gleam. The statue was the golden Buddha, now on display in Bangkok. To protect it from the marauders, the monks had covered it with stucco. Presumably none of them lived to reveal what they had done. Also on display in Bangkok is the emerald Buddha, which, I believe, is made of jade. It is a tiny figure picked out by a spotlight and is exquisite.

We returned to Bangkok by riverboat on the River Proya. Two dainty Thai hostesses presided over several large barrels of chilled Thai beer. We gained the distinct impression that they expected severe chastisement if any of this was brought back to Bangkok. There were many Americans about on leave from Vietnam. Taking a taxi was hazardous. The standard of driving, at excessive speed, was low.

During the period in which I was Financial Secretary, Bim Davies was Chief Secretary and Sir Robert Foster High Commissioner. He had long District experience in Northern Rhodesia before being responsible for Native Affairs there. He became Chief Secretary and Deputy Governor in Nyasaland before his Pacific appointment. He went on to become Governor and Commander in Chief in Fiji and Governor General for a short time after Fiji became Independent. He had a relaxed style but knew everything that was going on in the Service. He expected his Chief Secretary and Financial Secretary to do their jobs without running to him for advice on matters delegated to them. They should also know when he should be consulted in advance. Lady Foster was held in great esteem by my wife. On one occasion the French High Commissioner from Noumea was making a visit and there would be the usual formal dinner the night before the visitor left. Meeting Lady Foster a week before the function, my wife said, 'Lady Foster, I am afraid I'll have an attack of social malaria on the night of your dinner.' 'Why, my dear?' was the reply. 'Because there will be a toast to President De Gaulle, and with my Franco-Algerian background, I can't drink to that man.' A hoot of laughter came from Madge Foster. A few days later she accosted my wife when she was shopping. 'I've solved your problem,' she said, 'I am going to make the evening informal, with small tables and there will be no toasts.' Her directness also endeared her to the Fijians.

CHAPTER THIRTEEN

Chief Secretary

AT THIS JUNCTURE I must record some of the changes which took place at senior level.

In 1970 Val Andersen, who had been Resident Commissioner of the Gilbert and Ellice Islands Colony, retired. He had formerly been Secretary for Protectorate Affairs in the Solomons. Sir John Field, a previous Governor of St Helena, replaced him. Bim Davies, the Chief Secretary, was posted to the Bahamas as Deputy Governor. I took his place as Chief Secretary. John Smith, most of whose service had been in Nigeria, replaced me as Financial Secretary. He brought considerable expertise with him and three years later was promoted Governor of the Gilbert and Ellice Islands. At that stage the Colony separated from the Western Pacific High Commission. Reg Wallace succeeded him as Financial Secretary. After service in senior posts in the Gold Coast, he had been Financial Secretary in British Somaliland. He then had eight years in Whitehall, serving in the War Office and the Treasury. In 1978 he was to succeed John Smith as Governor of the Gilbert and Ellice Islands. He concluded a varied career by becoming Financial Secretary for Gibraltar.

In 1972 Roy Davies, the Deputy Chief Secretary in the Solomons, retired. His place was taken by Trevor Clark, who had served throughout Nigerian Independence. He came to us from Hong Kong, where he had served in a variety of posts, including that of Director of Social Welfare. He was to succeed me as Chief Secretary in 1974. The post was later redesignated as Deputy Governor.

In 1973 Sir Michael Gass, the High Commissioner, retired. He was succeeded by Sir Donald Luddington, whose previous service had been in Hong Kong. In 1976, after I left the Pacific, he returned to Hong Kong. He was replaced by Sir Colin Allen. After his initial years in the Solomons, he had been Resident Commissioner in the New Hebrides. He was later Governor of the Seychelles at the time of Independence.

By shrewd posting policy, when the Protectorate was about to become Independent, the High Commissioner and Deputy Governor of the Solomons had both been through the Independence process. This policy also applied to the Governor of the Gilbert and Ellice Islands.

Nevertheless there were too many changes at senior level in the few years before Independence.

I had acted for more than six months in the post of Chief Secretary and knew the ambits of the job. Fiji had become Independent in 1970 and Papua New Guinea would achieve Independence in 1975. There was a noticeable quickening of political expectations in the Solomons.

A Legislative Council was created only in 1960. Direct elections were not introduced until 1967. The 1970 Constitution had broken new ground. The usual format was that of a Legislature and an Executive Council comprising Ministers with responsibility for certain subjects and Departments. The 1970 Constitution endeavoured to incorporate the Melanesian tradition of reaching decisions by consensus. The Governing Council headed towards the usual model. But it still included up to six public officers appointed by the High Commissioner in addition to the three *ex-officio* members, the Chief Secretary, the Financial Secretary and the Attorney General. The other seventeen members were elected. The constitution departed from the orthodox model in that the Executive Council was replaced by all members of the Governing Council sitting in private. Instead of Ministers, the High Commissioner established committees of members of the Governing Council, which would be given responsibility for subjects such as education or communications. This had been tried before in Ceylon, where the system was known as the Donoughmore Constitution.

At the end of 1971, I was appointed as Chairman of a Select Committee of all members of the Governing Council:

'to submit proposals for the amendment or replacement of the British Solomon Islands Order 1970.'

The proposals were, in effect, the pre-Independence Constitution for the Protectorate. The principal recommendations were:

- Governing Council to be renamed Legislative Assembly.
- The Assembly to consist of twenty-four elected members and the three *ex officio* members.
- High Commissioner to be renamed Governor in his relations with the Solomon Islands. The Chief Secretary to be renamed Deputy Governor.
- Replacement of the Governing Council meeting in private as the Executive by a Council of Ministers chaired by the Governor. The *ex officio* members to have the status of ministers. There should be a Chief Minister who would recommend Ministers to the Governor for appointment, The Financial Secretary to be replaced by an elected Minister at some time in the future.

- Elected Ministers not to exceed six in number. The Chief Minister to recommend members of the Legislative Assembly to the Governor for appointment as Ministers.

With some minor amendments, the Report was adopted by the Governing Council in July 1973. Prior to the 1973 elections, the number of elected members was increased by Order in Council to twenty-four, in readiness for the new proposals to be introduced.

During the proceedings of the Committee, the possibility of introducing a Bill of Rights into the revised Constitution was discussed. A model was obtained from London. This was at a late stage, when there was pressure to bring deliberations to a conclusion. Solomon Mamaloni, who was to become the first Chief Minister, airily dismissed the model. 'No,' he said, 'We must have a Bill of Rights based on Melanesian principles.' This was not so bizarre as it sounds. Freedom of movement is a desirable aspiration. In the Solomons, however, how did one reconcile this with an embargo on any movement for forty days within a certain area after a chief has died? Did freedom of religion allow any obscure cult the right to enter the Solomons to proselytise the inhabitants? A Bill of Rights could well be deferred, however, until the next Constitutional change. I suggested that Solomon bring a draft of what he had in mind to the next meeting. My suggestion remained unheeded. We concluded our Report.

I was invited to attend an annual academic Seminar, known as the Waigani Seminar, at the University of Papua New Guinea in 1971 and 1973 to deliver papers on Constitutional development. I was accompanied on the first by Fred Osifelo, who had been with me when I was District Commissioner, Malaita. Francis Bugotu, a New Zealand-trained teacher, came with me on the second visit and delivered a hard-hitting paper of his own. It dealt with the problems of Solomon Islanders during the decolonisation process. He went on to be the Solomon Islands Ambassador to the United States and later to be the Secretary-General of the South Pacific Commission. I first met him on a visit to Pawa school, where he and Baddeley Devisi were teachers. A group of dancers, semi-naked and smeared with mud, cavorted before the visitors. He and Baddeley were two of the dancers. I have mentioned Francis's career. Baddeley, as Sir Baddeley Devisi G.C.M.G., ultimately became Governor-General.

The Solomon Islands politicians and senior civil servants were responding well to the challenges which lay before them. Politicians such as David Kausimae, Willie Betu and particularly Solomon

Mamaloni showed remarkable initiative in policy-making. The Liquor Regulation had been amended to remove the embargo on Solomon Islanders drinking. This eased social relationships at public functions and in private homes. Melanesian male orientation still made it difficult for the wives of Solomon Islanders in authority. They might well have been educated to a lower level than their husbands. Their knowledge of English might be limited. At receptions, the men would move from one group of males to another. Their wives would stand shyly together on the fringe of the room. Their faces would light up if they were addressed in pidgin English. Language and unfamiliarity with the strange government rite of receptions were the obstacles. If they were talking in a medium which they knew, and to someone familiar, they often made shrewd observations on the issues of the time.

The work schedule of the Chief Secretary included weekly meetings of the Executive Council and four meetings of the Legislative Council each year. These could last from two to three weeks. Preparation for these meetings and reporting them to London were time-consuming. Consequently, when I acted as High Commissioner, I took the opportunity to visit the Districts. On one of these tours to Malaita, I walked with the District Commissioner, Bob Finnimore, halfway across the island. I wished to see the new cross-island road for myself. Toiling up a muddy slope, after two hours, I realised that the years were catching up with me. Bob, totally unperturbed, patiently awaited me at the top. My wife and I also visited Lord Howe, also known as Ontong Java. Like Sikaiana, Lord Howe is a Polynesian outlier, with its own welcoming ceremony. We had to transfer from the ship to two large canoes each containing a large basket-chair decorated with flowers. We were instructed to remove our shoes. On reaching the shore, we were confronted by a double line of comely damsels. They were wearing grass skirts and anointed with perfumed coconut oil. The line stretched for about a hundred yards towards the village. An older woman then approached me with a small basin containing a brew of oil and turmeric, a bright orange colour. She smeared my face and arms with the concoction. At least that was her intention. My shirt and shorts also received a generous contribution. I was then led to the front of the waiting girls. Each had gripped the wrists of the opposing girl, with both hands at waist level. This formed a square of the four hands, creating a series of steps along which I was to walk. The two girls at the front knelt down and I stepped on to their hands, climbing on to the hands of the next two girls in the line. I had to place my hands on their heads for balance. As their hands were liberally smeared with oil, I frequently slipped, to the merriment of the participants and onlookers. I noticed that the girls whom I had passed left the line to resume position at the back. My wife also ran the gauntlet. It seemed a long way to the village for both of us. After this welcome, formal business was conducted.

Perhaps the most memorable visit was to the Western District, where I had served twenty years before. Nostalgia might have been stronger than the wish to record development. Whatever benefits we brought, it was important that the Melanesian way of life survived in the villages and this was so. There were more schools, clinics and signs of affluence such as sewing machines, outboard motors and chainsaws. Housing was still mainly of thatch; dugout canoes were pulled up on the beach; foodstuffs came mainly from the gardens and the sea. We left the Marovo Lagoon for Choiseul. On landing on one of the beaches, I found that the dignitaries of the village had been lined up to be introduced to me. Among them was one wearing an ill-fitting, creased suit with a row of war-medals. He broke ranks and said, 'Your Excellency, Tommy.' We embraced. It was Sergeant Tamburi who had been my staunch support at Malu'u. He had aged prematurely, as many Melanesians do, and died a few years later. I remember him in his thirties, sinewy, straight as a ramrod, black, proud, bare chested. He wore the police uniform of a khaki lavalava, or skirt, with a scarlet cummerbund and black leather belt. As he turned away after saluting, I used to see the scar where a Japanese bayonet had failed to kill him. We spoke of old times late into the night.

There were two Royal Visits during this period. The first was by Prince Philip in 1971, when I was Acting High Commissioner for the Western Pacific. The second, in 1974, was by the Queen, Prince Philip, Princess Anne, Captain Mark Philips, soon after their marriage, and the Earl Mountbatten.

In 1971 Prince Philip arrived on a Sunday evening, coming ashore in the Royal Barge from H.M.Y. *Britannia*. I greeted him on the wharf, in uniform. I introduced him to my wife and the senior members of Government and their wives. After Prince Philip had inspected a guard of honour, we set off for the Anglican Cathedral Church of St Barnabas. On completion of the service, we escorted H.R.H. back to the wharf to re-embark on the Royal Yacht. That concluded the programme for the first day.

However, on reaching the wharf, Prince Philip said to myself and my

Greeting Prince Philip on his Visit to the Solomon Islands.

wife, 'Come on board for dinner to-night. He then turned to my Royal Air Force Aide de Camp and said, 'You come along too'. We did not have a great deal of time to change and return to the wharf. Some of this was taken up preparing the Aide de Camp for the occasion. His fly buttons had come off his evening uniform trousers. My wife was busy with a needle and thread before donning her evening dress. We had a relaxed dinner for a party of ten. Prince Philip poured the drinks. Dinner was followed by attendance at the Sunday night cinema show. We then returned ashore. This was an unforgettable gesture. Prince Philip was indicating at the start of the Visit that I should not be too uptight about it.

The next morning Prince Philip met District Council representatives from all Districts. This was followed by a display of dancing before visits to the Central Hospital and workshops of the Public Works Department. He then came to Government House for a swim and a private luncheon. A varied programme was arranged for the afternoon. During this he was escorted in turn by the leading politicians. He then returned to Government House for a Reception in his honour. In the evening he had a formal dinner party on H.M.Y. *Britannia*. Before retiring, he had been on duty for fifteen hours.

I boarded the Royal Yacht at seven o'clock the next morning to accompany the Royal party to land at Malu'u in the north of the island of Malaita. It was about five hours' sail. We had to land on the beach in Gemini inflatable boats crewed by 'Yachties' from H.M.Y. *Britannia*. Prince Philip was received by Bob Finnimore, the District Commissioner. He was challenged ceremonially as he stepped ashore by an old man dressed in scanty traditional nether garments. He came close to the Duke of Edinburgh with a short diamond-shaped club with sharp edges. Carried away by the occasion, he brandished this very close to Prince Philip's face. Having faced challenges of this kind before elsewhere in the Pacific, in New Zealand and Papua New Guinea, Prince Philip stood his ground. He was then presented with the club. He passed this to his police officer to carry. The President of the Malaita Council joined us. After visiting a school, we boarded landrovers to visit a Catholic Mission station at Takwa and on to Fouia village. Here an even more aggressive challenge took place, with the same type of club. I remarked to the police officer: 'At least you'll be fighting on equal terms!'.

We then embarked on canoes for a relatively short journey to Sulafou Island. Sir John Gutch and I had broken the news of the Poole murder there many years before. This is one of the oldest of the artificial islands in the Lau Lagoon. It typifies the Melanesian housing and way of life. Some of the islanders had begun to make basket chairs for sale. They used rattan creeper from the bush. They had constructed a very large one. This stood with uneven legs and misshapen arms in the middle of the village. Prince Philip was invited to be seated and was garlanded with strings of native shell money. Above his head was a large caption which read: YOUR ROYAL HIGHNESS'S THRONE. We then boarded two large canoes to take us a relatively long trip up the lagoon to Matakwalao. H.M.Y. *Britannia* awaited us there at anchor. Admiral Trowbridge commanded my canoe. Bob Finnimore accompanied Prince Philip and other members of his party in the second canoe. We had rehearsed the trip before the visit. Normally the water inside the fringing reef of the lagoon is flat calm. On the day of the Visit there were breakers on the reef and a heavy swell in the lagoon. Our canoes were some distance apart. If both canoes went into troughs at the same time, the other one disappeared. I could but hope that the royal canoe would come into view again. We duly arrived at Matakwalao. About forty stocky Malaitans rushed into the surf. They hoisted Prince Philip's canoe with its passengers to shoulder height. It was carried ashore and deposited on the beach. There Bob Finnimore and I took our leave. H.M.Y. *Britannia* left Solomon Islands waters. I believe that this was the highlight of Prince Philip's visit.

The 1974 visit, the first by Her Majesty the Queen, encompassed four days. During this time the Royal party visited all four districts. Entry to the Protectorate took place on Monday 18th February, at Star Harbour in Eastern District. On the following day, Tuesday, 19th February, the programme was arranged for Honiara in Central District. On Wednesday, 20th February, Princess Anne, accompanied by her husband, opened the Solomon Islands Fair in Honiara. They then joined the Queen, Prince Philip and the Earl Mountbatten to visit Auki, in Malaita District, by an Andover of the Royal Flight. H.M.Y. *Britannia* left for Yandina in the Russell Islands. The Andover brought the Royal party to Yandina, where they boarded the Royal Yacht. It then sailed for Gizo, in the Western District, arriving on Thursday, 21st February. The programme ended at 14.30 in the afternoon, The Royal Yacht then sailed for Papua New Guinea.

My involvement in the Visit was much less than on the previous occasion. Sir Donald Luddington had by then replaced Sir Michael Gass as High Commissioner. The latter had been on leave at the time of Prince Philip's Visit in 1971. Although I chaired the Central Planning Committee for the 1974 Visit by the Queen and Prince Philip, the detailed arrangements were in the hands of the Deputy Chief Secretary, Trevor Clark. He has a keen eye for detail and is a good organiser. I was closely involved with the rehearsals. I attended the events when the Visit took place in Honiara and Gizo.

My personal memories of the Visit began with the rehearsal for the landing at Star Harbour. A special wharf had to be constructed to accord with the tides. It had to be at the right height when the Royal Barge came alongside. The wharf had been constructed with thick planks, with a gap of about an inch between them. Francis Talasasa was the Solomon Islander District Commissioner. His wife took the part of the Queen for the rehearsal. When she stepped on to the wharf, we were alarmed to see the point of a spear appearing through one of the cracks near her heels.' What on earth is this?' I said to Francis. 'Well, Sir, this is where the Queen first steps on to Solomon Islands soil. I would like to mark the spot so that we can put a plaque there afterwards'. We prevented Royal security officials from having heart attacks by forbidding this. It also drew attention to the unsuitability of the wharf, in its current condition, for high-heeled shoes.

One of the ceremonies in Honiara was the planting of a *kauri* tree by the Queen at Vatakolaa village on the outskirts of Honiara. I was standing next to one of the ladies in the entourage. She was being very fidgety during the ceremony. When I looked down I discovered that she was standing in a red ants' nest. I drew her to one side. Then, unobtrusively, I removed each shoe from behind, one by one. I shook the ants out and restored her decorum.

My wife and I attended the dinner on board H.M.Y. *Britannia* on Tuesday, 19th February. This was preceded by drinks and followed by a Reception for which the dinner guests remained. Gifts presented to the Duke of Edinburgh on previous visits were on display. The remarkable efficiency of the Royal Yacht crew was demonstrated by their management of two consecutive functions. One boards the Royal Yacht by entering a central reception area. To port is the lounge and to starboard, of equal size, is the dining-room. We had drinks in the lounge and then crossed to the dining-room. The tables were decorated with ornate table-pieces. Cutlery, china and glassware were meticulously placed. After dinner we repaired for coffee to the lounge, which had been largely cleared of furniture. When the time came for the reception, the Royal party withdrew and formed a line facing the lounge. At the end of the line an aide ushered the guests into the lounge. When half the guests had entered, the Royal reception line quietly moved over to stand facing in the opposite direction. By this time the staff had totally cleared the dining-room, into which the remaining guests were ushered. When all guests were assembled, there was freedom of movement throughout both of the rooms.

I was also invited to lunch on H.M.Y. *Britannia* at Gizo and had the honour to be seated on the Queen's left. Royal protocol decrees that one does not address the Sovereign until she has spoken to her subject. I was given my signal by the words, 'Would you like the salt, Mr Russell?' I soon discovered that the Queen's knowledge of the islands was far deeper than could have been acquired from last-minute briefing. After lunch, those of us who had been associated with the planning for the visit were invited individually to take leave of the Queen and Prince Philip. We returned ashore before the Royal Yacht sailed. Again there was a sense of silence now that the busy four-day programme had come to an end. Fourteen days later I was to leave the Solomons after twenty-six years of service. February, 1974 was a month of departures.

We occupied a new Government House when I acted as High Commissioner. Michael Gass was the first occupant. He was a keen gardener and had designed the grounds personally. There was a swimming pool, with the scarlet blooms of a New Guinea creeper hanging from a pergola. Trees were hosts to great bunches of white orchids. Colourful Wanda orchids grew in beds to decorate the house. This had been designed in timber by New Zealand architects to reflect one of the country's main industries. There was a large dining-room with a table and chairs for twenty-four. It opened on to a spacious verandah. This had to be large enough to accommodate the guests at a reception. Functions would normally be held on the lawn adjacent. But a tropical downpour could quickly send the guests scurrying indoors. The roof of the house had to have special bolts to be proof against hurricanes. Earthquakes were another problem. On one occasion there was a rumbling like an approaching tube train. The direction of the earthquake was unmistakable. The building creaked in protest but remained erect. Each of the bedrooms on the first floor had a verandah overlooking the lawns and the sea.

Breakfast was served individually on the verandahs. The minah birds put on their morning display. The Barringtonia tree has a large leaf which it drops. The leaves cover the ground each morning. The minah bird would approach a leaf. It would lift one edge three inches off the ground. If there was a slug hiding from the sun, breakfast for the minah bird; if not, it dropped the leaf and went on to the next one.

The High Commissioner's office was in a wing of Government House. The Solomon Islands were perhaps large enough to justify this. Practice in larger Colonies, Fiji, Ghana, and Hong Kong may have influenced the decision. This led to 'despatch-box' government. The High Commissioner was isolated from the Secretariat, his senior officers and politicians. 'Government House Meetings' were not regarded as routine. Papers for the High Commissioner's attention were carried to Government House in red despatch boxes. The High Commissioner wrote in red ink. The style of the commander of an aircraft-carrier inevitably has to be different from that of a frigate. The question was: What was the size of the ship? Was it appropriate for a future Chief

Minister to enter the High Commissioner's office like a schoolboy summoned to the Headmaster's study?

At the level below, that of Chief Secretary, Financial Secretary, Attorney General, we had inevitably to be more approachable by politicians, Permanent Secretaries and Heads of Department. Yet our personal assistants knew the pressures and were adept at gauging whether immediate access was necessary. Tilda Vitorovic, when I was Financial Secretary, and Pat Twomey, when I was Chief Secretary, were shrewd judges in deciding when access should be postponed. Relations between the three officials holding the posts above had to be close. The Attorney General, who was also the Director of Public Prosecutions, had a special role. Very often, because of pressure of work, he could also be involved in legal drafting. He could be called upon to advise on constitutional matters. As the opposition in the Legislative Council had no legal representative, he might be expected to give informal advice to them. He was under no strict obligation to do so. Renn Davies, our Attorney General, became a judge in the New Hebrides in 1973. He was replaced by his able Solicitor General, Jerry Nazareth, who, in turn, became a judge in Hong Kong. Senior law officers played a significant personal, as well as professional, part in the years leading to Independence.

At the end of 1973, Donald Luddington, who was now High Commissioner, asked me for my response to a telegram received from London. This was to ask whether I should allow my name to go forward for consideration as Governor of the Cayman Islands. After discussing this with my wife, I agreed. Time went by. I had postponed my leave until conclusion of a visit of the Queen and other members of the Royal family in February, 1974. In January I was told that I had been recommended for the post but nothing could be said publicly until the appointment had been approved by the Queen. It had not been approved fourteen days before I was due to proceed on leave. This might be my final departure from the Solomons, in which I had served for many years. Eventually I obtained agreement to say that I would be leaving the Solomons finally. I was not allowed, however, to say where I was likely to go. A number of farewell functions was hastily arranged. One of the most memorable was that given by the Solomon Island Speaker and the members of the Legislative Assembly. Solomon Mamaloni, who was soon to be Chief Minister, spoke. He was visibly moved by the occasion and said: 'We will try to make the Solomons the place you have tried to create.' He was not someone to have made the remark simply as a courtesy.

An announcement was eventually made before departure. I handed over to the capable hands of Trevor Clark.

'Were you sorry to leave?' The answer to that question is that it was like tearing my right arm off at the shoulder. But it was time to move on. I took with me a breadth of experience for my new job which I could have obtained nowhere else. I had served under two Resident Commissioners and seven High Commissioners. I had acted in the equivalent of a Governor's post. I had witnessed the superb performance of many officers in many Departments. I would aim for similar standards. I would not be disappointed.

CHAPTER FOURTEEN

Governor of the Cayman Islands

The first term of three years

THE CAYMAN ISLANDS are a relatively new country. Comprising three islands, Grand Cayman, Cayman Brac and Little Cayman, they were uninhabited until 1658. The total land area is a hundred square miles. Early inhabitants included buccaneers, shipwrecked sailors and deserters from the English army in Jamaica. Probably most of these were of European stock. With the emancipation of slaves in 1835, the population developed into the multi-racial society which it is today. It is English-speaking, self-confident and vibrant. Until 1962, when the federation of the West Indies broke up, the Cayman Islands were a Dependency of Jamaica. Since 1832, however, they had had a legislative body. This was composed of the magistrates and vestrymen, elected by adult male suffrage. The islanders petitioned the United Kingdom to become a Colony of Britain in 1962. They considered this preferable to becoming a Dependency of Jamaica. They already had a history of largely handling their own affairs. Moreover, they were accustomed to living within their means. They had never had outside help to balance their modest budget. Nor had there ever been direct taxation.

The 1962 Constitution established an Executive Council to advise an Administrator, appointed by London, and a Legislative Assembly.

Until the Second World War, the islands were isolated. They had few exports. Caymanians had a proud reputation for seamanship. They plied this craft on the world's oceans. At one time there were as many as three thousand Caymanians employed by foreign shipping companies. The remittances which they sent home boosted the modest national income. The terrain was unsuitable for commercial arable farming. Peasant farming, however, provided basic foodstuffs. Fishing, and especially turtling, also reduced the necessity for a cash income. Sailing on small vessels in search of turtles on long sea voyages had two effects. It produced a very hardy breed of men. It also engendered a fierce devotion to their homeland.

With the majority of the working male population at sea, Caymanian women took over many of the responsibilities which were formerly a male preserve. They did not wholly surrender this role when the men returned to work in the developing economy. Hence the introduction of women into politics, the Civil Service, the private sector and the Churches has never been a problem in the islands.

After the Second World War international airfields were developed on Grand Cayman and Cayman Brac. The one on Cayman Brac, 'the Brac', was largely built voluntarily by the 'Brackers' as the warm people of that island are called. As civil aviation developed, the pre-war isolation died. The Cayman Islands lie five hundred miles south of Miami in Florida. Cuba lies a hundred miles to the north; Jamaica a hundred miles to the south-east. The nearest part of South America, Nicaragua, is two hundred miles to the south-west. The islands had now come into the modern world. Tourism began to develop.

In the mid-1960's it became apparent both to the government and the private sector that the absence of direct taxation might offer advantages in developing an offshore financial industry. The Caymanian Financial Secretary at the time, Sir Vassel Johnson Kt. CBE, spearheaded this initiative, stipulating that it must be under Government control. Credit is also given locally to Caymanian attorneys, including Arthur Hunter, Bill Walker, Warren Connolly and Charles Adams. Among the accountants Michael Austin played a prominent role. Tourism and offshore finance both prospered, with ancillary industries of real estate operations and construction following in their wake. The community benefited substantially from the job opportunities created and the expertise which these industries attracted.

The total population in 1974 was about 20,000. This was much smaller than that of my first district in the Solomons. Yet it had a larger budget than that of the Solomons. More importantly, it did not have the administrative restraint of budgetary control from Whitehall.

I received about ten days briefing before leaving England. It did not do much to prepare me for the job in hand. I had lunch with representatives of the West India Committee. I met representatives from Cable and Wireless and Sir Robert McAlpine. These all had connections with the Colony. I looked at various files. By far the most relevant discussions were with the Bank of England, which had a representative on the Cayman Islands Currency Board. This briefing was knowledgeable and up-to-date. My wife and I also arranged to meet my predecessor, Roy Crook, and his wife for dinner. This was a private arrangement as the convention at the time was that incoming and outgoing Governors had no contact. This convention has now been abandoned.

I was also granted an audience with the Queen. This privilege is customary for Governors before assuming appointment. Although it is a routine formal occasion, the Queen quickly exhibited both interest in, and knowledge of, the Colony. She was to visit it, together with Prince Philip, a few years after I had returned to England.

My wife and I flew out to the Cayman Islands via Jamaica, where we spent the night. I was to be sworn in shortly after arrival. This required garbing myself in full Colonial white uniform with plumed helmet, sword and medals. My sword, in a plastic cover, would not fit into my suitcases. I was not allowed to take it in the cabin. It was classed as a dangerous weapon. It was thus consigned to the baggage compartment of the plane, nestling in a long cardboard tube containing my wife's umbrellas and a plastic Christmas tree. While we disembarked at Kingston, Jamaica, it was to carry on to Mexico. The British High Commission staff were very concerned by my predicament. As I was about to step on to the plane taking us to Grand Cayman, I was handed a Naval sword, of much larger dimensions than mine. It seemed to be festooned by chains. I was reminded of Cicero's quip when a small senator, Lentulus, entered the Roman Senate wearing a large sword. 'Here is a sword, wearing Lentulus!' I declined. I was consequently sworn in without a sword. I do not believe anyone noticed.

On arrival I was greeted by Desmond Watler, the Caymanian Chief Secretary. After inspecting a Guard of Honour of the Cayman Islands Police, I was introduced to Members of the Executive Council, Legislative Assembly, the Judge, and their wives. In the airport lounge were the Clerks to the Legislative Assembly and Executive Council, and Heads of Department. I recognised Andrew Greiff, the Commissioner of Police, as an old Pacific hand. As Chief of Police in Tonga, he had attended a Pacific Police Conference in Honiara before subsequently being posted to Belize.

Before the swearing-in ceremony, there was a brief interlude at Government House. This had been constructed following the separation of the Cayman Islands from Jamaica. It was a modern one-storied building based on the design of a Provincial Commissioner's house in one of the South African High Commission Territories. At that time it did not have air-conditioning. It was relatively small, with three bedrooms. It was, however, sited in its own grounds on the edge of Seven Mile Beach. I arrived not long after the Governor had been shot in the grounds of Government House in Bermuda. An edict had gone out that the security of Government Houses should be improved.

In Governor's uniform.

Consequently a six-foot wall had been build round the landward boundaries of Government House grounds. There was an entry gate and guard-house. I learnt subsequently that a wrought-iron fence of the same height was to be erected between the front of the house and the sea. As the wall itself was no more than a token deterrent, I substituted for the wrought-iron fence large plant pots joined with ropes. This was largely respected by tourists as defining the bounds of the beach area. A pleasing feature of Caymanian land law was that the public had free access along any beach or shoreline. Individual property-owners on the coast could neither fence off, nor claim as private property, the beach frontage of their properties.

I had taken considerable care in crafting my speech for the swearing in ceremony. This would be held in the George Town Town Hall. The first impressions Caymanians would form were very important. I identified the five strands in the community with which I should have to co-operate and which I would have to persuade to work together. These were the people, their elected representatives, the Civil Service, the private sector and the Churches. I also pledged that whatever policies I endorsed, I should keep constantly before me the need to preserve the Caymanian way of life. As I was to be head of the Civil Service, I undertook to keep their interests at heart. The reply was given by the senior member of the Executive Council, Berkeley Bush. His welcome nevertheless suggested that I would not find my new assignment a bed of roses.

We then adjourned to Government House for a reception. The Chief Secretary, who had been acting as Governor after Roy Crook's departure, was the host. There were several hundred guests. I was immediately impressed by the calibre of the businessmen, the politicians, senior civil servants and Heads of Department. The atmosphere was cordial. Even on this first social occasion, however, I was aware of certain tensions between the members of government and the opposition. These had to be sensed. Caymanian politicians do not wear their animosities on their sleeves outside the parliamentary building.

I was driven to the office the next morning. The old government office building, which had also housed the former Commissioner, had burnt down in 1972. Since then, most of the government administration had been conducted from rented accommodation in the West Winds Building near George Town port. My office was modest but functional. To my surprise, however, I found that the four elected members of Executive Council, of Ministerial status, shared one office, sitting around a large table. Their principal secretaries, on the other hand, had individual

Delivering the address at the swearing in ceremony at George Town Town Hall.

offices. This situation was to be corrected in the new office building, for which the contract was soon to be placed.

Some three weeks after my arrival, one of the many Banks, Interbank, shut its doors. The Managing Director abruptly left the country. The Bank had run into severe cash flow problems. Criminal activity was suspected. I had been briefed by the Bank of England that they had worries over the operations. The suddenness of the collapse nevertheless took the community by surprise. It had opened a mortgage subsidiary only a few months earlier. This was publicised as a means of support for Caymanian entrepreneurs and home-owners. There were also substantial Caymanian deposits in the main bank. Police investigations revealed that charges should be brought against certain officers of the Bank. One of these had to be extradited from Monaco. Arriving under escort by air in

Jamaica, he was flown by charter flight to Grand Cayman. Security was tight. The populace expressed surprise that it had been possible to place him behind bars in George Town without prior rumours circulating. In a small island, gossip was rife. Gossip was known locally as 'on the marl road'. Usually there was fire behind the smoke.

Before my arrival I had agreed a programme with the Chief Secretary, and this had been arranged. After the first meeting of the Executive Council, I held an informal meeting with the members of the Legislative Assembly. I then made visits to each of the constituencies in the company of the elected members for the area. The first of these visits was to the two sister islands, Cayman Brac and Little Cayman. I wished to establish the understanding that I would give them the same degree of attention as Grand Cayman. This was not difficult for me, as I quickly developed a special affection for both islands. The 'Brackers' were industrious. They had a justifiable reputation for looking after their own interests. They had raised the funds locally to build a hospital and airfield. They had organised their own electricity supply. The amenities, for a population of eleven hundred, compared favourably with those in some of the islands in the Outer Hebrides in Scotland. I stayed at the only hotel at that time, the Buccaneer's Inn. I was accompanied on the trip by a police orderly. The bedrooms were sited on an open verandah. As I was about to enter one, my orderly stopped me and said: 'Not yet, Sir.' He then entered and looked in the bathroom, the wardrobe, and under the bed. When he was satisfied that no assassins were lurking about, he said 'It's all right now, Sir'. He left me to unpack. When I left the room, I realised that there was no lock on the door. After touring the island, I held a well-attended public meeting which was followed by refreshments. The atmosphere at such functions was far less artificial than that at receptions for which invitations had been issued. The degree of frankness was encouraging. Problems would be brought into the open and not allowed to fester.

On returning to Grand Cayman, I continued similar programmes in the other constituencies. I had meetings with the executive committees of most of the associations in the community. These included the Chamber of Commerce, the Red Cross, organisations such as the Lions and Rotary, Scouts, Boys' and Girls' Brigade. I also arranged to meet professional associations for banking, accounting, real estate and construction. An important body was the Ministers' Association, as religion was deeply embedded in the Caymanian Community. Presbyterianism was the main religion on Grand Cayman. Baptists formed the principal denomination on Cayman Brac. I also visited all offices in the Secretariat and all

Government Departments. I arranged receptions at Government House each week for the Civil Servants of the Departments which I had visited. This proved popular with their wives. Families were scattered island-wide. Opportunities to get to know each other were then infrequent.

During this programme I was taking stock. I had to arrange my own priorities. It was twelve years since the Colony had been established on separation from Jamaica. Some of the procedures of Government had remained relatively unchanged. There was a backlog of legislation urgently required. There was no Government Gazette, which is the authority for publication of laws as they are made. Publication was made by pinning a copy of the laws with a drawing-pin to a notice board outside Post Offices. Archaic practices included reading the Riot Act at formal openings of the Grand Court. The reason for this was that it had been the practice in Jamaica. I arranged for a Gazette Law to be debated and enacted four months after arrival. I established priorities, after discussion with the Executive Council, for a legislative drafting programme. This was announced in my first Throne Speech opening the Legislative Assembly.

I gave personal attention to revising main and subsidiary legislation governing the Public Service Commission. I discussed improvements in the administration of the Civil Service with the Chief Secretary and Principal Secretary (Personnel). I decided to introduce a revised Guide to the Operations of the Executive Council and a Register of Interests for all members of the Executive Council at the next elections in 1976. I started work on these.

The 1972 Constitution established cabinet-type government with a unicameral Legislative Assembly of fifteen members, twelve elected and three *ex-officio*. The *ex-officio* members were the Chief Secretary, the Financial Secretary and the Attorney General. Until the Assembly determined to elect a Speaker, the Governor presided over the Assembly. Immediately following an election, the twelve elected members selected four of their number to be appointed Members of Executive Council. The Governor then allocated subjects – Education, for example, or Departments, such as Public Works – to individual members as their responsibility. National policy and decisions to place laws before the Legislative Assembly were a responsibility of the Executive Council. I was normally obliged to accept the advice of the Executive Council on all subjects for which Members were responsible.

One of the elected members of the Executive Council, Trevor Foster, who was responsible for the Sister Islands, lived on Cayman Brac.

Consequently only the three Grand Cayman elected members of Executive Council were available to take full responsibility for portfolios. Take responsibility they did. They led from the front.

Warren Connolly, an Attorney at law, was responsible for the portfolio dealing with Natural Resources, Land and Tourism He was actively promoting and laying the foundations for the tourist industry. There were then about fifty thousand visitors by air. With the professional assistance of Dr Giglioli, an entymologist who had a global reputation, he fought a robust campaign for funds to control mosquitoes. These had long been a virulent pest in the islands. Their reduction to negligible limits was important for the comfort of the Caymanian population as well as for the development of tourism.

Warren had also to promote the adoption of a Physical Development Plan and the completion of a Cadastral Survey. This entailed survey of the boundaries of all parcels of land in the territory. Boundaries were determined by judicial process if these were contested. All parcels and their ownership were registered after the survey. Absolute freehold title was then granted to the owners of individual parcels of land.

The only riots in Caymanian history had taken place a few years before against the legislation for these projects. There was still some public resentment and suspicion. Warren Connolly was an effective performer in the Legislative Assembly. He had made a study of the evolution of parliamentary democracy in the Cayman Islands. The Liquor Licensing Law and the Tourism Law were two pieces of legislation which he steered through the Assembly. His wife Islay was Chief Education Officer. She had made a similar study of the development of education in the islands.

Berkley Bush was the Member responsible for Communications and Works. He was an ex-seaman who was the proprietor of a cinema, now demolished. The upgrading of the Owen Roberts International Airport had been completed. He was turning his attention to the airfields on Cayman Brac and Little Cayman. Following his introduction of the Roads Law, he had set in train the tar-sealing of the main roads on Grand Cayman. He had organised the purchase of the heavy equipment which enabled the Public Works Department to do this. He gave priority of attention, however, to planning and commissioning the work of installing a modern port in George Town. This was completed after the 1976 elections, in which Berkley Bush lost his seat. He was succeeded in his portfolio by Captain Charles Kirkconnell. It is a mark of how politics are conducted in the Colony that at the opening of the port, Berkley Bush was given pride of place. Although he had lost his place in the hierarchy, the Port had been his brainchild. I know how much he appreciated this.

The holder of the third working portfolio was Benson Ebanks, who had been Manager of Barclays Bank and is still a Director of the Cayman National Bank. He also had a hardware business in West Bay. He was in charge of Education, Public Health and Welfare. The Health Services Law and the Health Practitioners Law, enacted in 1974, owed much to his personal input and drive. He also left behind him a renovated Central Hospital, an extended and improved High School and Primary School buildings. He introduced GCSE and CSE examinations. He was also responsible for inaugurating the National Council of Social Services.

My *ex-officio* members were Desmond Watler, the Chief Secretary, Vassel Johnson, the Financial Secretary and Gerald Waddington, the Attorney General. The first two of these were Caymanian. Gerald Waddington was a Jamaican. He and Desmond Watler were to retire two years after I assumed duty. Vassel Johnson, however, was to remain as Financial Secretary for all of the time I served in the Cayman Islands. He pioneered the financial services industry and cannily husbanded the country's economy through good days and bad. He astutely built up reserves to enable the Government to undertake labour-intensive projects when unemployment threatened. His staff appreciated his qualities. They were far fewer in number than in the Treasury in the Solomons. Although in 1974 they had no access to computers, they could produce revenue and expenditure figures for the past month within ten days of the month's end. Vassel was knighted for his outstanding service when the Queen visited the Cayman Islands in 1983.

With the assistance of the British Development Division in Barbados, he was also responsible for drawing up the Colony's first Five-Year Development Plan. Upgrading of the Owen Roberts Airport and improving landing facilities at the George Town Port were top priorities. The Plan also included a substantial building programme. This embraced, among other projects, the Legislative Assembly and Grand Court Buildings, the Comprehensive School, installation of water and sewerage systems and improvements to the Central Hospital. The second phase of the Plan provided for British Aid funds to be supplemented by local bank loans. This phase was in the planning stage when I arrived. It included the Government Administration Building and the tar-sealing of the road system. The George Town port project was to be financed for the most part by a loan from the Caribbean Development Bank. The financing for these major projects was put in place with commendable speed.

The Attorney General, approved by the Foreign and Commonwealth Office to replace Gerald Waddington, was David Barwick CBE, QC. He was an ex-Pacific colleague and a personal friend. A New Zealand solicitor, he came to the Solomon Islands as Solicitor General in 1953. His wife Margaret was my son's first school teacher in Honiara. His three children and my son Malcolm knew each other well. In 1956 he transferred to the Gilbert and Ellice Islands as a judge. Before coming to the Cayman Islands in 1976, he had been legal adviser to the Independent Government of Malawi for nine years. He was to be appointed Governor of the British Virgin Islands in the year in which I left the Cayman Islands in 1982. His wife, a keen artist, also specialised in tropical gardening. While in the British Virgin Islands, she designed the Botanic Gardens there. She pursued her painting and tropical gardening after they retired to the Cayman Islands in 1988. My friendship with them continued, both in the Cayman Islands and in the Lot, in France, where we both had houses. Sadly, not long after their permanent move to France last year, David died. He had wide interests, with a sharp, legally-trained mind. A family man, he was proud of his son, Simon, his two daughters and grandchildren. Simon had founded a business in graphic design in the Cayman Islands. Jan, his elder daughter, is an accomplished artist, living with her husband in France. His younger daughter Miranda has *cordon bleu* qualifications. She is married and lives in Atlanta.

A Governor leans heavily upon his official members of the Executive Council. I was peculiarly fortunate. Having a trusted friend with an impeccable legal pedigree helped me enormously with my assignment.

I was also fortunate in having an efficient Clerk of the Executive Council, Jenny Manderson MBE, JP, who subsequently served as Permanent Secretary (Personnel) and as District Commissioner of the Sister Islands. Mrs Sybil McLaughlin MBE, JP was the able Clerk to the Legislative Assembly. Some time after I left, she was appointed as Speaker. I accompanied her on several occasions to Commonwealth Parliamentary Association Regional Conferences for Speakers and Clerks of Parliaments in the Caribbean. This was always a pleasant and informative interlude, as the Conferences were held in different Caribbean countries. I wondered at first how the eminent Speakers of Independent countries such as Jamaica and Trinidad and Tobago would accept me, a Colonial relic of the past. They were amused. As one of them put it, I had to suffer the same problems of the job.

Governors' Conferences were also held annually. These were usually in Barbados, which was the headquarters of the British Development

Division. The Cayman Islands were not heavily involved in a British aid programme. For such aid as we received came by the way of loans rather than grants. In 1976 we were advised that loans too would be phased out in a few years' time. Normally, if I had any argument with London, it would be on behalf of the Cayman Islands. On this occasion I argued strongly that it was in British interests to keep a small quantum of aid coming into the country as part of an agreed aid programme. This would enable the United Kingdom to send advisers who could have some impact on policy. If aid was discontinued, as suggested, Caymanian politicians would occupy the high ground. Members of Executive Council had constitutional responsibility for spending their own money. If they wanted advice they would ask for it. This argument, however, carried no weight against plans to economise in British aid funds. British aid towards Development Plans ceased shortly afterwards.

A general election was held in November 1976. There were no political parties. There were, however, two groups of candidates, each with a slate of common aims. Unlike the voters in the Solomons, Caymanians knew exactly what to do. Indeed, they were so familiar with electoral practice that petitions were not uncommon. There were six electoral districts. In four of these there were multiple votes. George Town had three seats. The voter placed three X's on the voting slip against three of the names. Canvassing began about two months before the elections. It increased in intensity, so that political meetings could be taking place in several constituencies on the same night. Candidates from the same group would all make speeches. They would proceed from one meeting to another. So did a large number of the crowd. I arranged to have a short synopsis of each political meeting. I could thus determine from speeches and questions what were the issues of most importance to the electorate. As the campaign wore on, my assessment that change was in the air seemed to be confirmed. In the event, all four members of the Executive Council lost their seats. The opposition in the previous Assembly, led by Jim and Haig Bodden of Bodden Town, took eleven seats out of the twelve. Jim and Haig Bodden were then elected to Executive Council with Truman Bodden and Charles Kirkconnell. The former was a well known lawyer from George Town and Charles Kirkconnell was one of the leading business-men in the community. Their style was less conservative and more mercurial than that of their predecessors. They were, however, to achieve much in their four years of office.

My first experience of mercurial behaviour was on the issue of Caymanian passports. Jim Bodden suggested to Dennis Foster, the Chief

Secretary, that we could derive substantial revenue by vastly increasing passport fees. The Passport Law could be changed to ease the qualifications for obtaining a Caymanian passport. Residents of Hong Kong would be willing to pay as insurance against the changes expected in the Colony. I advised Dennis Foster to reject the proposal out of hand. Shortly afterwards, Jim and Haig Bodden asked to see me on a matter of great importance and urgency. When Jim Bodden said why he had come, I said that Caymanian passports were not for sale. After banging the table and loudly reiterating his arguments, he passed the ball to Haig Bodden, his colleague. There was an equally loud and voluble presentation from Haig. I simply said that they were wasting their time. I awaited the next verbal assault. Suddenly a broad grin broke over Jim Bodden's face. 'Well, you know, we had to try it, Sir!' They both left the office in surprisingly good humour.

The expression in Solomon Islands Pidgin English for such an attempt was 'Me tryim no more' – 'I was only trying!'.

One Caymanian, Sheppie Brandon, was renowned for this technique. He was well educated, had been abroad for long periods, and could talk persuasively. He had lived in England, Jamaica and the United States. He impressed one of the Heads of Department in the Foreign and Commonwealth Office with his proposals for development. At the end of the discussion he professed to have forgotten his wallet and borrowed ten pounds. Recovery engendered some correspondence with London.

He had some problem with the Cayman Islands Police. Together with another Caymanian he stole a small boat. They put to sea. A message was sent to the authorities of surrounding counties. Two Caymanians had stolen a boat. Their destination was unknown. On their arrival in Mexico, they were apprehended and sent to prison. I subsequently received several telephone calls from Mexico to Government House asking whether I would accept the charges for a telephone call. After being caught out once, I declined the subsequent calls. Towards the end of their sentence, they were transferred to an open prison. Inexplicably, within days of their sentence ending, they escaped and walked through Mexico to Guatemala and through Guatemala to Belize. They were apprehended on the border of Belize by a British Army patrol. Sheppie Brandon then pulled a notebook out of his pocket. He said that he was a reporter from one of the English tabloid newspapers. He was writing an article on the hardships endured by British Army personnel in Belize. He must have been convincing. He was then said to have talked the patrol into giving them Army boots to continue their long march to freedom.

Shortly afterwards, I received a telegram from a junior officer in one of the British Consulates in South America. It asked for agreement to issue emergency one-way passports to two Caymanians. They had applied for travel documents and passages back to the Cayman Islands. They had also asked that a message be transmitted to the Governor of the Cayman Islands. This said that they would only return if granted an amnesty for any minor misdemeanours committed before leaving. They would have no funds and would like several thousand dollars to be made available for them on return. Sheppie also suggested that some employment would not come amiss. The posts of Commissioner of Police or Chief Immigration Officer were suggested. If it were inconvenient to meet such requests, it was possible that some mercenaries might arrive subsequently in the Cayman Islands. There were several oil depots near the capital which could be attractive targets for them. The message then went on to say: 'What answer should be given to them?' Apart from agreeing to their repatriation and issue of one-way passports without amnesty, my reply was suitably laconic. When they returned, Sheppie must have talked the owner of the boat into withdrawing the charge of stealing it. I do not recall his being imprisoned on return.

Official entertainment and the social round were very much part of the job. Financial services and tourism were expanding, bringing a stream of high-profile visitors to the islands. There were visits from London. One of these was Patrick Duff, the Head of the West Indian and General Department which dealt with the affairs of the Dependencies in the West Indies. We had a high mutual respect for each other. I was left, in large measure, to run my own ship, provided that I kept him fully and regularly informed. In the early months there were about three receptions a month at Government House for between one and two hundred guests and formal dinners for up to eighteen at ten-day intervals. Whenever possible, I insisted upon a fifty per cent Caymanian presence. The Cayman Islands were their country. Caymanians paid for Government House. They paid the Governor's salary. They provided the funds for entertainment and to maintain the building. Sometimes the function was for a special occasion. It might be a seminar for doctors interested in the medical repercussions of diving accidents. A large group of tour operators might be visiting to see what the islands had to offer. In such cases the policy had to be adjusted. In addition, nearly every night in the week there were private receptions to which the Governor and his wife were invited. Among invitations received were those to Caymanian weddings, funerals, and christenings. These presented some difficulty as it would have been impossible to attend all of these occasions. I hoped that I steered a middle course and did not cause offence when invitations were declined.

During the year, there were several large drinks parties which were preferably held in the garden. The Queen's Birthday party and those held for Civil Servants and their families at Christmas and on New Year's Day were standard each year. A few were held in the early evening. For those my wife had two worries. First, she hoped it would not rain. There was insufficient room in the building for all the guests; transferring bars and catering arrangements from the garden to the house was a nightmare for the staff. Secondly, she hoped the mosquito sprayers kept away. When there was a reception for the tourist fraternity held in the garden, Dr Giglioli was anxious to prohibit any insect guests from attending. This was achieved either by fogging or aerial spray. A truck would appear with what looked like a horizontal V1 flying bomb on the back. This belched a mixture of kerosene vapour and insecticide. If the timing was wrong, it descended on the glassware and any food which had been laid out for the party. The aerial spray plane flew at an astonishingly low altitude, skimming rooftops and electricity power lines. It drenched the ground below its flight-path with a mixture similar to that distributed by the fogger. On reception nights, take-off seemed to be timed for the beginning of the reception and the guests to be the target. (The reader should allow for the exaggerations of retrospection.) The pilots who helped to make the anti-mosquito campaign so successful had to be men of extreme dedication. They took their life in their hands each night. Francois Lesieur, the senior pilot, had to make a forced lading near Lime Tree Bay, opposite Government House, on one occasion. He walked away unscathed. He was flying the second Thrush aircraft the following evening.

There was also reciprocal entertainment with visiting warships. We had calls at irregular intervals from British, French and American naval ships, including the American Coastguard. These were popular. Sporting and social functions were arranged in advance. Many local residents invited groups of sailors to their homes. George Town could offer rugby, soccer, tennis, squash, golf, netball, basketball and shooting. Swimming and barbecues on the beach, called 'banyans' by the Navy, were popular. One of these went disastrously wrong. My wife and I were among local guests to be invited aboard the Royal Navy aircraft-carrier H.M.S. *Hermes* for lunch. In the middle of lunch a klaxon sounded the alarm. A helicopter took off. It returned with an unconscious sailor who was immediately sent below to the ship's infirmary. He subsequently recovered – a very lucky young man. Along with others, he had been swimming off Seven Mile Beach. He approached a yacht at anchor. The owner said: 'Hi, son. Come aboard for a drink.' The sailor required no second invitation. After several drinks, he dived off to return ashore. Seconds later, one of the ship's officers who had been snorkelling shouted to a colleague: 'That looks like a body down there.' They brought up the unconscious sailor. Efforts to resuscitate him on the beach failed. The helicopter was called for. He returned to the world by sitting up in bed aboard the *Hermes* and asking for something to eat.

The subject of ships leads to two developments of the economy appropriate for a country with a long marine heritage. The first of these was the expansion of the British Shipping Registry. The Cayman Registry had been in the doldrums as a spare activity for the Collector of Customs. It was transferred to the Department of the Registrar-General, R.C. (Bobbie) Bodden and has since expanded under new legislation as part of the Red Ensign group of British Registries. The second development was the promotion of an oil transfer operation in the waters between Cayman Brac and Little Cayman. The depth of water in southern United States ports is insufficient to allow supertankers alongside. Until an offshore pipeline and berthing facilities had been built in Louisiana, oil had to be transhipped from large vessels into smaller ones. The shallower draught of these vessels allowed them to come alongside. But under maritime conventions the documentation for the transferred oil could not be issued at sea. As Cayman Brac could issue manifests if transfers took place in Cayman Island waters, its proximity to the Gulf ports of America offered advantages. In addition there were sufficient qualified officers and seamen in the Lesser Islands to conduct the transhipment operations. Contracts were signed and transhipments began to take place. Two smaller tankers came alongside massive supertankers of four hundred thousand tons burden and were tied up. The three ships then drifted while the oil was being transferred. The size of the supertankers was impressive. They were fully automated and carried small crews. Because of their bulk, they lay motionless while the small tender coming alongside bobbed and rolled in the swell. Going on board for lunch, I had to leap on to a rope ladder descending from the top deck. The ladder was on wheels. It rolled forty feet up the side. I then manoeuvered myself on to the deck, conscious of the fact that I should have to return by the same route after pre-luncheon drinks. I was, however, in good company with the members of the Legislative Assembly. These included the intrepid Miss

Annie Huldah Bodden, a lady of ample girth. She must have reached the top deck by the power of prayer.

Before the elections, the approval of the Physical Development Plan and the completion of the Cadastral Survey provided copious supplies of political ammunition. The Lesser Islands regarded planning as an impediment to development. Not far away, in Texas in the United States, a factory, a church and a public house could be built next to each other at the whim of the developers. I attended a spirited meeting on Cayman Brac during a gubernatorial visit with my wife and son. There was a mild demonstration at the airfield as we left.

The Cadastral Survey had been completed on Grand Cayman in the West Bay, George Town and part of the Bodden Town areas of the island. There was a large swamp known as the Duck Pond Swamp opening to the ocean. Under local custom, a landowner owned the swamp adjacent to his land up to the median line of the swamp. This was as far as his neighbour opposite could claim. As Government owned the seabed up to the high-water mark, the Chief Surveyor had claimed the part of the swamp adjacent to the high-water mark on the seaward side. This was considered below the belt. Demonstrations were held in George Town immediately before Christmas. The leaders announced that they wished to deliver a petition to the Governor at the Administration Building. I discussed with the Commissioner of Police whether there should be any visible police presence. We decided against this. A police officer in civilian clothes was on the scene. Conveniently, the police headquarters were adjacent to the Administrative Building. Compared with my experiences in the Solomon Islands, the demonstration was very orderly. A lone drum beat time as the marchers came into view. There were placards. One read 'GIVE US BACK OUR SWA' Unfortunately the message would not fit on to the banner and the letters 'MP' could just be determined below the 'SWA'. I went down to receive the marchers and invited the leaders to accompany me to the Executive Council meeting room. I received and read their petition. I promised that the Executive Council would consider it. I should reply in accordance with their advice. Having read it, I could not, however, hold out a great deal of hope. I then accompanied the leaders to the front of the building, where they wished me, my wife and son a merry Christmas and left. They accepted reluctantly, later in January, the dismissal of most of their requests.

Of greater concern for the completion of the survey was the view of an economist at the British Development Division in Barbados. She argued that to complete the survey would not be a cost effective use of British funds. The first Governor of the islands, Athel Long, had had much more serious demonstrations involving the despatch of a British warship. The populace had reacted strongly against the survey taking place. Assurances were given that the survey was not the precursor of a land tax or rating. There would be very positive effects on the economy, as indeed proved to be the case. Thirdly, the whole cost of the survey would be borne by the British Government. The economic argument for discontinuance was that the eastern end of the island contained swamp land incapable of development. There was also a large uninhabited area on the East End side of the transinsular road to which surveyors could not gain access. The benefits of survey would go to a limited number of landowners. I discussed this unexpected development with Executive Council. We agreed that discontinuance was politically untenable. To strengthen my hand, they agreed to pay with Cayman Islands funds for a road to be built into the middle of the inaccessible land at East End. I was thus able to demolish one of the main arguments for discontinuance. But the British Development Division in Barbados held their ground. Funds would not be available to complete the project. I deployed the political arguments to Patrick Duff in London. These won the day and the survey was completed. It has been of immeasurable benefit to development. Under the land registry system which followed, every piece of land has a title. Land can be bought and sold in hours rather than days. The real estate market, which gives the government a minimum of 5% stamp duty on every sale on Grand Cayman, is one of the strengths of the economy. The road, which was built for eighty thousand dollars, has provided access for the largest quarry on the island and led to the development of the largest arable farm on Grand Cayman.

I naturally had my ear to the ground on constitutional change. The message emanating from both groups in the 1976 election was clear: no constitutional change. Nevertheless the United Kingdom was under constant pressure, in the United Nations Committee of 24, to grant Independence to its remaining Colonies. As far as the Caribbean dependencies were concerned, the stock reply was that this was there for the asking. Great Britain would, however, be guided by the wish of the inhabitants. To make its own judgement, the Committee regularly sent a Mission to one or two Dependencies each year. The Cayman Islands' turn came in 1977. I warned the Assembly that this was possible in the Throne Speech in March. Putting the Mission together took time. I received very little warning that the visit was to take place. The date of arrival came late on a Friday might and was released to the Press on the

Monday morning This was to lead to press comment afterwards that I had delayed publicity about the visit. Ratu Vunibobo was the sympathetic Fijian Chairman of the delegation. The Mission was very thorough. We had nothing to hold back. It was given every facility to hold public meetings and consult individuals. I doubt whether in 1977 they found one Caymanian who wished for any change in the constitution or desired Independence. I later accompanied Truman Bodden, Member of the Executive Council, and George Smith, a Member of the Legislative Assembly, to New York for presentation of the Mission Report. We joined the British Delegation to United Nations. The Committee was strongly against colonialism. It was now faced by a report from its own Mission advocating that the Cayman Islands remain a colony. There was a face-saving recommendation that the United Kingdom should discuss with the Cayman Islands whether the constitution could be advanced to a point short of internal self-government. This did not alter the main conclusion. Truman Bodden spoke. It was a hard-hitting lawyer's speech. He quoted back at them the United Nations Resolution which laid down that all people have the right, freely, to determine their political status. George Smith's simplicity was equally effective. He supported his colleague on economic and social grounds. He was on his feet for no longer than two minutes, concluding:

> To contemplate a change in the constitution now would stir up unrest. I therefore affirm my loyalty and the loyalty of the Cayman people to the Queen and confirm the people's desire to remain a Crown Colony with no constitutional change at this time.

Although Truman's hand was no doubt involved in the script, it was a virtuoso performance.

There was considerable debate in the Committee, concentrating on the diplomatic nicety of whether the report should be 'approved', or 'noted'. It was finally 'accepted'. Even further discussion as to whether to amend the constitution was too much for some members of the public. A petition to the Queen not to alter the *status quo* received wide support. 'Recall the Governor,' said one speaker. 'Replace him with someone capable of holding the reins'. The message was clear. No constitutional change.

Nor was there to be a change of Governor at the time as my term of office was extended three times. I was to serve for seven years and four months in total, until January 1982.

CHAPTER FIFTEEN

Governor of the Cayman Islands: Final Years of Office

BY NOW THE work pattern for the year was familiar. The year started with the New Year's Day Reception at Government House. Executive Council Meetings took place every Tuesday afternoon. These entailed preparatory work. Draft papers were submitted through the Clerk by the Permanent Secretaries and official Members of the Council. Sometimes they required discussion or reference to the Financial Secretary or Attorney General. Following meetings, the Minutes were referred to me for approval. It was very seldom that they required amendment. Minutes of Public Service Commission meetings were also sent, at that time every fortnight, for my approval. These contained recommendations for promotions, transfers, disciplining of Civil Servants. They had to be examined with care. Approval was not automatic. On occasions the Commission was asked to reconsider. The Minutes could also be sent to the Attorney General or Chief Secretary to obtain their views. Each week there was a steady stream of files asking for my guidance or decision from the Chief Secretary, Attorney General or Financial Secretary. I encouraged any member of Executive Council, official or elected, to come to see me at any time when I was not otherwise committed. Permanent Secretaries were always in attendance in discussions with Heads of Department. They represented the elected member of the Executive Council, to whom responsibility for the Department had been delegated.

The Constitution decreed that the Governor would preside over the Legislative Assembly in the role of Speaker, if the elected Members had not voted to create the post of Speaker. I duly presided for my full term of office. There were four meetings a year. Exact times varied from one year to another. In February or March, June, September and November was the normal annual pattern. The June meeting, when the Governor delivered the Throne Speech to open the next annual Session, and the Budget meeting, were the longest. March and September meetings might last for eight to ten days. The Budget meeting could last three or four weeks, with the advent of Christmas acting as a stimulus to conclude.

The other landmarks in the year included the Agricultural Show on the Public Holiday of Ash Wednesday. There were annual functions at Easter. The Queen's Birthday in June was marked by a parade at which the Governor took the salute in full uniform. The Queen's Birthday Honours were read out by the Chief Secretary. Previous Honours were presented. Normally it was possible for a Royal Navy Frigate to be in port at the time. A detachment from the ship usually supported the Cayman Islands Police Force on parade. The Cayman Islands Veterans Association, of which I was a founder member, led a supporting contingent of voluntary organisations such as the Boy Scouts and Girls' Brigade. In November, Remembrance Day was celebrated at the War Memorial, next to the Elmslie Memorial Church. In the same month a national festival, Pirates' Week, was held. This was a brainchild of Jim Bodden, who was the Member of Executive Council responsible for tourism. It was in the tradition of carnivals held elsewhere in the Caribbean. It involved the capture of the Governor by marauding pirates. The pirates and their wenches then governed the country for a week until they were put to flight by law and order. Participants dressed for the part and the Pirates' Landing became an annual spectacle. I was on leave for the first one. Dennis Foster, who was acting Governor, was duly captured in full colonial uniform. When the next occasion came round, I was approached by the organisers to play my part. I drew the line at appearing in uniform. Hence I was duly captured in what a Miami theatrical costumer imagined Governors wore three hundred years ago. I was then paraded in a tumbril leading a procession of floats through George Town. As the vehicle was lurching from side to side, I put out a hand to steady·myself. I found that I was clutching a large hangman's noose. This festooned the vehicle together with skull-and-cross-bone flags and other piratical symbols. The death penalty still existed in the Colony. Gordon Brown has not a monopoly of prudence. I persuaded the organisers the following year that the part of Governor was tailor-made for the local drama society. In later editions of Pirate's Week I attended as a spectator. The festival was extended to include programmes in each settlement on Grand Cayman and in Cayman Brac. The accent was on craftwork and days of yore. It has a useful subsidiary role in preserving old customary practices such as rope-making, boat-building, weaving and basket-making.

Between these landmark occasions, I aimed to tour Cayman Brac and Little Cayman at least twice annually. I visited all other constituencies, in the company of the elected parliamentarians, once a year. In addition I paid annual visits to Departments in the company of the Permanent Secretary responsible. I also made occasional visits to the local press, tourist premises, businesses and small industries. Larger labour-intensive projects were few. The population was small and wage levels comparatively high.

Overseas visits had to be fitted into the annual calendar as they arose. For these the Secretary of State's permission to be absent from the Colony had to be obtained. The first of these took place three months after my arrival. My wife and I were asked to accompany the Cayman Island delegation to a Caribbean Tourism meeting in New York. We were to attend the ball given for the occasion. Thus my first request to absent myself from the Islands was to go to a dance. There were regular Commonwealth Parliamentary Association Conferences of Speakers and Clerks, which took me to St Lucia, Montserrat, St Kitts and the Turks and Caicos Islands. On the Montserrat visit I stayed afterwards with Wyn Jones, the Governor, and his wife Ruth. They were old friends from the Solomons. After the St Kitts Conference I visited David Le Breton, the Governor of Anguilla. The island was not dissimilar to Cayman Brac. In the Turks and Caicos the Governor, with very limited resources, was coping with the Commonwealth Parliamentary Conference, a Diplomatic Service inspection of his office, and a Constitutional crisis. The Chief Minister, Jag McCartney, had been killed in an aircrash in the United States. Until he had been formally identified and death had been established, no replacement Chief Minister could be elected. The Governor had accordingly to assume direct responsibility for government. The reasons for this this were not readily understood by politicians.

As well as attending the Committee of Twenty-Four proceedings in New York, I also paid official visits to Houston, Miami, New Orleans and Dade County in Florida. The first of these was to attend the inaugural ceremonies for the initial flight of Cayman Airways into Houston. I was presented with the key to the city and a Texan stetson by the Secretary of State on arrival. Garth Davies, Managing Director of the Cayman Islands News Bureau, had arranged a packed four-day programme. Together with the Cayman Islands delegation, I visited the NASA Space Centre, Galveston and Austin. It was not all sightseeing. I made four promotional speeches in the course of the four-day visit. These included well-attended meetings at the Exson Building and at the World Trade Centre.

In January 1978, together with a delegation from the Cayman Islands, I attended the Second Caribbean Conference on Trade, Investment and

Wearing the Stetson presented to me on arrival in Houston, Texas.
On the left of picture is Superintendent Kevin McCann.

Development held by the American Government in Miami. It was of sufficient significance to be attended by President Balaguer of the Dominican Republic and President Odiber of Costa Rica. I was programmed to address a plenary session of the conference, numbering about six hundred businessmen and government representatives. My usual technique in public speaking, where eye contact with the audience is vital, was to memorise the speech and appear to speak *ex tempore*. I recorded main headings on the back of a business card concealed in my left hand.

I confess to some butterflies in the stomach when I was introduced in front of a larger audience than usual with radio microphones and television cameras. My theme was the Cayman economy, which I described as being on the point of lift-off. At the banquet following the conference, security was tight. There were two State Presidents present. Each of them appeared with their own security. Guests were searched on entry. Security officers stood at ten metres intervals round the curtained banqueting-hall. We were seated at the Cayman Island table when the President of the Dominican Republic entered with his wife. They were both relatively small and were surrounded by bulky security guards of impressive stature. After taking his seat at the top table, the President rose and was escorted out of the room by the phalanx of security guards. One of our party, Alex Sanguinetti, the managing director of Cayman Airways, had left the room to pay what the Americans term a comfort visit. He reappeared very quickly. He said 'That's the first time I have been flushed out of the toilet at the end of a sub-machine-gun!' We now knew the reason for the President's departure. During the dinner a security guard knelt before the top table with a sub-machine gun pointed to the floor. I did not stoop to recover a dropped napkin. The President's after-dinner speech, made in Spanish, was a delight to listen to. He was a poet and the cadences and diction translated words into music.

The United States Oceanographic Survey had been charting Cayman Islands waters by agreement with the Admiralty. 1981 was the year of their one hundred and fiftieth anniversary. I was invited to participate in the festivities in Bay St Louis, not far from New Orleans. As we could incorporate promotional work in the New Orleans and gulf ports area, I accepted. My collection of keys to American cities grew. The architecture of the old French areas of New Orleans impressed me as much as its modern jazz reputation. We visited another space station and the ports of Biloxi and Gulfport. A number of Caymanians are settled in this area. They were invited to the reception, which I hosted in one of the older gracious hotels in New Orleans. The visit again called for promotional speeches about the opportunities for investment in the Colony. It was always pleasant, however, to return to Grand Cayman after four or five full days of representational duties.

In July 1981 I returned to Florida on the invitation of Mayor Clark, the Mayor of Dade County. I collected another key, this time to Miami. Dade County was twinned with the Cayman Islands and the Mayor and I signed a joint Proclamation. I did not mind being kissed by a sea-lion on a visit to Marine World. I was more apprehensive when we visited the

Everglades. We were ceremonially welcomed by Seminole Indians still living in the swamps. I was told that I was to be presented with a traditional bead-embroidered waistcoat. The place of presentation was in the middle of a fenced area containing about twenty alligators. They looked fairly somnolent, but the crocodiles in the Solomons could move at speed. If my host could look nonchalant, I concluded that I should survive the experience. The reptiles were still sleeping as we left the stockade. This duty was not mentioned in my letter of appointment.

These last few paragraphs may give the impression that I was a perpetual tourist. Not so. The visits were undertaken over a number of busy years.

More numerous than the visits abroad were visits to the islands by leading businessmen, government officials and celebrities in different fields. Businessmen were coming and going throughout the year. Social functions allowed me to mix with the field which they represented. This could be construction, accounting, tourism, banking, insurance, law or development. In the government sphere, I had several visits by Michael Macoun, the Overseas Police Advisor, a man of vast overseas police experience. Sir Richard Posnett, who was Governor of Belize, took advantage of a visiting Royal Navy ship to compare our respective jurisdictions. It was a pleasure to welcome Sir Robin Vanderfelt, the Secretary General of the Commonwealth Parliamentary Association, whom I had known in my Pacific days, Sir Richard Stratton, Assistant Under-Secretary of State. Patrick Duff, Head of Hong Kong and General Department, David Dale, and Walter Wallace were visitors from the Foreign and Commonwealth Office. Among non-official visitors I recall Buzz Aldrin, the second man to land on the moon. He gave my wife a copy of his book *Return to Earth*, which left the impression that he had been programmed to get to the moon but not to return to his own planet. Fred Perry came to open the new courts of the Tennis Club and many Rugby Internationalists appeared with the Golden Oldies. This constant tide of newcomers to the community negated the feeling of insularity often felt in small communities.

In 1980 the oil transfer operations on Little Cayman had grown to a volume of ten million barrels a month. The promoters, Cayman Energy Ltd, had planned, and had entered into contract to construct, a shore-based storage terminal on Little Cayman. This was costed at ten million dollars. It was welcomed by Government as constituting less risk to the environment than transfer at sea between tankers. Unfortunately for the developers, but before money was sunk in the project, the Loop in

Lousiana came into service. This was a long piping system. It ran out into the Gulf to mooring facilities in deep enough water to allow the super-tankers to berth. These carried oil of different quality in separate tanks. Oil of different properties had to be stored in separate tanks ashore. When the oil was unloaded into the pipe, a plug of water separated one consignment of oil from the next one of different grade. The consignments could then be unloaded into separate tanks. A problem arose when the tanks for a specific grade were full. The unloading process was then blocked. When this difficulty was eventually overcome, there was no reason to tranship oil en route to America. Accordingly the need to transfer or store oil offshore disappeared.

We had necessarily devised detailed plans for dealing with oil spillage. Had the beaches on Grand Cayman become polluted, the burgeoning tourist industry would have been crippled. Although the immediate effects on the economy were adverse, there was, nevertheless, some consolation in that a potential danger had been removed.

Attempts to diversify the economy were not very successful. High wage rates and a small population were disincentives. As there was no direct taxation, we could not offer tax incentives to developers. There was a hydroponic venture in George Town. A tropical fish farm foundered as the ground water was too brackish. The Turtle Farm, originally brought to maturity by the Commonwealth Development Corporation, changed hands several times. Undoubtedly the original stock had come from the wild. However, farmed turtles now laid their eggs on a beach constructed on the farm in West Bay. The eggs were hatched in polystyrene boxes. The baby turtles were then reared in ponds through which fresh seawater was pumped. A mass of scientific data was accumulated on the green turtle and the few loggerhead turtles on the farm. More were released into the wild for conservation purposes than would have survived naturally. There was an international treaty, CITES, (Convention on International Trade in Endangered Species). When this was negotiated, an exemption was made for farmed turtle. The Convention scheduled both protected species and endangered species. It allowed countries to have tighter restrictions than were specified in the Convention. The United States consequently passed domestic legislation which effectively banned the import of any green turtle products. This stopped sales to tourists returning to or through the United States. It also prevented sales to, or shipment through, the United States. Despite vehement protest, this was a battle which we lost. The farm was sold and purchased by the Cayman Islands Government.

The aim was to keep the breeding stock alive until a possible reversal of the ban. The farm became a tourist attraction. Its contribution to science is now recognised.

The success of the Cayman Islands in offshore finance was not achieved without increasing vigilance by the Government and the commercial community. Following the demise of Interbank, a Banking Inspectorate was established. 'Know your client' philosophies had long been a principle of Caymanian bankers. Normal confidentiality between professionals and their clients was preserved and enshrined in law. Legislative changes were progressively introduced, however, to allay, as far as possible, the concerns of the metropolitan powers. This process has continued through the years, with United Nations, the European Community, the O.E.C.D. and the Financial Action Task Force, all scrutinising Caymanian laws and practises to ensure that these conform to international norms. Amendments have been made to legislation as necessary. The basic problem is that there has never been direct taxation in the Cayman Islands. The outside world is the wolf without the tail trying to persuade a very happy bushy-tailed wolf to be the same. In 1980 we enacted insurance legislation to broaden the base of financial services. There was immediate growth in this sector in the years before I left.

Domestically, the government machine was adapting to power the expanding economy. Radio Cayman came on stream in 1977. Initially it was a Government Department. Access to the radio by politicians, particularly in the run-up to election, had to be defined. Government Departments were expanded. Monitoring financial services and the promotion of tourism were allocated additional resources. By 1978 there were sometimes three cruise ships a day off the port of George Town. Plans to improve cargo handling on Cayman Brac came to fruition. A new containerised port became operational in 1981. Additional revenues allowed improvement of the educational system and a Middle School and a Community College were opened. A Law School was inaugurated in conjunction with the University of Liverpool. This allowed Caymanian law students to obtain degrees recognised by Liverpool University. Consequently, over the years, an impressive number of Caymanian solicitors and barristers have joined the legal profession. Many are employed in the financial services industry. Much was happening in the social services field. Drug consumption was on the increase. Hard drugs, particularly crack cocaine, came on to the illicit market. Draconian penalties were introduced for pushers. Even for possession penalties were severe. A parallel social programme was, however, put in place for rehabilitation and education. Staff of the Social Services Department was increased.

The facilities in the Central Hospital were complemented by opening up clinics in the main population centres. Greater emphasis was placed on preventative medicine. A study by the University of Colombia in the United States analysed a significant proportion of handicaps suffered by Caymanian children. A hereditary Caymanian disease was identified. This combined motor problems with congenital deafness and other deformities. A storage disease was difficult to identify until the child reached puberty, when there was a complete breakdown in health. The reason for these ailments was the small size of the community and some degree of inbreeding. A Caymanian, Angela Ebanks, was sent to Colombia University for training in constructing genealogical trees. It was then possible to counsel Caymanians before marriage as to whether either party had serious disabilities in the family tree. The campaign was eventually incorporated in the health programme. Angela later became Director of Tourism.

Meetings of the Legislative Assembly, over which I continued to preside, kept me in intimate touch with the business and law-making of the country. There were three occasions which I remember particularly. Jim Bodden was in full flood during a debate. One of the members, Captain Reid from Cayman Brac, appeared to nod off. Jim Bodden looked at him and said, 'I must be failing in my delivery, Sir, if members fall asleep in the middle of my speech!' Immediately Captain Reid leapt to his feet. 'On point of explanation, Mr Speaker'. Jim Bodden gave way and sat down. 'I am an old salt, Mr Speaker. I was at sea in the days of sail. Any monotonous continuous noise, the wind in the rigging, or, in later days, the pulse of the engines below deck, have always tempted me to fall asleep. The Honourable member's speech has the same effect.'

The second occasion also involved Jim Bodden when he was in Opposition. When the new Legislative Building was opened, an appeal was made for quality ornaments to embellish what was a gracious structure. After consultation, the Bank of Nova Scotia commissioned from Spinks a specially designed mace. This must be in place, as in the House of Commons, whenever the House is sitting. I presided when the the Right Honourable Donald Fleming PC, QC, a former Minister of Finance in Canada, presented the mace on behalf of the Bank and its local Trust Company. It was a formal occasion. There were three taps on the door to admit strangers. The presentation speech was made and Berkley Bush made a speech of thanks. It was then open to any member to speak. Jim Bodden rose and the tenor of his remarks was: 'I've never seen such a blatant piece of advertising in my life. If we need a mace, why can't we buy one?' Another Executive Council member rose and hastily poured water on the embers of the previous speech. That night, at the reception at Government House in honour of the presentation, Donald Fleming and Jim Bodden were the best of friends. Fleming had been a parliamentarian. He had realised that Jim Bodden had been trying to score a political point.

The third occasion took place long after I had left the Assembly and had been representing the Cayman Islands in London for more than ten years. I thought that I was leaving the job. I wished to leave some memento behind. After discussion with the Governor, who was still Presiding Officer, and the Clerk of the Assembly, I again commissioned Spinks. This time it was to make a ballot-box in silver. It would be engraved with the Colony Coat of Arms to replace the battered wooden ballot box then in use. It was mainly used for electing members of the Executive Council after an election. Although I suggested that the presentation be made low-key, it was virtually a re-run of the presentation of the mace. I made the presentation speech. One of the members was deputed to make the reply. All went well for the first part of the speech. The tenor of a remark in the second half was: 'But you said that the ballot-box was symbolic of the democracy which the Cayman Islands enjoy. But we don't enjoy it now while you are sitting up there,' pointing at the Governor in the chair. I was highly embarrassed. The Governor knew, however, that the allegation was none of my making. Another political point. The ballot-box survives.

In 1979 I realised that the Proclamation summoning meetings of the Legislative Assembly had to specify the place, as well as the date and time. The Legislative Assembly Building was a gracious new building, specially designed for its prestigious purpose. It occurred to me that there might be merit, however, in taking Parliament to the people and holding a meeting on Cayman Brac. This would help in reinforcing the unity of the three islands. As all parliamentarians would have to live in the same hotel, it could assist in reducing some of the tensions which were surfacing before the 1980 elections. The meeting would coincide with the opening of the Aston Rutty Community Centre on the Brac, where the Assembly would sit. It actually drew a greater attendance of the general public than was usual on Grand Cayman.

Despite the heavy additional administrative burden this placed on the Clerk and her staff, I decided to repeat the performance in 1981 after the elections. On this occasion the disadvantage of operating away from base became apparent. The Government was introducing a controversial Housing Development Corporation Bill. It was strongly contested by the Opposition, led by Benson Ebanks. The Standing Orders of the Assembly decreed that a Bill should be gazetted and circulated to members by a specified number of days before the meeting. He alleged that this had not been done. We substantiated the exact day on which the Bill had been gazetted. Proof of this was more difficult, however, as gazettal took place on Grand Cayman and not on Cayman Brac. I was satisfied that the Bill had been properly introduced and later assented to it. This led to a petition to the Secretary of State. The petition was dismissed by him. In a minority, the Opposition was entitled to use all legitimate means to prevent a Bill to which it objected from passing into law. It failed.

I was ably supported by Rese Bodden as Secretary. When she transferred to higher office, I had a succession of efficient Diplomatic Service Secretaries. In addition to their secretarial duties, they managed my social calendar as well as the finances of my office and Government House. Work has since increased to such a level that the Governor has a Staff Officer and Social Secretary as well as a Governor's Secretary. I had a Jamaican butler and cook at Government House. Sergeant Fredance Ebanks was my police driver and Superintendent McCann acted as an honorary Aide de Camp on overseas visits to America. American officials looked for some contribution to security on these occasions.

The Civil Service is a living organism. New entries, retirements, promotions, departures at end of contract, happen each year. Apart from the changes of Chief Secretary and Attorney General early in my tour of duty, I was fortunate in having stability at senior level. Judge Moody, a Jamaican, retired at the end of 1978. He was replaced as Chief Justice by Sir John Summerfield, previously Chief Justice in Bermuda. Andrew Greiff, the Commissioner of Police, left in 1978. He was succeeded by Jim Stowers, who had been an Assistant Chief Constable in the Devon and Cornwall Constabulary. He had previously served for two years as Head of the Criminal Investigation Department in the Cayman Islands force. James Ryan, the Headmaster of the Cayman Brac High School, was appointed District Commissioner of the Sister Islands in succession to Garland Jackson. He was the third District Commissioner during my tour.

These changes were tolerable as they did not all happen at once. A General Election, on the other hand, was a considerable shock to the system. In the 1980 election the Unity team, which had received eleven votes in the previous election, only secured eight. The opposing group, named Progress with Dignity, secured four. Executive Council remained the same except for the replacement of Charles Kirkconnell by John McLean. With Charles Kirkconnell now on the Opposition benches, the Opposition was a strong team. For the first time there was no Executive Council member from the Sister Islands. This was not a constitutional requirement; it had merely been a convention to vote one of the members from the Sister Islands on to the Executive Council. As the Chief Secretary, Dennis Foster, came from Cayman Brac, I transferred responsibility for the Sister Islands to his portfolio. The Brackers were not very happy to lose political representation. Having an official member in charge of their affairs was, as one resident said, 'Like putting a one-legged man into an arse-kicking contest'.

Changes which were most noticeable and welcome were the numbers of Caymanians coming into the Civil Service and the private sector with full professional or academic qualifications. The government was generous to the point that its Scholarship Board awarded scholarships to universities to any Caymanian student who gained entry. Qualified accountants, nurses, doctors, a surgeon, lawyers, teachers and engineers were now coming through the system in greater numbers. Many, after completing a period of up to four years for which they were bonded to serve in the Civil Service, left to join the private sector. They were not lost to the economy. In the private sector there were already many highly successful Caymanian businessmen in the professions, in law, accountancy, real estate, architecture and banking. There were also many in business who had come from the United States, Canada, the Caribbean, United Kingdom and Europe. They had worked in the community for many years and hoped to stay there. The ratio of expatriates to the number of indigenous Caymanians was, however, constantly growing. A work permit system was in place. Permanent residence with the right to work was difficult to obtain. Even today this is an area of concern. The expanding economy cannot be maintained by the current numbers and skills of the local work force. An expatriate work force must be attracted by adequate incentives. One of these is to put roots down in an attractive country which they have helped to prosper.

I mentioned earlier the fierce feeling of identity Caymanians have for their homeland. This partly explains some reluctance to dilute their ownership. It also explains the astonishing degree of self-help which they bring to their community. The people of Cayman Brac, impatient with Government delays, built their own airfield and hospital. The Government then took them over. A prosperous Bracker, Linton Tibbetts, might have been expected to focus on the United States where he conducts his business. He has built two hotels on Cayman Brac and another on Little Cayman. He promoted the Red Carpet Air Service between Cayman Brac and Florida when connections by air were poor. The Kirkconnell family, one of the leading business firms on Grand Cayman, have founded an old peoples' home on Cayman Brac. There are a number of service clubs constantly active in the community. The Lions have for many years promoted a programme for those with problems of sight. Rotary founded a boys' home, Bonaventure House, and also a library building on Cayman Brac. Their Christmas party for the elderly is one of the regular events on the social calendar. Fundraising for sports and good causes, as well as sponsorship by banks and business houses, are on the grand scale. Foreign residents who have made their home in the islands are usually generous in their response to appeals.

There was little time to relax. Seven Mile Beach was, however, in front of Government House. A swim in the early morning or at the weekends was always available. There were attractive walks on all the islands and caving, particularly on Cayman Brac. We played bridge with American friends, Bill and Maud Littleton, with Sir John and Patricia Summerfield and with Vassel and Rita Johnson. My wife had a lady's foursome. The last of them, Dorothy (Dee) Stevenson, died very recently. I looked forward to seeing her when I used to visit the islands.

I was awarded the C.M.G. in the Queen's Birthday Honours in 1980. I came home for the Investiture at Buckingham Palace. On arrival in London, I had to obtain a black topper to match my morning-suit This was difficult to arrange at short notice. I was able to procure one for what seemed a large amount of money. When I was forming up in the appropriate line before the event, I was hailed by Sir William Hesseltine, the Queen's Private Secretary. I had had dealings with him when the Queen visited the Solomons in 1974. He invited me for a drink in his office at the conclusion of the investiture. After the presentation by Her Majesty, the medal is removed by the palace staff. It is placed in a box, which is handed to the recipient. I repaired to Sir William's office. I partook of his sherry, recovered my expensive hat and gloves and left. As I was about to enter the car hired for the occasion in the palace court-yard, a side door of the palace opened. Sir William waved to me. 'Tom, I think that this is what you came for!' In remembering my expensive hat, I had forgotten the C.M.G.!

The last three months before I left were a frantic round of visits and farewell functions. It was really a reversal of the initial visits which I had made on my arrival. My successor was to be Peter Lloyd, then Deputy Governor of Bermuda. I had met him in the Pacific when he was Colonial Secretary in Fiji. We agreed to meet in Miami before he assumed office. Briefing was easy as he knew the routine. I was asked to delay my departure slightly so as to conform with his departure from Bermuda. We left Grand Cayman on the second of January 1982, our thirtieth wedding anniversary. I had completed thirty-four years of service. A few months later I should be sixty-two years of age.

CHAPTER SIXTEEN

Representational Duties in London

W E RETURNED TO England via Philadelphia, where we spent a week with our friends the Littletons. We enjoyed gracious American hospitality, visiting museums, art galleries and theatres. We then journeyed on to our flat in Farnham, in Surrey, which we had purchased when my son Malcolm was at Edgeborough Preparatory School there. He graduated from Cornell University in Hotel Management shortly after our arrival in England. He has remained in the United States since.

We had to adjust to returning to a new way of life after thirty-four years abroad. The flat was too cramped for a permanent home. We sold it and, within a few months, moved into a new, spacious house on the outskirts of Farnham. Much of my retirement leave was taken up in converting old woodland into a garden.

Family circumstances had changed. One of my two brothers had died in a drowning accident a few months before I came home. Working in Scotland, he had been a prop to my parents, who were both in their eighties. I felt that this responsibility now passed to me. My wife's mother had died during our months in England before leaving for the Cayman Islands. Her father now lived alone in Pau, near the Pyrenees. As an only child, my wife, too, had an extra mantle of care. I love the French for 'only daughter': 'Une fille unique'. Sadly, during the next few years my second brother died in Canada, leaving a widow and six children. Worse was to come as my father died in 1984 and my wife's father in the following year. Two of my father's sisters, Jenny Lawrie and May Graham, survived him and went on to pass their hundredth birthdays. May, surprisingly bright and active, has now reached the age of one hundred and one.

We were very happy to move into a house of our own after so many transitory residences through the years. Women are by nature homemakers. Only families who have led the nomadic life which we had led in the Overseas Services can appreciate fully the deprivation felt by wives and mothers constantly on the move.

Before leaving the Cayman Islands, however, I had been given hints that I might be asked to perform some unspecified services for the

Cayman Islands Government. Indeed in one organ of the press there was speculation to this effect:

> His knowledge of the territory and our way of life which he so readily adopted can be put to further benefit . . . He would be in the right position in the United Kingdom to tell the Cayman Islands story if called upon to do so.

The Cayman Islands Department of Tourism had engaged John Enright and Associates to open a tourist office in London. He rented accommodation in Curzon Street. I found out subsequently that he had been asked to leave space for additional government use. Eventually I was asked if I would agree to assume representational duties, primarily and initially for business promotion, for an experimental period of one year. I agreed subject to three qualifications. Approval had to be obtained from the Secretary of State to assume such duties immediately following my departure from the territory. My successor had to approve the arrangement. Thirdly, I should be answerable to the Governor, through the Chief Secretary, rather than to a political portfolio. All of these conditions were met and I assumed duty in London on conclusion of my retirement leave on 1st July 1982. I little thought that I should be in harness for a further eighteen years.

There were at that time three Representative Offices of British Overseas Territories in London: Hong Kong, Gibraltar and the Falkland Islands. Robert Peliza, a former Chief Minister of Gibraltar, had visited the Cayman Islands while I was there. He had spoken to Jim Bodden, the leading politician, and Dennis Foster, the Chief Secretary, about the advantages and the importance of having a territorial presence in London. With considerable foresight he also advocated the formation of an Overseas Territories Representative organisation in London. This later came to pass as the Dependent Territories Association.

Initially the impact of the office was minimal. I shared a secretary with the Cayman Islands News Bureau within the Department of Tourism complex. Deirdre Kirwan-Taylor, who assisted John Enright, was soon to take over responsibility for the Tourism activities. The total staff was four in number but we all worked for the Cayman Islands and cooperated well. When Deirdre Kirwan Taylor was directly employed by the Department of Tourism, with John Enright in the wings as a consultant, I assumed responsibility for accounting for the office as a whole. My first year went by. I was re-engaged on contract for a further two years with the title of the post designated as Cayman Islands

Government Representative in the United Kingdom. It took time for me to adjust to a role in which I was no longer in the decision-making process. As Governor, I was effectively executive head of state and personally involved in all major decisions. I had necessarily to change gear.

I then had the good fortune to recruit Mary Chandler, who had been my last Diplomatic Service Secretary when I was Governor, as Secretary in the London Office. She had returned to the Foreign and Commonwealth Office at the end of her assignment and had decided to leave. I had reservations about her decision to leave a pensionable post in which she had a career of world-wide appointments ahead of her. But once she convinced me that she had decided to leave Foreign and Commonwealth Office employment, I obtained approval to engage her on contract.

I brought with me two defects for the job I was doing. First, I was acutely conscious of the need to keep a low profile politically. In no sense did I wish to give my successor any concerns that I retained any influence in governmental decisions. Secondly, I was old-fashioned in my philosophy towards decision-making by British Ministers. The Governor, having consulted his Executive Council, would put recommendations to the Foreign and Commonwealth Office. The officials would consider and put a proposal to the Minister or Secretary of State. The decision would be taken and conveyed to the Governor. Initially it seemed to be hitting below the belt to lobby to have a Parliamentary Question asked on the subject or to endeavour to get press backing for the proposition. The Foreign and Commonwealth Office might well have advised against the recommendation. I was never instructed to follow this route. As the years of representation went by, however, I came to the point of view that once I knew what the Cayman Islands Government wanted, I was entitled to use any legitimate means to secure the desired decision. An attribute which I did bring to the job was my total commitment to my employer, the Cayman Islands Government. While I was fully prepared to advise the Foreign and Commonwealth Office on factual matters and on personalities, I eschewed any advice or comments on policy or political matters. For one thing, I was not fully briefed or up to date. For another, this would have strayed into the Governor's domain.

Towards the end of my first year, I was asked if I could assist with recruitment of staff in the United Kingdom. Success in this field led to my taking over responsibility for recruitment of all staff required. This had several benefits. The first was that by direct recruitment, the London Office saved the substantial fees demanded by the recruitment agency which we had previously employed. This saving was of such dimensions that in a heavy year of recruitment I defrayed the total cost of my office from savings in recruitment charges. The second advantage was that Heads of Departments, to whom applications were sent by the Public Service Commission, could select the persons they wished to interview. Normally I chaired the selection panels. These included the Head of Department concerned and usually a member of the Public Service Commission. A specialised member of the panel had sometimes to be co-opted, where the post was of a technical nature. The variety of the posts required eliminated any tedium from this facet of the job.

We recruited teachers, doctors, nurses, consultants, surveyors, marine engineers and surveyors, commissioners of police, judges, accountants, computer staff, lands officers, law lecturers and legal draftsmen. Mary Chandler, my secretary, quickly developed an affinity for this work and for duties of an executive and administrative nature. This was to earn her promotion to the post of Deputy Representative. In the recruitment field, advertisement, referral of applications to the Cayman Islands for short-listing, arranging interviews and travel, advising candidates of the results of interview, making job offers and arranging airfares to the islands entailed fast, accurate and detailed work. At times we were dealing with up to two thousand applications and were obliged to bring in temporary staff to cope with the volume of paper. When the cost of temporary staff escalated, it became cheaper to engage a third and eventually a fourth member of staff.

In the Cayman Islands our recruitment work was materially helped by the Chairman of the Public Service Commission, Athel Long, and the Permanent Secretary, Personnel, Mrs Jenny Manderson. Athel Long had formerly been the first Governor of the Cayman Islands, when the post of Administrator was renamed. Mrs Manderson had formerly been Clerk to the Executive Council and had readily adapted to establishment duties.

Once it was known that the Cayman Islands had an office in London, requests for information on banking, company formation, immigration and purchase of property began to arrive in increasing quantity. These were made by telephone, fax and letter. E-mails were not then in use. In 1982 there were no booklets on these subjects. One of my first tasks was to draft these, refer them to the Department concerned to vet and approve, and produce sufficient copies for our use in London. The

Cayman Islands News Bureau, which was contracted to provide the Government's Public Relations and Information, realised that these fact-sheets filled a general need. They agreed to take them over, have them printed in a uniform format and keep them up to date. When a Government Information Service replaced the News Bureau, it took over this responsibility and latterly transferred them to the Internet. Keeping them up to date, as legislation, fees, charges and factual statistics change, has proved difficult.

Requests for commercial information could well lead to inward investment. Many requests, however, were simply for information. Journalists, students, academics, statisticians could absorb considerable research time, which contributed little to the country's economy. Self-administration, dealing with the running of the office, payment of salaries, completing office budgets, producing monthly accounts took up considerable further time. No-one was looking over my shoulder. I had, however, to assess, on a regular basis, not only that the office was cost-effective, but that it was making a positive contribution to the country's well-being. In representative duties, the benchmarks for making such a judgement will not be found in textbooks.

In 1988 we had a fire in the premises in Curzon Street. It proved the value of fire drills. We could only watch from the pavement as the fire raged in the lower floors of the building. Our offices were on the fourth floor and our files and papers escaped damage. We identified a company in Knightsbridge which specialised in letting accommodation in such circumstances. We moved temporarily until we were able to lease suitable accommodation, which was also in Knightsbridge. Some repartitioning and carpeting was required before the move. Again the Government Office shared common premises with the Department of Tourism. In 1995 the property, which was owned by an insurance company, was purchased by Harrods, directly opposite. We judged it timely to move, which our lease then allowed us to do without penalty. After viewing a considerable number of properties, we leased offices at 6, Arlington Street, near the Ritz Hotel. There were two suites adjacent to each other. This separated the Government and Tourism offices for the first time. We shared common telephone facilities. The same friendly relationship and willingness to help each other survived the partitioning between us.

Developing a network of helpful contacts took time and improved through the years. The Commonwealth Parliamentary Association office, off Westminster Hall in the House of Commons, was always helpful in arranging meetings between visiting Parliamentarians from the

In my office at 6 Arlington Street.

Cayman Islands and United Kingdom Parliamentarians. Many of the latter had a special interest in the Colony or in United Kingdom Overseas Territories. Disappointingly, visiting Cayman Islands Ministers seldom gave themselves time on visits to Europe for specific purposes to take full advantage of this opportunity. While it was possible to arrange briefing meetings for interested Members of Parliament, they preferred to have face-to-face discussions with other parliamentarians. The Falkland Islands Government Office and the Gibraltar Government Office manned stands promoting their territories at the Conservative and Labour annual Party Conferences. Both of the territories which they represented had particular political problems, the Falklands with Argentina, and Gibraltar with Spain. It would have been difficult to justify this level of expenditure for the Cayman Islands, but I found it useful to attend International Day at both Conferences, when a special programme is arranged for foreign dignitaries. Parliamentarians were more approachable on their own turf and in the relaxed atmosphere of the Conferences. I took every opportunity to describe the pressures on our financial services industry from various international agencies such as the European Union, O.E.C.D., and the Financial Action Task Force. I could also describe the barriers already in place against money-laundering and tax evasion.

Inevitably the profile of the Executive Council, the Legislative Assembly and the civil service changed. Sir Vassel Johnson, the Financial Secretary retired from the Civil Service in 1983. A year later he was elected to the Legislative Assembly and appointed a Member of the Executive Council, a post which he held for a further four years. He was succeeded as Financial Secretary by Tom Jefferson and he, in turn, by George McCarthy. The latter has borne the brunt of the attack by overseas agencies on financial services in smaller countries. He has enjoyed sound legal advice. He has been assisted by astute analysis of the external criticisms by the Cayman Islands legal, accounting, banking and insurance professions. He has thus ensured the buoyant survival of the financial industry.

James Ryan, who was previously District Commissioner on Cayman Brac, was the current Chief Secretary, while David Ballantyne served as Attorney General, the only expatriate in the Executive Council and the Legislative Assembly. Elections have taken their toll of many of the politicians with whom I previously worked. Gilbert McLean and Linford Pierson, both former Permanent Secretaries, now serve on Executive Council as Elected Members. Mr McKeeva Bush has replaced Mr Kurt Tibbetts as Leader of Government business. This position is likely to be renamed Chief Minister in the near future. The cadre of permanent secretaries has seen many changes. Joy Basdeo, Andrea Bryan, Kearney Gomez, Harding Watler and Leonard Dilbert had close relations with the London Office during my term in London. It will be evident that, apart from the Governor and the former Attorney General, the whole political machine and the top reaches of the Civil Service are capably administered by Caymanians.

In London contacts were developed with Whitehall Ministries which had interest in our affairs. The shelf-life of officials was sometimes relatively short. I had often to revert to a most valuable publication which lists the individuals, the subjects for which they are responsible, addresses and telephone numbers in all Government Ministries and Agencies.

Other Overseas Offices in London were, however, using professional help in contact-building and image-improvement. I sought approval to do likewise. My recommendation was accepted, except that the firm, Profile Communication, was engaged directly by the Financial Secretary to assist him with his financial services problems. This meant that the Managing Director of the firm, Susan Eastoe, was directly responsible to an office in the Cayman Islands instead of one in London. Nevertheless I benefited substantially from the arrangements. New press, political, and business contacts were established and enhanced. It was important to deal with negative press comment promptly. But immediate access to the Financial Secretary was occasionally difficult. The opportunity for rebuttal was sometimes lost.

Susan Eastoe had also been engaged by the Falklands and Gibraltar Offices in London to organise a conference on what were then called British Dependent Territories. I was co-opted on to the organising committee. It was a high level occasion, taking place in the Queen Elizabeth Conference Centre in 1995. It was opened by Douglas Hurd, the Foreign Secretary. A number of the other Dependent Territories which had no offices in London were nevertheless represented by persons living in the United Kingdom. When the Conference finished, we met to discuss its effect. We concluded that it had done much to alert the general public to our existence, our contribution to the world's economy, and to some of our problems. It would be a pity to allow the initiative to die with the demise of the Conference. We resolved to meet regularly and, with the later approval of our governments, established the Dependent Territories Association (D.T.A.), later renamed the United Kingdom Overseas Territories Association. (U.K.O.T.A.). Susan Eastoe, as Secretary, drew up terms of reference which were accepted by our governments. In the interests of open government, I suggested that a representative of the Foreign and Commonwealth Office should be invited to all our meetings and this proposal was adopted. The Association has provided a useful think-tank, where various papers have been put forward and discussed. The similarity of our responsibilities, and our compatibility, assisted us in understanding problems peculiar to individual territories. Sukey Cameron represented the Falkland Islands; Albert Poggio, Gibraltar; Bill Samuel, the Turks and Caicos Islands; Janice Panton, Montserrat; Stephen Dickinson, the British Virgin Islands; Cathy Hopkins, St Helena and myself the Cayman Islands. The group as a whole has given support for individual territories faced with dire problems, such as St Helena in its demand for an airport or Montserrat confronting the volcanic eruption there. The chairmanship of the Association rotated annually.

I was also a Council Member of the Royal Commonwealth Ex-Services League, representing the Cayman Islands Veterans Association and the Turks and Caicos Legion. The League was founded by Earl Haig in 1921 after the first World War. He had the backing of General Smuts in South Africa, the British Legion in England, Canada, Australia, South

Africa and New Zealand, who became the founder members. Its aim was to ensure that no ex-servicemen of the Commonwealth or their dependants should ever be in need; this became a greater challenge after the Second World War. The present Grand President of the League is Prince Philip, who succeeded Earl Mountbatten of Burma. I was elected as a member of the Executive Committee and in 1993 appointed Chairman of the Standing Committee on Welfare Programmes. This is responsible for distributing aid for benevolence and projects throughout the Commonwealth. Duties involve about twelve meetings a year and attendance at Triennial Conferences in different Commonwealth countries. I have retained these appointments since I retired. It is a charity which I can serve with dedication because of my Army and Commonwealth background.

RCEL wreath-laying ceremony in Barbados.

For five years, from 1982 to 1987, I was Chairman of the Council of the Pacific Islands Society of United Kingdom and Ireland. The Society was formed of persons who had served in the Western Pacific, of Pacific Islanders who had immigrated to this country, and Pacific Island students. I continued to serve on the Council until the year 2001. The main social event of the year was Pacific Day, held on the occasion of the Annual General Meeting. This usually embraced a Pacific feast followed by Pacific singing and dancing. We took the latter cultural activities to the Dome on one occasion.

I was an official member of the West India Committee, an organisation with a very long history. It involves all the West Indies High Commissioners in London and a number of Members of both Houses of Parliament with a particular interest in the West Indies. It has a strong interest in trade links between Britain and the West Indies and organises trade fairs and conferences. It has extended its activities into Europe and I attended conferences organised by its European offshoot, the Council of Europe, in Brussels and in Aruba in the Dutch Antilles.

As a life member of the Royal Commonwealth Society and a member of the Caledonian Club, I used their facilities to entertain visitors from the Cayman Islands. I was always sure of a warm welcome and excellent service in both clubs. I had been Honorary Representative for the Royal Commonwealth Society in the Solomon Islands. I had also taken an interest in their essay competition in the Cayman Islands.

The visit to Aruba was by no means the only visit abroad. In 1984 John Enright and I visited Hong King to arrange to take a stand at a Tourist Fair. This could also serve as a base from which to issue information on financial services. The British Government at the time was discouraging efforts to attract capital out of Hong Kong. But some of the older business houses were prudently forming companies in offshore jurisdictions. They believed that the Hong Kong economy would remain strong after the Chinese take-over. If not, a contingency plan would be sound business practice. Our intention was simply to make known what services were available in the Cayman Islands. Alex Sanguinetti, the Director of Tourism, Mary Chandler and Deirdre Kirwan-Taylor helped us to survive a very busy visit. We were greatly assisted by the Hong Kong Chamber of Commerce in identifying potential business contacts. Despite recommendation to engage an agent to maintain a Cayman Islands presence there, this was not followed up. It was left to one of the leading Cayman Islands law firms to establish an office there much later. An enduring memory of the visit was a day spent with the Royal Navy on their annual picnic for families. Coincidentally, Alex Sanguinetti was related to Peter Booth, the Naval Commander who offered us this hospitality. Shortly afterwards the same team, apart from Mary Chandler, visited the International Tourism Bourse in Berlin. Alex Sanguinetti was now Director of Cayman Airways and the Director of Tourism, who joined us, was Rudi Selzer, an Austrian. The cheapest way to travel was to hire a minibus. We had the excitement of travelling along the Berlin corridor and passing through the Russian checkpoint. Rudi was distinctly nervous about this experience. Alex, who had a son in the American Marines, did little to allay this feeling, as he prominently displayed American and Marine emblems and did his best to emulate General Patton. On our return trip, we toured the battlefield at Arnhem. Our guide depressed me. A parachutist, he had dropped at Arnhem and had subsequently married a Dutch wife. His life consisted of reliving each day, and describing, the short period in which he had been in action. He was, however, happy to do so and his presentation showed no sign of staleness.

The Cayman Islands were an associate member of the European Community. I was unable to determine exactly what our privileges and obligations were. Through the Foreign and Commonwealth Office, I arranged a fact-finding visit to Brussels and did my own research. It was reassuring. A British Overseas Territory (other than Gibraltar, which is a member of the Community) is not subject to Directives. The rub is that the Community can say to Britain, as a Member, 'We would like you to use your best endeavours to apply the gist of this Directive to your Overseas Territories.' Under our Constitutions, the United Kingdom is responsible for External Affairs. Let me quote a Decision of the Representatives of the Governments of the Member States of 27th November 2001:

> The member States concerned commit themselves to promote the adoption in the Caribbean dependent or associated territories referred to in Annex A of Council Decision 2001/822/EC of 27 November 2001 on the association of overseas countries and territories with the European Community, of the same measures that the Member States adopt and implement under the Community rules to be adopted on the taxation of savings.

The Cayman Islands have, of course, no laws for direct taxation.

I subsequently visited Brussels on several occasions. On one occasion, organised by Susan Eastoe, who accompanied me, we had a very useful round of meetings. Our travel plans for return to London had to be altered rapidly, however. It was the day of the fire in the Channel Tunnel. I paid subsequent visits to Brussels and Paris with Cayman Island delegations to the European Union and the O.E.C.D.

I travelled to the Cayman Islands once or twice a year to update my knowledge and for discussions. Occasionally I extended my trip privately to travel home via Houston, where my son was now working. Over the years I visited New Zealand, Australia, South Africa and Barbados on the triennial Royal Commonwealth Ex-Services League Conferences. After both the Antipodean Conferences, I arranged to visit the Solomon Islands. They were bitter-sweet visits. I was warmly received. The Governor-General arranged receptions for me on both occasions. I met many old Solomon Island colleagues and visited my old haunts in the Western Solomons and Malaita. But there were signs that the inter-island rivalries which have led to recent armed confrontations were surfacing. There was an air of dilapidation and shoddy maintenance. Individuals grumbled about corruption, maladministration and politicians stepping out of line. Yet in the villages, apart from some extra clinics and village schools, Melanesian way of life had not changed much. The gardens and the fishing grounds would endure. The jungle would soon overlay derelict bridges and roads unused through lack of vehicles and lack of fuel.

After the South African Conference, I stayed for ten days with Bob Finnimore in Anerley, Natal. Transferred from Kenya to the Solomon Islands, he had been a District Commissioner on Malaita. He was now retired in South Africa He is a renowned host. He escorted me to two game parks. Distance did not deter him from driving me to see other retirees from the Solomon Islands These included Brian Twomey, who had been Commissioner of Lands, and his wife Pat. She had been my Secretary when I was Chief Secretary in Honiara. John Bee, a former District Officer on Malaita, was now farming. Jock Elliot, who had been a foreman in the Public Works Department, invited us to lunch. He was a gentle, friendly Scot, who had been very popular during his working life. Not long after my visit, his house was burgled. He was assaulted, admitted to hospital and died. We were not to know this at the time. I had tasted Africa. I could now appreciate, to some extent at least, the spell which it cast on those who served there.

In May 1989, after a short period in hospital, my wife died. There was time to alert my son who flew from America. He simply took control of affairs. Although he had to return to Houston after the cremation ceremony, his presence did much to bring me through a period of life which all of us dread. Later in the month another event took place which helped to restore my mental equilibrium. Mary Chandler was married to a friend to whom I had been introduced, Adam Allen. Her father had died when she was young and I offered to give her away. This was a commitment which I knew my wife would have wanted me to honour and gave me great pleasure. After a few years I realised how fortunate I was at this time to have to return to duty and to become immersed in challenging work.

The flat which her father had occupied in Pau formed part of my wife's estate. She had let it unfurnished to a widow who had befriended her when her father died. My son and I discussed renovating the flat for our own use when the lease expired. Our French lawyers then revealed that the occupier had rights of renewal. She could not be dispossessed. The escape hatch was that if we wished to put the flat up for sale, we could do so. The occupier had to be offered first refusal. After discussion, we decided to do this and use the funds towards purchase of a house in the Lot, slightly nearer to the United Kingdom. Although my son has British citizenship, he is half French by blood and bilingual. I felt that it was important for him to continue to have a stake in France. We visited the Cahors area together and selected an old farmhouse with a manageable garden and a barn attached. It was in a small village called Flaynac, about eight kilometres from the city. Our friends the Barwicks had property near Villefranche du Perigord, about thirty kilometres distant. There is a circle of close friends in the area.

With their help I identified a French architect, obtained planning permission and put in hand the conversion of the barn into living quarters and a double garage. The conversion yielded a large lounge with the original beams and stone walls, a double bedroom and bathroom. We were pleased with the result. I paid brief visits during the conversion, travelling by air to Toulouse and onwards by train, some eighty minutes journey, to Cahors. I should like to have spent more holiday time there but had, very willingly, to pay frequent visits to my mother, who was now in her nineties. Most of my leave allocation was necessarily spent in Scotland. She enjoyed car travel. Hence in successive years I drove her to the Outer Hebrides and to various stretches of Western and Northern coastlines. She was remarkably resilient and good company for her years. The end inevitably came, at the age of ninety-nine years and nine months, in August 1995. My son inherited Hassendean, which dated back to 1760. It required renovation and he asked me to arrange this with

My house in Flaynac.

the help of a local architect. After renovating the house at Flaynac, I was used to frustrations and delays. The process took the best part of two years.

Meanwhile, when I was not in the London Office, I was managing my own house in Farnham. I was also looking after houses and gardens in France and Scotland. Sometimes these commitments made me realise that I was in my late seventies. I made it known that I should step aside from my post whenever a suitable replacement had been identified. But at the end of each contract I was requested to carry on for another two years. I still assessed that I had something to contribute.

It became my turn as Cayman Islands Government Representative to take over the chairmanship of the Dependent Territories Association. This was extended to cover a second Conference in February 1998, We had been pressing for extension of British citizenship to the inhabitants of all Dependent Territories to whom this had not been granted. Gibraltarians and Falkland Islanders already enjoyed this privilege. It allowed visa-free entry to European Community countries and entry, residential and working rights in the United Kingdom. We argued that this should not be reciprocal. Unfettered rights of entry and residence to small island territories could rapidly erode fragile ethnic balances. We had also discussed amendment of the term 'Dependent Territories' to

'British' or 'United Kingdom' Overseas territories. We knew that the Foreign and Commonwealth Office was conducting an in-house study of relations with the Dependent Territories and that Governors and Chief Ministers had been asked to submit their views. In parallel, the House of Commons Foreign Affairs Committee was conducting a Dependent Territories Review.[7] During this I was summoned, as Chairman of the Dependent Territories Association, to give evidence. It was an educative experience. The scene is familiar from television. The witness sits in the jaws of a horseshoe of the committee members. He or she is treated with the utmost courtesy. In the august precincts of the Committee rooms, however, responses have to be made with care. I was duly asked about the citizenship issue, the appropriate name for Dependencies, the procedure for the selection of Governors, relations between Governors, officials and elected Ministers, how these could be improved, mechanisms for apportioning British aid, my own qualifications for Governorship, and sundry other matters. Consequently the Foreign and Commonwealth Office published a White Paper on *Partnership with the United Kingdom Overseas Territories*. This was to be our new name. Suggestions in my testimony to the Committee did not materially differ from many of the procedures introduced. I was particularly pleased that my suggestion that there should be regular meetings of Chief Ministers was in line with the creation of an annual Forum. This has rectified an important political deficit. The final decision on British citizenship, which has since been approved by legislation, was not taken in time to be announced at the February Conference. Nevertheless the Secretary of State, who opened the Conference, gave a very positive indication that this was likely. In a paper written for the Dependent Territories Organisation, I had used the phrase 'Qualified nationhood' to describe the relationship a Dependent territory had to the international community. I was gratified to hear the term used by the Secretary of State at the Conference.

The Cayman Islands is a young, dynamic country. I felt increasingly that it was inappropriate that it was represented in London by a non-Caymanian approaching his eightieth birthday. I agreed to accept finally a year's extension of contract to give time for a successor to be appointed. There were also some frustrations. The extent to which the London Office could help in allaying international concerns about financial services was not fully appreciated. In addition, the pressure of work on

7. See *Foreign Affairs Committee. Second Report. Dependent Territories Review*, Interim Report, HMSO, London, 1988.

the Financial Secretary and his team was oppressive. It became increasingly difficult to obtain timely decisions. Profile Communications, the Public Relations company contracted to the Financial Secretary's portfolio, had sometimes to let important responses to press criticism go by default. Junior staff at the Cayman Islands end were over-protective of their own sphere of work. Information could not be released without higher approval. To my dismay, without reference to me, the decision was taken that the public relations company dealing with American affairs on the other side of the Atlantic should be responsible for United Kingdom affairs. Profile Corporate Communications still retained the Secretaryship of the United Kingdom Overseas Territories Association. It was, however, no longer responsible for the public affairs of the Cayman Islands in the United Kingdom.

Representation inevitably involved attendance at various seminars, conferences, receptions, dinners and ceremonial occasions. Most of these were work-related rather than social occasions. It would be tedious to précis an eighteen-year programme. Most memorable, perhaps were:

- Dinner at the Guildhall for the 75th anniversary of the Commonwealth Parliamentary Association.
- Ceremonies in Westminster Hall, attended by H.M. the Queen, for the 50th anniversary of United Nations.
- Annual attendances at the Labour and Conservative Party Conferences.
- Attending as a representative of the Royal Commonwealth Ex-Services League the 50th anniversaries of VE and VJ Days.
- Annual receptions given by the Gibraltar Representative, Albert Poggio, by the Falkland Islands Representative, Sukey Cameron, and the Cayman Islands, which had a stronger social element and were always enjoyable.

Jennifer Dilbert, a Caymanian graduate in Economics, who had been head of the Cayman Islands Currency Board, was selected to take over my post. Her father had been one of my Permanent Secretaries. She had also served in the private sector as head of Deutsche Bank operations in the Cayman Islands. She was on sabbatical leave in Canada when she applied for the post. She had wide experience in banking and financial services. She was an admirable choice. For various reasons, however, she was not immediately available. So much for the finality of my extension. I agreed to serve until September 2000, when I said goodbye to the office.

Hassendean, in Scotland, was standing empty. I now had no reason to

Hassendean.

remain permanently in the south. If I had to attend meetings in London, I would have no difficulty in finding accommodation. I had my house in France. I arranged with my son to lease Hassendean from him and put the Farnham house on the market. By June 2001 the house was sold. I returned to Scotland on the 1st July. The profile of the village has changed. I have been virtually absent since I went to St Andrews University in 1937 – a long gap of sixty-four years. I have been made to feel welcome. I am at home.

CHAPTER SEVENTEEN

Reflections

On the Past

Decolonisation of the Solomon Islands

In the last few years the Solomon Islands have descended into near-anarchy. They are still struggling to return to some semblance of order. Simplistically, past administrators can shelter behind the thought that at the time of Independence the country was well administered. Realistically they must acknowledge some of the blame.

Independence was granted in 1978. Fiji became Independent in 1970 and Papua New Guinea in 1975. Solomon Islands politicians were impatient to shake off the colonial yoke. Britain was content, if not eager, to remove it.

Yet in retrospect, the inheritance of the new administration was tarnished. Parliamentary government had existed for less than twenty years. Initial ministerial appointments were not made until 1974. The first general elections were held in 1967. Progress had been made in appointing Solomon Islanders to senior posts in the Civil Service and in the private sector. On Independence, many vacancies at senior level had to be filled by Solomon Islanders. The Civil Service had already been diluted by members who had stood for election and were now politicians. The Central Bank and Statutory Boards had to be serviced. Diplomats and senior staff for a new Ministry of Foreign Affairs had to be found. Pressure on the new government would increase to replace expatriates by local officers. Consequently Solomon Island Civil Servants were promoted into high-level posts before they had the training or the measure of experience required. These problems were foreseen in a percipient paper by Mr Kenneth Younger of Nuffield College, Oxford, in 1959. In this he advocated the formation of a Commonwealth Overseas Service.[8] Standards of financial control inevitably declined. Although the British Government undertook to fund the anticipated deficit in the budget for the three years following Independence, this support was finite.

There were other deep-seated problems. The Preamble to the Pre-

---

8. See PRO File CO 1017/522.

Independence Constitutional Conference in London lists six basic principles These include:

> Solomon Islands is a united nation in which different cultural traditions are recognised and respected.

and

> a commitment to decentralisation of legislative and executive power.[9]

The first of these is inaccurate; the second is misguided.

As events have proved, we had not had the time, before Independence, to weld the different islands and island groups into nationhood. Until 1918 the Shortland Islands, Choiseul and Ysabel had been under German rule. Before the British assumption of responsibility for the Protectorate in 1893, there had been traditional headhunting raids between different islands. Historic enmities and inter-island suspicions remained. Communications between islands were poor until before World War II. Improved shipping services and the introduction of air travel between islands brought a greater sense of cohesion. The numbers benefiting from these services were, however, small. The island dweller's social boundaries were those of his 'line' or lineage, and then of the language-speaking area in which it was based. Beyond that was the island or island group on which he was resident. There were about eighty different languages. It was difficult to contact those living in the interiors of the larger islands. The islands were distributed over thousands of square miles. These factors ran counter to the concept of the Solomon Islands being a united nation in 1978. They were administered as a territorial unit. They were recognised as such by the outside world. Drawing lines on maps, however, does not create a country, as history has shown.

If the Solomon Islands were not united at the time of Independence, the premature decentralisation of legislative and executive powers has contributed to disunity. Until Independence the Solomon Islands were administered by a strong central government divided into four districts. Each district had a District Commissioner, who was responsible for coordinating Central Government policy in his district. Under a system of Local Government, Councils were established in each district. These had power to make regulations on local issues. At Independence, district administration was scrapped. With the abolition of District Commissioners, the Central Government lost its executive and visible representation among the people. This was not a role which could be taken over completely by elected representatives of the national parliament. Of

---

9. See *Report of the Solomon Islands Constitutional Conference*, Cmd 6969. HMSO, London, 1977.

greater divisive significance, however, was the division of the Solomon Islands into nine Provinces with Provincial Parliaments replacing the District Councils. While the limits of legislative and executive powers were laid down, the ability of the periphery to take a line independent from that of the centre was immeasurably strengthened. This was to be shown later in confrontations on timber concessions.

The Solomons are well endowed with natural resources. Fertile soils have long fostered a strong peasant-farmer base of indigenous crops These, allied with fishing, largely support the rural community. The Government, at Independence, was left with substantial exports of copra, the dried flesh of the coconut. This depended as much on plantation production as on peasant farming. Part of the Independence package, however, was agreement for the new Government to convert all freehold land into leasehold. This had the effect of signalling to expatriate copra producers that their days were numbered. There were substantial exports of cocoa. Rice was being produced as a commercial crop on the Guadalcanal plains. A cattle industry was thriving. Timber concessions had been negotiated. To sustain the industry, concessionaires had to pay a royalty to Government, from which the deforested areas were replanted by the Forestry Department. Alternatively, they could opt not to pay a royalty. If so, they had to carry out replanting themselves to the satisfaction of the Department. Tuna fishing had been established on a commercial scale. A Japanese company was given the concession. This was subject to close inspection of its activities and the financing and operation of a cannery in the islands. Mining concessions had been negotiated but placed on hold because of adverse market conditions. Gold mining was to come on stream shortly after Independence.

Income from these activities did not keep pace with increasing expenditure and political aspirations. Honiara, as the capital, increasingly became a mecca for small Melanesian businesses, labourers and unemployed on the look-out for work. Many of these came from Malaita. Matters came to a head in 1999, when the Guadalcanal Province sought substantial reparations from the Government for placing the capital in their Province. Some of the Guadalcanal people styled themselves as the Isatabu Freedom Movement. They raided the police armoury in Honiara and forced members of the community from Malaita to return to that island. This could only provoke one result. Malaitans formed an opposing movement, the Malaita Eagles. They similarly raided the police armoury on Malaita and returned to Honiara in force. By mid 2000 there was armed warfare in Honiara. Wanton destruction of property took place, including bridges on the main coastal road leading to the capital from both sides. The airport was besieged. Flights into Guadalcanal were suspended. Workers were prevented from working at the Gold Ridge gold mine. The Commonwealth Development Corporation oil palm plantations on the Gudalcanal Plains and the associated oil mill were closed. Production ceased. Exports declined. The treasury coffers were soon empty. Imports of oil, foodstuffs, and medical supplies dried up. Many Civil Servants were laid off as there was no money to pay them. The Prime Minister was effectively prevented from discharging the duties of his office for a period. Road blocks were set up on each side of Honiara by the Malaitans. Consumption of drugs and alcohol fomented the situation. There were gratuitous shootings, including one incident at the main hospital. A wounded man had been brought in for surgery. His assailants burst in to the operating theatre to finish him off on the table.

The Roman Catholic and Anglican churches were a moderating influence upon the situation The international community eventually succeeding in arranging a conference in Australia, the Townsville Peace Agreement, at which some semblance of agreement to cease the violence was obtained. But implementing this and restoring the authority of the police force has proved difficult. Much of the money contributed from overseas in the hopes of restoring the economy has been spent to compensate the relatives of victims of violence on both sides.

The Townsville Peace Agreement can not be said to be a landmark on the route to normality. Indeed, according to an ABC News Report, the Australian Defence Association has said that it will take more than a decade to reorganise financial and administrative infrastructure in the Solomon Islands. Lawlessness has spawned further insurrection. On the weather coast of Guadalcanal, the Guadalcanal Liberation Front has been formed. Its leader, Howard Keke, and his armed followers are reported to have committed a number of murders, to have seized hostages, burnt at least one large village, and displaced up to 1,500 islanders.

Pacific countries, led by Australia, have realised that a destabilised island nation could rapidly develop into a haven for international criminals. Consequently they have resolved, with legislated approval by the Solomon Islands Government, to send in a multi-national peace-keeping force of about 2000 strong. As at 25th July 2003, the advance party has now landed. The contingent will include a strong element from New Zealand and others from Fiji, Tonga, Samoa, Papua New Guinea and Vanuatu.

The armed component of the Force is to support police sent in to stiffen a demoralised and indisciplined local Force, to quell the insurrection, and restore order. The peace-keeping force will also contain a strong contingent of experienced expatriate civil servants and administrators to assist a crumbling local Civil Service, to restore the economy and an effective administration. The following months will determine whether reinforced local police units or extraneous armed forces will be required to quell the insurrection and lawlessness.

Undoubtedly it will take many years before the economy and an effective government can be resurrected. The damage to a 'united government' is incalculable.

Ironically, the Solomon Islands were declared a Protectorate in 1893 to stop the excesses of the indentured labour trade and headhunting. This was being exacerbated by distribution of arms and liquor. In the year 2000, the fracas between the Guadalcanal and Malaita people was exacerbated by the arms obtained from looted police stations and from imported supplies. Liquor and drugs also inflamed the situation. Now, however, there is no pax Britannica.

On the Present

The Cayman Islands and the remaining United Kingdom Overseas Territories.
Of Britain's vast colonial heritage, it is now responsible for only ten inhabited territories. These still span four of the world's oceans. In the Atlantic there are Bermuda, St Helena and the Falkland Islands. In the Caribbean are situated the Turks and Caicos Islands, the Cayman Islands, the British Virgin Islands, Montserrat and Anguilla. Gibraltar lies at the gateway to the Mediterranean. Pitcairn is the only Dependency left in the Pacific. The total population of these territories is probably under 200,000. Gibraltar, which has its constitutional future inhibited by the Treaty of Utrecht, would like closer association with Britain, like the Isle of Man or Channel Islands. The Falkland Islands, because of Argentina's claims on their sovereignty and the Falklands' War, have special reasons for retaining current links with Britain. Pitcairn, with a population of less than one hundred, could not be independently viable. The remaining seven Overseas Territories have evinced no wish to become Independent. Bermuda and the Cayman Islands are nevertheless mature and further advanced politically and economically, than any of the Pacific territories when they espoused Independence.

There was a noticeable détente in the policy of accelerated decolonisation in the late 1970's. The last of the Pacific Territories were en route to Independence. The Seychelles and British Honduras were on track. There was some mopping up to do in the West Indies. In 1983 Brunei became Independent at the end of the main historic span of decolonisation which had begun in 1948. Perhaps because the remaining territories were small, with individual populations below 60,000, viability seemed less certain. A review of policy towards the remaining Caribbean territories and Bermuda took place in 1987. It was recommended that Britain should not press Territories to become Independent. The previous United Kingdom policy had been: 'Independence is our goal. But we will not grant this if your people are not ready to go. They can choose the time'. The new policy was: 'If you want Independence, we will do everything to assist you to obtain this, provided that we are sure that your people want it. But if you wish to remain an Overseas Territory, that is acceptable'. The United Kingdom was, to all appearances, now committed to the possibility of retaining the remnants of empire in perpetuity. Future governments, however, are not bound by the policies of their predecessors.

In the break-up of the West Indies Federation, it was recognised that there was a danger in advancing constitutions too far before a date for Independence had been agreed. Britain was then left in the position of having surrendered power but retaining responsibility. The rule of thumb was that if a Territory was granted full internal self-government by constitutional change, Independence would follow about eighteen months later. There was some concern over Belize, which, as British Honduras, was granted Independence in 1981. Having been granted full internal self-government as a prelude to Independence, it held elections. The Opposition favoured remaining a British Colony. Had it won the elections, the question would then have arisen whether the existing constitution had gone too far for a continuing colonial relationship.

In 1999 the Foreign and Commonwealth Office published a White Paper, *Partnership for Progress and Prosperity*.[10] This was a review of relationships between Britain and its Dependent Territories. These in future were to be known as United Kingdom Overseas Territories. It was a recognition of the need to reach an understanding on what could possibly be a long relationship.

The new partnership was to be based on the principles of self-determination and freedom for the Territories to run their own affairs to the greatest degree possible. Suggestions for constitutional modernisation were to be considered.

---

10. See *Partnership for Progress and Prosperity. Foreign and Commonwealth Office White Paper*, Cmd 4264, HMSO, Stationery Office.

The White Paper on Partnership grants full British citizenship to the residents of the Overseas Territories which did not have it. This is not reciprocal. British residents will not be able to enter, reside and work in the Overseas Territories without control. Nevertheless it is patently obvious in the White Paper who is the senior partner. As the administering power, the British Government deems itself responsible for the Good Governance of Overseas Territories. It retains legislative powers. Her Majesty, under current Overseas Territories constitutions, reserves the right, on the advice of Her Privy Council, to make laws for the peace, order and good government of the Territory. If agreement cannot be reached, it can dictate what it expects of the junior partners. The subject on which disagreement has arisen may well have been delegated under Overseas Territory constitutions to elected Ministers. The British Government contributes to budgetary finance in only two of the territories. A number of them have ceased to qualify for British aid.

In parallel with granting greater devolution of powers to United Kingdom Overseas Territories, there is evidence of a greater hands-on approach by London. This stems both from using modern management techniques in the delicate field of political relations and from international pressures. In the area of financial services, pressure is brought upon the British Government by the European Union (EU), the Organisation for Economic Co-operation and Development (OECD) the Financial Action Task Force, United States Government Agencies and United Nations Agencies. The Treasury and Inland Revenue in the United Kingdom are likely to press the Foreign and Commonwealth Office to enforce similar measures in the Overseas Territories to those agreed for the United Kingdom. In respect of the Caribbean Territories, a Ministerial group meets regularly to co-ordinate British policy across a wide range of subjects. Many of these affect matters for which elected Ministers are responsible in the Territories.

The Treasury clings grimly to its powers to intervene in Overseas Territory affairs. Initially, when British funds are used to supplement local budgets, it has a legitimate right to approve them. It can thus control the extent to which the United Kingdom contributes. Usually when a Territory succeeds in coming out of Grant-in-Aid, as budgetary assistance is known, it will still be receiving development grants. The Department for International Development (DfID) and the Treasury can then influence economies through Development Plans and Country Papers. This continues to the stage at which a country prospers further and no longer qualifies for Development grants. It may, however, qualify for Development loans. When its Gross Domestic Product rises to the level when it no longer qualifies for loans from British funds, the case for outside interference with the Territory's finances becomes tenuous. Yet borrowing of any kind has to be enshrined in local loans legislation. This must be approved by the Foreign and Commonwealth Office. Such procedure stems from the liability of the British Government to repay the loans if for any reason the Overseas Territory defaults on the loan. In recent years, although many Overseas Territories are standing on their own feet financially, their finances are still subject to detailed scrutiny by the United Kingdom. The right to do so is justified on grounds of 'contingent liability'. In 1997 a study of the five Caribbean Dependencies was undertaken by the National Audit Office.[11] It endeavoured to assess the United Kingdom's commitment if financial or other disasters struck. In the light of the Montserrat volcanic eruption and subsequent heavy financial input by the United Kingdom, it can be argued that the review was prudent.

It is however a bold policy to decrease constitutional controls for an indefinite period while attempting to impose an increasing level of policies from London. Many of these are the result of international treaties to which the United Kingdom is a signatory. On some of these the opinion of the Overseas Territory may not have been sought.

One must ask whether the local Executive Councils, Cabinets, or Councils of Ministers, the captains of their constitutional vessels, will indefinitely accept the advice of the Foreign and Commonwealth Office as the pilot. Problems are certain to emerge. It may be useful to endeavour to determine what these might be.

The most likely area of conflict is that of external affairs. This is reserved to Her Majesty's Government through the Governor. But the interests of the Overseas Territory and that of United Kingdom are not always compatible, as the current situation in Gibraltar illustrates. As a member of the European Union, United Nations and a host of international bodies, United Kingdom is a signatory to many international agreements and conventions. It is often expected to bring its overseas territories into line. When I was Chairman of the Dependent Territories Association, I received a letter in 1998 from the Hon. Pamela Gordon, Chief Minister of Bermuda.[12] This followed a meeting of Chief Ministers of the Caribbean. It was brought to my attention that:

---

11. *Report on Contingent Liabilities in Dependent Territories*, National Audit Office, 1997.
12. *Foreign Affairs Committee. Second Report. Dependent Territories Review. Interim Report.* Published by HMSO, 1998.

During the course of the discussions the delegates were unanimous in expressing their grave concern at the increasing tendency of the British Government to impose decisions on the Dependent Territories in the Caribbean, without consultation in some cases, without the agreement of the countries concerned.

The pace and complexity of international affairs, and the absence of representatives of Overseas territories at many Conferences where their interests are being discussed, are likely to compromise the partnership arrangements in the White Paper.

Despite the commitment to partnership in the White Paper, the second area of concern is that of trust. It is not difficult to draw the conclusion that the United Kingdom regards its relationship with the larger metropolitan countries as of greater national importance than the partnership arrangement with her Overseas Territories. Although Gibraltar does not fall within the ambit of the Partnership White Paper, the recent attempt by Britain to reach agreement with Spain on the future of Gibraltar, without the agreement of the elected government of Gibraltar, adds credence to this thesis.

Another goal of the White Paper is Good Governance in the Overseas Territories, particularly in the fields of financial services, human rights, the ecology and drug trafficking. This, as already stated, is assumed as a British responsibility. Good Governance in the United Kingdom is determined by the electorate. In the Overseas Territories some political parties may have campaigned for election on human rights issues such as the death penalty and homosexuality. Elected Ministers may also have been assigned responsibility, under their constitutions, for a subject such as the ecology. Under the reserved power to legislate for Overseas Territories, the British Government has used Orders-in-Council to annul the death penalty in the Caribbean Territories and also to legalise homosexuality between consenting adults. When there are conflicting views between Overseas Territories in the Caribbean and the British Government, it may be hinted that use of an Order-in-Council is a trump card held by the senior partner. This can lead to a souring of the relationship.

I have mentioned the continuing interest of the Treasury in the finances of the Overseas Territories. Contingent liabilities are a concern. In the year 2000 the shortfall in Government Revenue in the Cayman Islands was CI$33.5 million. Expenditure was CI$10.2 million over budget and unpaid expenditure for the year amounted to CI$22 million.

While the current budgetary situation has improved, a recent Bond issue has raised for the Government the sum of $US163.5 million repayable over fifteen years. The introduction of Private Partnership Initiative programmes will lead to further expenditure which will not feature in the Government accounts. One estimate puts further capital projects at a level of CI$120 million. Bond servicing and rental of PPI facilities will, however, augment future recurrent expenditure where the root of the problem is embedded.

With the modernisation of Civil Services and the converting of Government Departments into Agencies and Statutory bodies, liabilities will increase sharply. Salaries are likely to be revised to private sector levels. Loans will be taken out. These may not have to be sanctioned by loans legislation. Pensionable liabilities will be augmented. If commitments cannot be met, the Local Government has to step in. If the cumulative debts are too much for the Local Government, the British Government is ultimately responsible. Many of the Caribbean Overseas Territories are dependent upon revenues from financial services, tourism and real estate. There is severe pressure on the regulation of financial services and exchange of information. The European Union is now pressing to introduce the Savings Directive to which I referred on page 209. This will oblige the governments of British Overseas Territories in the Caribbean either to report on deposits or investments by European Union citizens in their financial institutions, or alternatively to tax interest or dividends at a fixed rate. The right of the European Union to impose such a measure on a non-Member has been challenged by the Cayman Islands Government in March 2003 in the European Union Court of First Instance in Luxembourg. The *Caymanian Compass* reports that the Court ruled that the European Union cannot directly impose the Directive. Nor could it be argued that the United Kingdom was legally bound by the Directive to impose the same measures on the Cayman Islands. This however begs the question whether the United Kingdom, if so minded, could impose the Directive by Order in the Council. There is no direct taxation in the Cayman Islands. It is ironic that the American War of Independence began over an effort by the British government to tax the settlers in America against their will and without direct representation in the British parliament. Admittedly exchange of information is an alternative to taxation.

It is thus possible that revenues from financial services will decline. As the events on the 11th September, 2001 showed, revenue from tourism can also decline rapidly. This includes receipts from the Customs tariff on luxuries, food and drink consumed by the visitors. A proposal by the World Trade Organisation was to grade countries according to Gross

National Product. Import duty would be abolished or reduced in the richer countries. Some of the Caribbean Overseas Territories could be affected. They might not have delegates at the conference table to make their case. Although the proposal is unlikely to be adopted in its present form, it reveals a total disregard for countries which have chosen indirect taxation as their main fiscal impost. If revenues in Caribbean Overseas Territories declined, and contingent liabilities increased, there might be Treasury pressure to re-examine the current British policy of indefinite responsibility for Overseas Territories. Positioning Overseas Territories on the edge of full internal self-government increases their vulnerability to a future policy change to revert to decolonisation.

The United Kingdom Overseas Territories Association (formerly the Dependent Territories Association) held two successful conferences in London. It can claim much of the credit for bringing the Overseas Territories together into a mutually supporting group. It has strongly supported Gibraltar in its effort to divest itself of its constitutional straitjacket. It has urged the Foreign and Commonwealth Office to secure the funds to construct an airfield on St Helena. This country, and Pitcairn, share the melancholy distinction of dependency upon irregular shipping for their contacts with the outside world. The Foreign and Commonwealth Office now holds annual meetings of the Chief Ministers of the different Overseas Territories. As has been illustrated by the letter from the Chief Minister of Bermuda (p. 224), these can be preceded by pre-meeting discussions by the Chief Ministers. Should one of the Territories step too far out of line, the sanction in the past has been suspension of the Constitution. Now that individual territories keep in close touch with each other, such a step could provoke a united response. Overseas Territories have no direct representation in either the House of Lords or the House of Commons. There are however various Territory Interest groups in the House of Commons. The Foreign Affairs Committee there monitors relations between the Government and Britain's Overseas Territories. A united approach by the Chief Ministers acting in concert would attract immediate attention.

On the Present

The Cayman Islands

The White Paper had promised modernisation of constitutions There was still no wish to proceed to Independence in the Cayman Islands. Politicians, however, considered that it was time to examine the Constitution. This, with some amendments, had remained substantially unchanged since 1972. A Commission was established and made recommendations. These were considered jointly by representatives of the Foreign and Commonwealth Office and the Cayman Islands Government in late 2002. A draft constitution has been drafted and sent to the Islands in February 2003 for public comment. This indicates how far, within a United Kingdom Overseas Territory context, the United Kingdom Government is prepared to go to meet local political wishes for change.

The definition of the Governor's role remains substantially unchanged.

> The Governor shall, for the purpose of administering the government of the Cayman Islands, have such powers and duties as are conferred and imposed upon him by this Constitution or any other law and such other powers as Her Majesty may assign him.

The new Constitution has, however, to be interpreted against a background of substantial modernisation of administration and financial practice enshrined in local laws. The administration of the public service appears to be reserved for the Governor to determine in his discretion. In practice the Governor's powers to make substantial changes soon after new systems have been introduced, are limited.

The following are the main changes proposed:

- Fundamental rights and freedoms of the individual are described.
- A post of Deputy Governor, to be filled by a Caymanian is created. He will be head of the Civil Service under the authority of the Governor. It is likely that this post will replace that of Chief Secretary.
- An Advisory Committee will be established to advise the Governor on grants of pardon and remissions or respites of sentences.
- The Executive Council will be replaced by a Cabinet over which the Governor shall normally preside. This will consist of the Governor, the holder of the new post of Chief Minister, six other Ministers and the Deputy Governor and Attorney General *ex-officio*. The Chief Minister and Ministers will be appointed from elected membership of the Legislative Assembly.
- One of the Ministers will be designated Minister of Finance. He will preside over the Finance Committee of the Legislative Assembly.
- The post of Secretary to the Cabinet is created. In addition to existing functions performed by the Clerk to the Executive Council, he and his office will be responsible both to the Governor and the Chief Minister for developing and coordinating government policy.
- The duties of the post of Solicitor General are described. He will

directly take over responsibilities for prosecution which were previously the responsibility of the Attorney General.

- The number of elected members in the Legislative Assembly will be increased from fifteen to seventeen. The number of *ex-officio* members will be decreased from three to one, the Attorney General.
- The Speaker will be appointed from outside the membership of the Assembly. The Deputy Speaker will be elected from the membership.
- There will be a new appointment of Leader of the Opposition.
- There will in future be seventeen electoral constituencies with one elected member for each constituency, A Boundary Commission will be established to delineate the constituencies.[13]

The change to Ministerial government follows past precedent in the former decolonial process. It bears similarity to the pre-Independence constitution for the Solomon Islands on page 156f. It brings the Cayman Islands to the verge of full internal self-government. It is, however, not meant to be a staging-post, but a constitution which will define relationships with the United Kingdom for the indefinite future.

None of the controls exercisable by the United Kingdom in the original 1972 Constitution has been relaxed. All laws enacted in the Cayman Islands still have to be sent to London for non-disallowance, a clumsy euphemism for approval. The Crown still retains the right to legislate for the good order, public faith and Good Governance of the Territory. The Governor may, under certain circumstances and with the consent of the Secretary of State, return Bills or Motions which have been rejected by the Assembly, to be passed. If they fail to do so, he can deem them to have passed.

These are all sanctions for emergency situations The Constitution, however, purports to be the blueprint for the administration of the islands on a day-to-day basis. It may well have gone too far to endure as a permanent constitutional arrangement. I identify the following weaknesses:

- The discarding of two of the three *ex-officio* members from the Legislative Assembly, including the Chief Secretary or Deputy Governor, leaves no-one with inside knowledge to speak for the Civil Service or the other reserved subjects (Defence, external affairs, internal security including police).

---

13. See *Draft of the Cayman Islands Constitution Order 200 [3]*. Published by Cayman Islands Government Information Service, 13th February, 2003.

These will necessarily have to be assigned either to the only official in the Assembly, the Attorney General, or, as seems permissible under the new Constitution, to an Elected Minister *for the purpose of conducting government business in such matters in the Legislative Assembly.* In small territories there is little anonymity. Naming and hoped-for-shaming of Civil Servants is far more common than in the House of Commons. As naming may well have the political backing of the party in power, adequate defence by another member of the party will be difficult to demonstrate.

- Hitherto, although the Governor has presided over the Executive Council, he has not been a member, as, constitutionally, the Executive Council advises him. By making the Governor a member of the Cabinet, he is now in the position of being in a body which advises himself and the advice of which he can subsequently reject. There will be strong Ministerial objection to any decision by the Governor not to accept Cabinet advice. Ministers are bound by collective responsibility to follow decisions reached in Cabinet. Hence they may find the Governor's ability, as a fellow member, not to do so, particularly galling.

- The proposed new Constitution provides for each Minister *to be assisted by a board or committee . . . consisting wholly or partly of persons who are not public officers and established by a law made under this Constitution or by directions given in writing by the Minister concerned, and any such body shall have such advisory, consultative and administrative functions as may be conferred upon it . . . but shall be subject to the directions of the Minister concerned.*

  Appointees to such a board or committee will not be public servants and will bypass the Governor's sole right to appoint to the public service. Moreover, until a law is passed, a Minister will be able to circumvent his Permanent Secretary, whose powers will be greatly weakened by the establishment of such a body. Numbers and remuneration are not prescribed.

- While the Chairman of the Public Service Commission is to be appointed by the Governor in his discretion, the membership, a minimum of four, is to be appointed with the approval of the Chief Minister and Leader of the Opposition. The Civil Service Commission is appointed to ensure that Civil Service appointments are not politicised. This new provision gives a contrary indication. Moreover in any amendment to the Civil (now Public) Service Commission Law, there are indications that there will be significant decentralisation of powers to appoint without Commission and subsequent Governor's approval. This will leave the Commission largely as an appellate body for appointments and the authority dealing with disciplinary cases.

The new draft Constitution begins with a preamble stating the intention to be a country with sixteen aims. While this lists many attributes of the country, and the desire to continue them, it makes no mention of the dedication and contribution, past and present, of the Civil Service. This has been one of the strengths of the Cayman Islands. It has loyally supported whatever political régime has been in power. Permanent Secretaries have, to the best of their ability, served their political masters. They have also kept informed the managers of the service, the Financial Secretary, the Chief Secretary, and through them the Governor, of political priorities affecting the service, and of impediments to implementation. They have managed their portfolios of Departments with varying degrees of knowledge, efficiency and skill.

By increasing the powers of elected politicians, the draft Constitution has inevitably reduced the mechanisms for the defence of the Civil Service in the legislature, the ability of Permanent Secretaries to perform their traditional role, and possibly the ability of the Civil Service Commission to exhibit a non-political aspect.

Most importantly, however, the role of Governor is subtly changing It is true that the sanctions remain for the United Kingdom to have greater budgetary control should the Territory ever require financial help from United Kingdom. Day-to-day administration of the country's finances, however, will now be entirely in the hands of elected politicians. The numbers of *ex-officio* members have been reduced in the Legislative Assembly and the Cabinet. There are possible changes in the Permanent Secretaries' role. The result could be that the Governor's ability to intervene in decision-making before draft subsidiary legislation and Bills come before him formally in the Cabinet, is drastically reduced. Should relations with the Chief Minister sour, he will have no greater advantage in influencing policies than a High Commissioner in a Commonwealth country or an Ambassador in a foreign jurisdiction. His role will become largely representational and consist in reporting to London. With modern communications, he is unlikely to exercise any sanctions in the draft Constitution without prior concurrence or approval from London in times of crisis. Current practice of visits by senior officials and Ministers from London only serve to reduce the Governor's local standing. Increasingly he is in danger of being seen as a Regulator applying sanctions on instructions from London.

Thoughts. The practice and the realities will hinge largely on the personalities of the Governor and the Chief Minister and their commitment to making the Constitution work. This seems abundantly clear on both sides.

The introduction of a new Constitution has, however, been clouded by the delivery of a Judgement by the Chief Justice of the Cayman Islands, the Honourable Anthony Smellie QC, in January 2003. This has revealed matters which undermine the essential layer of trust which is the foundation of the concept of partnership.

Politics embrace the relationship of the individual to the State. When an individual consults professionally his lawyer, his doctor, his accountant, his banker, he expects confidentiality. The State is concerned only if the individual, or his consultant, or both, are transgressing the law. The professional bodies for each of the professions have elaborate codes of practice to ensure that their members operate within the law. In the Cayman Islands these are rigorously enforced. Police forces also endeavour to ascertain whether individuals and their professional consultants are operating within the legal framework. The Government, in close co-operation with the profession, repeatedly amends legislation to meet the sophistication of the global market in financial services. So far, so good, within the confines of the country's boundaries.

International finance, however, does not acknowledge boundaries. Crime prospers in countries with lax legislation, codes of practice, monitoring and inspection. Hence there is international agreement, spurred on by the spectre of international terrorism, to monitor more closely the international financial marketing system. Cross-border monitoring of monetary flows and suspicious transactions is vital. Impediments are the traditional client/professional confidentiality and the restriction on officials of monetary authorities and central banks from divulging information gained in the course of their duties. Legislation has been enacted to allow information to be passed, in certain circumstances, between the controlling authorities of banks and financial institutions. As a further development, there has been established a network of Financial Intelligence Units which liaise on international financial crime. The Cayman Islands organisation, called the Financial Reporting Unit (FRU), was commanded by an experienced ex-Scotland Yard Police Officer. The Unit was administratively responsible to the British Attorney General, David Ballantyne, an experienced law officer of probity and acumen, one of the three official members of the Executive Council. Its existence had come under political and press scrutiny. The case for its existence was acknowledged. Prophetically, attention focussed on its accountability.

A prosecution was brought at the end of 2002 against four individuals formerly employed in a bank which was closed on the advice of the Monetary Authority. Much of the evidence for the prosecution came from FRU sources. Reportedly it emerged from the trial that the head of the FRU received payments from a United Kingdom Agency which has been assumed to be MI6. The head of the FRU had an informant in the bank from whom much of the evidence had been derived and which had been reported to the Agency. The relationship between the head of the FRU and the informer was queried by defence counsel during the trial. His relationship to an Agency in London, where further evidence was understood to be available, then came to light. This had not been disclosed to the defence counsel. It is reported that an effort was made to weed certain evidence of any intelligence information which the authorities did not wish revealed to the general public. Some evidence was also reportedly destroyed on instructions from London by the head of the FRU. In face of these developments, and on a statement by the Attorney-General that the prosecution had no further evidence to present, the Chief Justice instructed the jury to bring in verdicts of 'Not Guilty' against the accused.

The political fall-out has been substantial. It is against a background of years of reform of commercial and financial legislation to comply with a relentless stream of international demands. The two main concerns are:

- That a covert operation was apparently mounted by British Intelligence in a British Overseas Territory.
- That this was apparently known by senior British officials of the Cayman Islands Government, while no elected politician was informed.

The head of the FRU has resigned and has left the Territory. Calls for the resignation of the Attorney-General were made. The local Bar Association and Law Society issued a joint statement advocating his resignation. A formal vote of No Confidence was passed by the Legislative Assembly. The situation merited discussion with Baroness Amos, then Overseas Territories Minister, during a visit. The *Caymanian Compass* reports that the outcome was that the Attorney General and the Cayman Islands Government agreed that his contract of employment be terminated by mutual agreement. The Attorney General would be entitled to the remuneration due for the remaining balance of his contractual period. Subsequently Questions were asked about the affair in the House of Commons.

It was reported in the *Caymanian Compass* that the Leader of Government Business, likely to be the Chief Minister when the new Constitution becomes effective, initially alleged that 'The United Kingdom has a plan to destroy us'. In a later statement, however, he made clear that his Government would continue to work with the United Kingdom. There was no desire to escalate matters to move towards Independence.

The official British line is that, while it regrets the turn of events, its actions were justifiable. In a statement made by Baroness Amos, the Overseas Territories Minister, on the 20th January 2003, she states:

> We have an international duty to deploy all the resources at our disposal in the global fight against financial and other crime. This will, of course, include our intelligence agencies. The very nature of this sensitive work means that it cannot be publicised, and that the appropriate safeguards must be in place to protect the integrity of operations and the safety of the individuals involved.

From the Caymanian point of view, it is difficult for one partner fully to trust another who has been caught searching his personal baggage. United Kingdom is responsible for the defence of its Overseas Territories. This subject is reserved under their constitutions. During the Cold War era, few would have queried the justification for covert operations for defence purposes. Using intelligence services in the commercial sphere in an Overseas Territory is not simply a matter of redefining targets. They will be operating in subject areas delegated under the Cayman Islands Constitution to Caymanian members of the Executive Council. Caymanians are now British subjects. If British-born officials have been advised in general terms of the operations, the question of trust again arises. The White Paper laid emphasis on the importance of the rule of law. A bank employee was engaged by someone purportedly in receipt of funds from a British Agency to break Caymanian Banking Law. This does not show the mother country in the best light to the Caymanian legislator.

On the Future

The Cayman Islands
Since 1972 there have been very few constitutional amendments of substance affecting the legislature. Elected members of the Executive

Council in the Cayman Islands have been re-designated Ministers. They and members of the Assembly have been increased in number. The duties of an independent Judiciary, Audit and Complaints Commissioner have been defined. These changes took place in the face of local concern that even minor change could trigger self-government and Independence. The people have repeatedly expressed the wish to retain existing ties with Britain as an Overseas Territory.

One of the proposals in the White Paper was the modernisation of Constitutions. A Commission consisting of three Caymanians from outside the Legislative Assembly was appointed. It took soundings from all walks of life and in all parts of the territory. Most of its recommendations have popular support. They have formed the basis for the 2003 draft Constitution. They are substantial. They will bring the Territory to the margins of internal self-government. They have sparked the formation of political parties. None of the devolutionary recommendations has been challenged. Dispute arose on whether the present system of voting for a block of candidates in the larger constituencies should be replaced by a system of 'one man, one vote'. This proposal was ultimately accepted. There was some pressure to have a referendum on approving the new proposals.

It is no longer unfashionable to talk about constitutional change. Indeed in April 2003 the Cayman Islands Chamber of Commerce invited the Chairman of the United Nations Special Committee on Decolonisation (The 'Committee of Twenty-four') to address them on the subject of decolonisation. He is reported to have said that there are three options – independence: free association: and integration. The United Kingdom appears to be veering towards free association to the degree that the United Nations will no longer regard its relationship with the Territory to be one of Colonial status. Time will tell whether this is a permanent solution.

There is still no wish for Independence. Once, however, politicians are virtual masters in their own house, one of the parties, as has happened elsewhere, could campaign in future on an Independence ticket. It could also happen that the United Kingdom demanded alterations to Cayman Islands Law or business practices which the financial community and the Government considered would wreck the economy. Independence could be seen as the only escape hatch. Although unlikely in the short term, United Kingdom policy towards Overseas Territories could change to renounce perpetuity of the relationship with its territories overseas.

Caymanians may be unaware that if a decision is taken to become Independent, the processes would be completed in less than a year. In Swaziland the resolution by the Swaziland Government to request Independence was made in September 1967. Independence was granted on 6th September 1968.[14] The Cayman Islands receive virtually no British aid. There would not be the complication of a compensation scheme for British staff losing a career. Hence the check list of 170 processes for Swaziland Independence might be shorter. The gap between a request for Independence and Independence Day could well be less than twelve months.

An election campaign is euphoric and brief. The electorate might well be induced to vote for a Party campaigning on an Independence policy. Voters, in voting for personalities, might not have full knowledge of the issues and of the irreversibility of the decision. This argues for a political awareness campaign where the advantages and disadvantages of Independence, in Caymanian circumstances, are dispassionately examined.

Some time after the introduction of the new Constitution, an option might be to follow this up with a second Public Enquiry. The terms of reference would state categorically that at the current time there was no wish for Independence. However, the scope of enquiry would be to assess the pros and cons of Independence. It should determine the optimum time scale needed, from a Cayman Island point of view, between a decision in principle to go Independent and casting off the hawser. It would be required to consult professional bodies In particular it should seek the views of leaders in the fields of banking, insurance, law, accounting, tourism, real estate and the Chamber of Commerce. Civil servants should be given freedom to express opinions. Witnesses should be allowed to give evidence anonymously, in camera, if they so wish. The problems for Defence and Internal Security should be assessed, as well as the extent to which there should be representation overseas. The effects on the economy should be evaluated. The Commissioners would be authorised to travel abroad to consult United Kingdom parliamentarians, Foreign and Commonwealth officials, the Commonwealth Secretariat and representatives of other Caribbean governments now Independent.

Such a study could not be undertaken secretly. This would give rise to the belief that Independence was being planned, The results of such a study would inform the Caymanian public of what the main advantages

14. PRO CO/106/33.

and disadvantages were. If, at some time in the future, what is now the bogey of Independence were raised, they would have objective information on the issues involved. The study might well reinforce the view that continued relationships with Britain for as long as possible were in the best interests of the islands. It could also be of value to other Caribbean Overseas Territories as a study commissioned by a sister government in circumstances similar to their own.

On the Present

Personal

I am back to my roots in Scotland, living in the house where I was born. Surprisingly, after thirty-four years in the tropics, I am not deterred by the Scottish winters. After six eye operations, I can no longer read a number-plate at twenty-three metres. Consequently, although my long-distance vision in reasonably good, I have had to surrender my driving licence. I have invested in an electrically-powered bicycle, equipped with capacious pouches on each side of the rear wheel. This allows me to do my shopping in Melrose, a mile distant from the house. My health is good, although my short leg has tilted the pelvis. One of the discs in my spine is below par. I have given up all civic commitments apart from my membership of Council on the Royal Commonwealth Ex-Services League. I also serve on the League's Executive Committee and as Chairman of the Welfare Committee. This takes me to London up to nine times a year for meetings, although a certain amount of work can be done by E-mail and fax. I visit my house in France two or three times a year and hope to winter there in future. I rely on public transport to get to London. I can be in my club in London about seven hours after leaving home. I keep up my Pacific connections through the Pacific Islands Society and Pacific reunions in Solihull and in Devon. There is still warm camaraderie among those of us who worked there. This year I visited my son in Texas. Thereafter I flew to the Cayman Islands to visit friends. Festivities were taking place for the 500th anniversary of the discovery of the islands by Christopher Columbus. Next year I have plans to go to New Zealand and Australia, where many ex-colleagues live. On a subsequent trip I hope to visit friends in America and my nephews and nieces in Canada.

My mother would have said, 'If I'm spared'. But for the time being I can still say,

I HAVE THE HONOUR TO BE.

APPENDIX 1

Table of Sources

p. 35 The Culture of Marovo. T. Russell *Journal of the Polynesian Society* Vol 57 No 6. 1948.

p. 41 Previous cult movements. Personal knowledge. See also Some Marching Rule Stories by the late Colin H Allan printed in the *Journal of Pacific History* Vol 9 1974.

p. 105 *On Crown Service* by Anthony Kirk-Greene published by I.B. Tauris 1999

p. 124 PRO File CO 1036/403.

p. 135 PRO File CO 1036/712.

p. 139 PRO File CO 1036/1291.

p. 214 *Foreign Affairs Committee. Second Report. Dependent Territories Review*: Interim Report. Published by HMSO 1998.

p. 217 PRO File CO 1017/522.

p. 218 *Report of the Solomon Islands Constitutional Conference*. London, 1977. Cmd 6969. Published by HMSO.

p. 222 *Partnership for Progress and Prosperity. Foreign and Commonwealth Office White Paper*. Cmd 4264. Printed for HMSO by the Stationery Office.

p. 223 *Report on Contingent Liabilities in Dependent Territories*. Printed by National Audit Office 1997.

p. 224 Quoted at p.81 of *Foreign Affairs Committee. Second Report. Dependent Territories Review. Interim Report*. Published by HMSO. 1998.

Appendix 3
Cayman Islands Government Statistical Abstract and Compendium of Statistics 1974, 1982, 1999 and 2000: Estimates of Revenue and Expenditure 1975, 1983 and 2000.

Appendix 2

Personal References

The Cayman Islands
Economic data indicating rate of growth

Monetary figures in Cayman Islands dollars
Rate of exchange CI$1 = US$1.20 (fixed)

	1974	1982	2000
Government Revenue	8,999,953	57,461,000	284,333,000
Government Expenditure (Recurrent)	7,527,000	46,763,000	258,874,000
Government Expenditure (Capital)	4,291,000	11,582,000	43,231,000
Customs Duty Collected	4,530,000	70,905,000	100,210,000
Total Value of Imports	21,851,000	107,000,000	558,700,000
Vehicles registered	3,394	9,251	25,061
Tourists – by air	53,104	121,214	406,600
– by sea	2,513	158,285	1,030,900
Number of cruise ships	8	179	605
Banks and Trust Companies	188	428	580
Registered Companies – Total	(1975) 6,618	16,712	59,922
Offshore Companies	(1975) 2,320	9,060	41,361
Population (estimated)	13,352	18,285	41,800
Work Permits	1,308	2,167	12,941
Civil Servants	712	1,139	2,985
Local Deposits in Caymanian Banks	23,678,000	70,905,000	887,542,000
Currency in Circulation	2,025,000	8,149,000	51,149,000
Per capita Gross Domestic Product	1,947	11,600	27,600
(not calculated annually)	(1972)	(1985)	(1997)

Note 1974 Year of assumption of duty as Governor
1982 Year of terminating appointment as Governor
2000 Last year in Cayman Islands Government Office in London